INTERNATIONAL RELATIONS LAW OF THE EUROPEAN UNION

International Relations Law of the European Union

DOMINIC McGOLDRICK

DIRECTOR, INTERNATIONAL AND EUROPEAN LAW UNIT,
FACULTY OF LAW, UNIVERSITY OF LIVERPOOL

LONGMAN
LONDON AND NEW YORK

Addison Wesley Longman Ltd
Edinburgh Gate
Harlow
Essex CM20 2JE
England
and Associated Companies throughout the world.

*Published in the United States of America
by Addison Wesley Longman Inc., New York.*

First published 1997

ISBN 0 582 28857 6 PPR

British Library Cataloguing-in-Publication Data

A catalogue record of this book is
available from the British Library

Library of Congress Cataloging-in-Publication Data

A catalog entry for this title is
available from the Library of Congress

Set by 7
Printed in Great Britain by Henry Ling Ltd., at the Dorset Press,
Dorchester, Dorset

*This book is dedicated with love to
April, Jessica, Christina and Agnes.*

Contents

Contents

Preface

This book was written at the kind invitation of Professor John Usher. I am grateful to him for that invitation and for his comments on the first draft of the manuscript. The book is part of a longer-term project on the interface between European Union law and public international law. I am increasingly convinced that it is intellectually indefensible for the disciplines, and those who teach them, to affect such distance from each other.

My colleagues in the International and European Law Unit, University of Liverpool, continue to provide a happy and constructive environment in which to research. In particular I wish to thank Professor Nanette Neuwahl and Fiona Beveridge for their comments on some chapters. Thanks are also due to Damian Chalmers, a former colleague, now at the London School of Economics, University of London. He has continued to be a source of constructive advice and discussion. Jessica and Christina McGoldrick provided valuable help in the final stages of completion. All responsibility for the views expressed is, of course, mine alone.

My work in academic life continues to be much supported by the McGoldrick and Owen families. I am profoundly grateful to them all. In particular I wish to acknowledge the support of my wife, April, and the inspiration of my brother, John. I hope that this book stands as some small measure of return on their faith in me.

Dominic McGoldrick
Faculty of Law, The University of Liverpool,
January 1997

General Editor's Preface

The Longman European Law Series is the first comprehensive series of topic-based books on EC Law aimed primarily at a student readership, though I have no doubt that they will also be found useful by academic colleagues and interested practitioners. It has become more and more difficult for a single course or a single book to deal comprehensively with all the major topics of Community law, and the intention of this series is to enable students and teachers to "mix and match" topics which they find to be of interest: it may also be hoped that the publication of this Series will encourage the study of areas of Community which have historically been neglected in degree courses. However, while the Series may have a student readership in mind, the authors have been encouraged to take an academic and critical approach, placing each topic in its overall Community context, and also in its socio-economic and political context where relevant.

As Dr McGoldrick indicates in his Introduction, the aim of this book is to examine the broad range of economic and political relationships that the European Union has with the rest of the world. These relationships are of increasing and inescapable importance, and raise legal questions of considerable complexity. I am most grateful to Dr McGoldrick for his willingness to contribute to this series; with his background in Public International Law as well as EC Law, he has provided a clear guide to the law and practice of the EU's international relations.

John A. Usher

Abbreviations

ACP:	African, Caribbean and Pacific States
AG:	Advocate General
AJIL:	American Journal of International Law
ASEAN:	Association of South East Asian Nations
BYIL:	British Yearbook of International Law
CCP:	Common Commercial Policy
CDE:	Cahiers de Droit Européen
CFSP:	Common Foreign and Security Policy
CMLR:	Common Market Law Report
CMLRev:	Common Market Law Review
COMECON:	Council for Mutual Economic Assistance
COREPER:	Committee of Permanent Representatives
EBRD:	European Bank for Reconstruction and Development
EC:	European Community
ECB:	European Central Bank
EC-Bull:	Bulletin of the European Communities
ECHR:	European Court of Human Rights
ECJ:	European Court of Justice
ECR:	European Court Reports
ECSC:	European Coal and Steel Community
EDF:	European Development Fund
EEA:	European Economic Area
EEC:	European Economic Community
EFTA:	European Free Trade Area
EIPA:	European Institute for Public Administration
EJIL:	European Journal of International Law
ELRev:	European Law Review
EMS:	European Monetary System

EMU:	Economic and Monetary Union
EP:	European Parliament
EPC:	European Political Cooperation
EU:	European Union
EU-Bull:	Bulletin of the European Union
Euratom:	European Atomic Energy Community
FAO:	Food and Agriculture Organization
GATS:	General Agreement on Trade in Services
GATT:	General Agreement on Tariffs and Trade
GYIL:	German Yearbook of International Law
Harv.ILJ:	Harvard International Law Journal
HL:	House of Lords
ICJ:	International Court of Justice
ICLQ:	International and Comparative Law Quarterly
ILO:	International Labour Organization
Int.Affairs:	International Affairs
JCMS:	Journal of Common Market Studies
JHA:	Justice and Home Affairs
JO:	Journal Officiel (of the Communauté Européenne)
JWTL:	Journal of World Trade Law
LIEI:	Legal Issues of European Integration
LQR:	Law Quarterly Review
Mich.JIL:	Michigan Journal of International Law
MLR:	Modern Law Review
MUP:	Manchester University Press
NAFTA:	North American Free Trade Agreement
NATO:	North Atlantic Treaty Organization
NILR:	Netherlands International Law Review
NYIL:	Netherlands Yearbook of International Law
OCT:	Overseas Countries and Territories
OECD:	Organization for Economic Cooperation and Development
OJ:	Official Journal (of the European Communities)
OJLS:	Oxford Journal of Legal Studies
OUP:	Oxford University Press
PL:	Public Law
PR:	Progress Report on the Intergovernmental Conference, Florence, June 1996
QMV:	Qualified Majority Voting
Receuil Des Cours:	Receuil Des Cours De L'Academie De Droit International

RG:	Report of the Reflection Group on the Intergovernmental Conference, December 1995
RGP:	Progress Report of the Reflection Group on the Intergovernmental Conference, September 1995
RMC:	Revue du Marché Commun
RMUE:	Revue du Marché Commun et de L'Union Européenne
SEA:	Single European Act
TEU:	Treaty on European Union (the Maastricht Treaty)
TRIPS:	Trade Related Intellectual Property Rights
UKTS:	United Kingdom Treaty Series
UNCLOS:	United Nations Convention on the Law of the Sea
VCLT:	Vienna Convention on the Law of Treaties
WEU:	Western European Union
WTO:	World Trade Organization
Yale LJ:	Yale Law Journal
YEL:	Yearbook of European Law

Table of cases

Introduction

The internal evolution of the EC has fascinated lawyers, economists and political scientists. It is a unique form of legal and political organization.[1] By contrast the field of the external or international relations of the EC (and now the EU) has been subjected to comparative neglect.[2] There are a number of possible explanations for this. First, the apparent uncertainty and delphic nature of the subject. There were relatively few judgments of the ECJ and these had tended to cloud the issues rather than clarify them. Some of the cases seemed to raise arcane discussion and merely reflect inter-institutional squabbling.[3] Secondly, the express provisions of the Treaty on external relations are badly drafted. Thirdly, external relations issues and consequences have been virtually ignored in major community reports[4] and texts on the internal market.[5] This may have been a deliberate policy decision.[6] Both practice and doctrine developed for which legal justification seemed tenuous, if not downright dubious. Legal precision also seemed unattainable if doctrine could be evolved merely to reflect the state of evolution of the EC.[7] Fourthly, the EC also appeared to be a unique creation from the perspective of international law.

1. See J.H. Weiler, 'The Transformation of Europe', (1991)101 Yale LJ, 2403–83.
2. See A.G. Toth, *Oxford Encyclopedia of European Community Law* (Oxford, OUP, 1990), pp. 256–71.
3. Indeed, there may be no objection to the substance of the matter at all. See, for example, Cases C-181 and C-248/91, *Parliament v Council and Commission* [1993] ECR I-3885 on humanitarian aid to Bangladesh.
4. See P.-H. Spaak, *Rapport des chefs de Délégations aux Ministries des Affaires Etrangères* (Brussels, Secretariat of the Intergovernmental Conference, 1956).
5. See Commission (1985); P. Checcini, *Research on the Cost of 'Non-Europe'* (Luxembourg, Office for Official Publications, 1988).
6. See P. Eeckhout, *The European Internal Market and International Trade* (Oxford, Clarendon Press, 1994), p. 340.
7. See *Ruling 1/78* [1978] ECR 2151; Case 283/81, *CILFIT Srl v Ministry of Health* [1982] ECR 3415.

Internationally, the EC was making claims for status and competence that challenged the traditional state-based paradigms of international law and international intergovernmental organizations.[8] Therefore, it was critical to observe the responses of non-EC states and other international organizations to this new creature. How could international law accommodate it?[9] Would international law itself have to change?

The scope and purpose of this book

This book seeks to provide a clear and user-friendly account of the law and practice of the EU's international relations. It sets those relations in the context of international law, community law and national law. It does *not* consider the substantive internal law and practice of the EC, general principles of EC law, or EC institutional law, *except* to the extent that reference to them is necessary to comprehend the law and practice of international relations. Similarly, treatment is confined to the EC and reference is only made to the European Coal and Steel Community (ECSC) and the European Atomic Energy Community (Euratom) when they provide relevant comparative law and practice.

The title of this book – *International Relations Law of the European Union* – was deliberately chosen. The more usual title – 'external relations' – is too closely associated with purely economic matters. This book is intended to reflect more accurately the broad range of economic and political relationships that the EU has with the rest of the world. Thus, while appropriate attention is given to international legal personality, competence and legal order (Chapters 2–7), this is balanced by a broader analysis of the development of a common foreign and security policy, other international aspects of the EU, and the EU's role as an international actor (Chapters 8–10).

8. See J. Groux and P. Manin, *The European Communities in the International Order* (Brussels, EC Commission, European Perspective Series, 1985); C. Vedder, 'A Survey of the Principal Decisions of the ECJ Pertaining to International Law' (1990) 1/2 EJIL, 365–77.
9. See H.G. Schermers, 'Community Law and International Law' (1975) 12 CMLRev, 77–90; K. Meessen, 'The Application of Rules of Public International Law within Community Law' (1976) 13 CMLRev, 485–501; J. Boulouis, 'Le Droit Des Communautés Européennes Dans Ses Rapports Avec Le Droit International Général', 235 *Receuil Des Cours* (1992–IV), 9–80, pp. 19–26; E. Piontek, 'European Integration and International Law of Economic Interdependence', 236 *Receuil Des Cours* (1992–V), 9–126.

This inclusive approach carries with it a problem of terminology. As will be explained in Chapter 2, the EC has international legal personality, but the EU appears not to have it. Thus, all international agreements are concluded in the name of the EC rather than the EU. Politically, however, relations with third countries are now presented as being with the EU, rather than the EC. The EU thus has relations with third states even if it does not have legal personality. Similarly confusing is that the Treaty on European Union (1992) introduces the concept of 'citizens of the Union' even though the relevant provisions are inserted into the EC Treaty. For the purposes of this book it becomes important to make clear whether it is the EC or the EU that is being referred to. I have used 'EC' when it is strictly necessary to do so, for example, when dealing with competence under the EC Treaty. I have used 'EU' more generally to express the European identity as a whole, embracing all three pillars of the TEU. For example, Chapter 10 deals with the EU as an international actor but it includes many activities that fall only within the competence of the EC. This use of 'EU' is more elegant than using 'EC/EU' but it should not be allowed to confuse or mislead.

The limitation on the size of works in this series means that this book is essentially concerned with the governing principles and policy considerations. I have sought to give examples from the major areas of practice but it is impossible to give extensive treatment to the international agreements or practice within substantive areas such as the Common Commercial Policy, international trade more generally, the environment, development assistance, or sanctions. A number of these will be considered in companion volumes in this series. They are also considered in detail in the excellent and compendious work by Macleod, Hendry and Hyett, *The External Relations of the European Communities: A Manual of Law and Practice.*[10]

The structure of this book

Chapter 1: The origins and development of the EC and the EU

An understanding of how the EU's rather complex international relations law has developed requires some appreciation of the legal and political evolution of the EC and the EU. The political and

---

10. (Oxford, OUP, 1996). I must acknowledge a substantial debt to that work.

policy issues have to be unmasked from the practice and the legal doctrine. At a simplistic level, the major political and legal issues relate to the distribution of power between the EC and the member states.[11] A tension has been evident since the inception of the EC. It was starkly reflected in the structuring of the Treaty on European Union (TEU) – the Maastricht Treaty (1992). It underlies the principle of subsidiarity, introduced as a general principle by the TEU.[12] The importance of the TEU lies not so much in relation to the EC itself – the stated aim was not to undermine it,[13] and, indeed, it was developed in a number of ways – rather that it fundamentally changed the organizational framework and structure around the EC. It introduced two intergovernmental pillars, one on Common Foreign and Security Policy (CFSP) and one on Justice and Home Affairs (JHA). International relations issues fall within these pillars as well. Their interrelationship with the EC pillar will need to be examined. The TEU also created a new entity, the European Union, the legal status and framework of which requires brief consideration.

Chapter 2: The international legal personality of the EC and the EU

This chapter looks at the status of the EC and the EU in the international legal community, that is, the broad question of their international legal personality.

Chapter 3: EC competence in international relations

Extensive consideration is given to the competence (or power) of the EC in the field of international relations. This chapter examines the different competencies, their legal bases, how they arise and how they are exercised.

Chapter 4: The nature of EC competence in international relations

This considers the nature of EC competence. If the EC has competence it can either be 'exclusive' or 'shared' with the member states. How is the nature of the competence determined? Can it change as the EC evolves?

[11.] This is a familiar issue in the development of federal constitutional systems and so analogies are often drawn with such systems.
[12.] See ch. 1, pp. 15–16 below.   [13.] Article M of the TEU.

Chapter 5: Mixed agreements

This chapter examines the phenomena of mixed agreements which have become central to the international relations practice of the EC.

Chapter 6: Practice and policy on EC competence

This chapter begins by examining the respective roles of the institutions in the negotiation and conclusion of international agreements and the importance of the correct legal basis for the conclusion of agreements. It then proceeds to consider, from a policy perspective, the range of strategies open in practice to member states, the institutions and third states concerning EC competence, both exclusive and shared.

Chapter 7: International agreements and the Community legal order

This chapter considers the legal effects of agreements in the EC legal order. In particular, it considers the circumstances in which either kind of agreement can have direct effect in the EC legal order. Consideration is also given to the effect of pre-existing international agreements from the perspective of the EC and from that of member states.

Chapter 8: From European political cooperation to a common foreign and security policy

This chapter considers the evolution of the EU's CFSP with all its political, security and defence dimensions. Proposals for reform are detailed.

Chapter 9: Justice and home affairs; international human rights; citizenship

This chapter briefly considers the international aspects of justice and home affairs, human rights and citizenship.

Chapter 10: The EU as an international actor

This chapter considers the variety of international roles played by the EU, and how the EU conducts and organizes its communication with the world. It outlines the different kinds of agreements and relations that the EU has with third states and groups of third states.

Chapter 11: Appraisal and prospectus

This seeks to draw together some of the themes that emerge from the preceding chapters. It offers a broad appraisal of contemporary EU doctrine on international relations. It also assesses the existing and future role of the EU as an international relations actor.

CHAPTER ONE

The origins and development of the EC and the EU

An understanding of the development of the EC and the EU is necessary to appreciate how their international relations law is determined.[1] The origins have to be understood in historical context. The Second World War had finished in 1945 but the Cold War and its Iron Curtain had descended. The economies of most of the European states, both the victors and the vanquished, had been shattered. The war had illustrated both the dangers of nationalism, and the limitations of the nation state, particularly in an increasingly global economic climate. The predominant considerations in the development of the European Economic Communities were thus political and security ones. There were economic motives, but these were subsidiary. If the nations of Europe could gather together their economic factors of production, and organize their resources on a common basis, they would present a strong challenge to the leaders in the world economy. There was also a broader *security* link, in the sense of the general argument that nations which trade together do not tend, as a rule, to go to war with each other.[2] Moreover, even in the origins of the EU there were strong tendencies towards a broader, more idealistic conception of the future of Europe as a group of states united in various ways.

[1.] See P.J.G. Kapteyn and P. Verloren Van Themaat, *Introduction to the Law of the European Communities* (Deventer, Kluwer, 1990), pp. 1–28; G.A. Bermann, R.J. Goebel, W.J. Davey and E.M. Fox, *Cases and Materials on European Community Law* (St Paul, Minnesota, West, 1993), pp. 2–21; D. Wyatt and A. Dashwood, *European Community Law*, 3rd edn (London, Sweet and Maxwell, 1993), pp. 3–15.

[2.] See E. Mansfield and J. Snyder, 'Democratization and War' (1995) 74(3) Foreign Affairs, 79–97. 'The Group emphasizes that this guarantee of prosperity and peace is not perpetual and that it would be a grave error to underestimate the Community's main contribution to the Member States and their citizens, namely a shared view of life that has ruled out war as a means of settling differences . . .', Reflection Group on the IGC, Final Report, Doc. SN520/95, 5 December 1995 (Brussels), p. 5.

There were undoubtedly different visions of Europe.[3] For descriptive purposes, a broad contrast between unionists, federalists and functionalists is helpful, but only on the understanding that there were many shades of opinion and many overlaps between them. *Unionists* saw enhanced development of the classical international law model of intergovernmental co-operation.[4] *Federalists* aimed for a European federation, but this of itself can mean different things. Concepts and definitions of a federation vary widely. It can be a descriptive term for a particular type of constitutional structure; so there are various kinds of federal states, e.g., USA, Germany, Australia. The EU is not a federal structure in this substantive sense.

However, 'federal' can also be a more general descriptive term for the distribution of constitutional power in a particular constitutional structure. There are an infinite number of possible models. In some states, federalism is associated with centralization of power, in others with decentralization. In the sense that the constitutional organization of the EU contains a certain distribution of constitutional power, it can therefore be described as a federal system.[5] When the meaning of a term can vary so much according to definition and context, it is dangerous to use it as a legal term without fairly precise definition. This partly explains the UK's objections to the Dutch draft of the TEU, which proclaimed a 'federal' goal for the EU. The other part of the objection lies in wishing to prevent the EU from evolving into a European federation in the substantive sense. The essential difference is between the EU being a single state for the purposes of international law, or continuing alongside fifteen or more separate states for the purposes of international law, but with those fifteen or more exercising some of their sovereign functions only through the EU or jointly with the EU. Critical analysis of the EU international relations is often based on federal state analogies, and, in particular, on how federal states conduct their international relations.[6]

Functionalists argued for a merger of sovereign national rights

3. This remains true today. See, for example, UK Government White Paper, *A Partnership of Nations* (Cm. 3181, London, HMSO, 1996).
4. See pp. 21–3 below.
5. See T.C. Fischer and S. Neff, 'Some Thoughts About European "Federalism"' (1995) 44 ICLQ, 904–15. The principle of subsidiarity operates within that constitutional framework as part of the power allocation machinery. See pp.15–16 below.
6. See J.H. Weiler, 'The Transformation of Europe' (1991) 101 Yale LJ, 2403–83.

in particular economic sectors. Ideas ranged from a single federal State, a 'kind of United States of Europe',[7] to a 'Europe d'Etats', but they all envisaged to greater or lesser degrees closer co-operation between states.

The first step: the European Coal and Steel Community

In May 1950 the French Foreign Minister, Mr Schuman, announced a proposal which would place all of the Franco-German coal and steel production under a common 'High Authority', in an organization open to the participation of European countries. This French-German axis is often stressed in analyses of the political development of the European Community and it remains of central importance.[8] The significance of the declaration lay in the vital importance of coal and steel as basic economic commodities in an economy. However, it was not just the fact of cooperation which was important, it was the nature of the High Authority. It was to be composed of independent persons and capable of taking decisions binding on all the participating states. Although there were various limitations on this High Authority, it established the pattern of an intergovernmental organization which contained an element of *supra-national authority*. That is, its decisions could be imposed down onto states and economic actors.

The European Coal and Steel Community (ECSC) was established in 1951.[9] The preamble to the Treaty refers to it as the 'basis for a broader and deeper Community among peoples long divided by bloody conflicts'. Another important aspect of the new Community was that it locked the Federal Republic of Germany into Western Europe. The basis of the ECSC was a common market for coal and steel. The law in the Treaty was very strictly defined (*traite-loi*), as were the powers of the High Authority.

---

7. The word 'kind' is often forgotten. See D. Wyatt, 'The United States of Europe' (1984) 4 OJLS, 256–65; 'If you sincerely want to be a United States . . .', *The Economist*, 23 March 1991, p. 23.
8. This remains the case but Germany increasingly appears to be the dominant partner. See A. Baring (ed.), *Germany's Position in the New Europe* (Oxford, Berg, 1994).
9. UKTS 2 (1973).

Extension of European cooperation into other spheres

Two notable, but unsuccessful, attempts were those in the 1950s to establish a European Defence Community and a European Political Community. The first reached the stage of a Treaty (1952) but it never came into force. The concept of a European Defence Community has recently emerged again in the TEU.[10] The development of Europe as a political community is again dealt with in that Treaty, but it was also the subject of developments within the existing European Community system. This principally took place under the provisions of the Single European Act 1986 (SEA) which made extensive provision for 'European Political Cooperation' (EPC).[11]

Towards the European Economic Community

Notwithstanding the setbacks on the creation of defence and political communities, various proposals towards greater European economic integration were made as part of the *'relance Européenne'* movement. Of major importance was the Spaak Report.[12] This report of an intergovernmental committee dealt with the questions of the establishment of a Common Market and with the development of the peaceful use of atomic energy. The report dealt with the concepts of Common Market, economic policy, the fusion of separate national markets, harmonization of laws, development of common policies, and competition laws. The very scope of these ambitious proposals raised a difficult problem in terms of drafting the Treaty. The *traite-loi* model of the ECSC could not be followed for a scheme as ambitious and wide ranging as this. A *traite-cadre* was needed. Matters of policy could be established in the Treaty, but the detailed practical functioning of the economic systems could only be dealt with by institutions that would need to be established, particularly if the communities were to be effective in achieving their aims. The report proposed that there should be four institutions – a Council of Ministers, a European Commission, a Court of Justice and a Parliamentary

10. See ch. 8 below, pp. 140–2, 170–1.
11. See ch. 8 below.
12. See P.-H. Spaak, *Rapport des chefs de Délégations aux Ministries des Affaires Etrangères* (Brussels, Secretariat of the Intergovernmental Conference, 1956).

Assembly. Particular stress was put on the proposal for a *Commission* which would serve the *Community* interest.

The substance of the report was accepted as the basis for drafting the Treaties. In 1957 the Treaties establishing the European Economic Community (EEC) and the European Atomic Energy Community (Euratom) were signed in Rome.[13] The Treaties entered into force on 1 January 1958. The next substantial leap forward came in the form of the Single European Act (1986).[14] This extended EC competence, made greater provision for qualified majority voting, and set the objective of achieving an 'internal market' by the end of 1992. This objective, often referred to as the 'single market', became the driving force behind the EC. Fears of a 'fortress Europe' led to a substantially increased interest in the EC from third states.

The EC gradually expanded. In addition to the original six there came the United Kingdom, Ireland, Denmark (all in 1972), Greece (1989), Spain and Portugal (both in 1986). From 1986 to 1995 the Community was composed of twelve members. After the Treaty on European Union (1992) created the EU, the existing member states are now members of both the EC and the EU. New member states accede to the Union and this includes the EC (Article O of the TEU).[15] Thus, on 1 January 1995 Austria, Sweden and Finland acceded to the EU, taking the number of member states to Fifteen.[16] Further expansion around the year 2000 appears likely.[17]

From the European Community to the European Union

As the 1990s began, the EC was at a critical juncture in terms of its development. Some of the broader political motivations for its establishment appeared to have served their purposes and could not serve as continuing justifications. In particular, the idea of

13. UKTS 1 (1973) Part II.
14. [1987] OJ L169/1.
15. See I. Macleod, I. Hendry and S. Hyett, *The External Relations of the European Communities: A Manual of Law and Practice* (Oxford, OUP, 1996), ch. 9.
16. Treaty of Accession concerning the accession of the Kingdom of Norway, the Republic of Austria, the Republic of Finland, and the Kingdom of Sweden to the European Union, [1994] OJ C241/1. After a negative result in a referendum Norway did not accede. See Council Decision 95/1 of 1 January 1995, [1995] OJ L1/1.
17. See D. Booss and J. Forman, 'Enlargement: Legal and Procedural Aspects' (1995) 32 CMLRev, 95–130. Slovenia is the most recent applicant.

limiting or controlling German economic power, and thereby preventing it from regaining the political and economic power which can flow from economic power, had to be reappraised. From a more positive perspective the EC had been a success. Many of the aims set out in the Preambles to the EEC Treaty 1957 and to the SEA 1986 had been achieved. Economic growth had been substantial both in absolute and relative terms. Germany was prosperous and firmly democratic. Indeed, a model of constructive treatment of the vanquished by the victors had been set. Politically and economically membership of the EC remained very attractive. For existing members to leave appeared inconceivable. New members were queuing to join. However, the development of the EC as a political community had been much less successful. It was little understood and little appreciated by the then 340 million (now 370 million) individuals who constituted the 'Peoples of Europe'.[18]

The Treaty on European Union 1992: The Maastricht Treaty[19]

It was in this context that two intergovernmental conferences were convened in December 1990.[20] One covered political union, the other economic and monetary union. After some dramatic negotiations in December 1991, the *Treaty on European Union* (TEU), the *Maastricht Treaty* (1992), was agreed and officially signed in February 1992.[21] After overcoming referendums in three member states and court challenges in a number of member states,[22] it came into force on 1 November 1993. The TEU is a further progression towards the concept of a 'union' of states in

18. See the preambles to the EC Treaty, the SEA and the TEU.
19. [1993] OJ C 224. An interesting historical point is that Guy Fawkes, famous for an unsuccessful attempt to blow up the UK Houses of Parliament, lived for a short period in Maastricht.
20. See A. Pijpers, *The European Community At The Crossroads* (Dordrecht, Nijhoff, 1992).
21. [1992] OJ C191/1. See R. Dehousse (ed.), *Europe After Maastricht: An Ever Closer Union?* (Munich, Law Books in Europe, 1994); D. O'Keeffe and P. Twomey (eds), *Legal Issues of the Maastricht Treaty* (Chichester, Wiley Chancery, 1994); A. Duff, J. Pinder and R. Pryce (eds), *Maastricht and Beyond: Building the European Union* (London, Routledge, 1994).
22. See especially *R v Secretary of State for Foreign and Commonwealth Affairs, ex p Lord Rees Mogg* [1994] 1 All ER 457; *Brunner and Others v European Union Treaty* [1994] 1 CMLR 57.

Europe.[23] One of the themes of this book is how that enhanced Union impacts on the international relations of the member states and of the rest of the world community.

What did the TEU do? [24]

Structural changes

The crucial significance of the TEU is that it radically altered the structural framework of the system.[25] The model adopted, strongly favoured by the UK and supported by a number of others, was a 'pillared temple' structure. The central pillar is the EC Treaty, as amended, which created the EEC.[26] Under the TEU the word 'Economic' is officially deleted. This simply reflected the fact that the Community has moved well beyond being merely an 'economic' community. Alongside the EC pillar, there are two separate intergovernmental pillars. The second pillar covers Common Foreign and Security Policy (CFSP), which replaces EPC.[27] This is provided for in Title V of the TEU. The third pillar covers matters of Justice and Home Affairs.[28] This is provided for in Title VI of the TEU. The second and third pillars formalized and developed the procedures for intergovernmental cooperation on EPC and on matters of justice and home affairs which had evolved outside the EC Treaty.

To avoid introducing a separate set of institutions, the pillars are linked by a 'single institutional structure'. The TEU also created a new overarching entity – *the European Union* – which includes all three pillars within it. It is helpful to illustrate the post-TEU structure diagrammatically.

---

23. See I. Campbell, 'From the "Personal Union" between England and Scotland in 1603 to the European Communities Act 1972 and Beyond – Enduring Legal Problems from an Historical Viewpoint', in B.S. Jackson and D. McGoldrick, *Legal Visions of the New Europe* (London, Graham and Trotman/Nijhoff, 1993).
24. I have drawn on the FCO Memorandum, *Europe After Maastricht*, House of Commons, Foreign Affairs Committee, 1992 (EC204), for this section.
25. See D. Curtin, 'The Constitutional Structure of the Union: A Europe of Bits and Pieces' (1993) 30 CMLRev, 17–69; U. Everling, 'Reflections on the Structure of the European Union' (1992) 29 CMLRev, 1053–77; P. Demaret, 'The Treaty Framework', in O'Keeffe and Twomey (eds), *Legal Issues of the Maastricht Treaty*.
26. The European Coal and Steel Community and European Atomic Energy Community are also part of the First pillar.
27. See ch. 8 below.
28. See ch. 9 below.

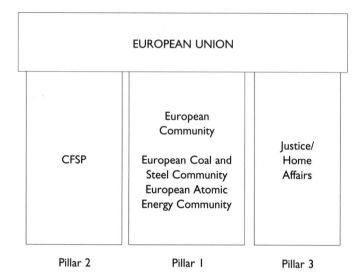

Changes to policies and institutions

The TEU made changes to the policies and institutions of the European Community.[29] The changes to policies included the codification and some extension of Community competence. The main policy areas are: visa lists;[30] education; youth; training; trans-European networks; industry; public health; culture; development; consumer protection; economic and social cohesion; research and development; and the environment. In each case there had already been some activity by the Community or by the 'Twelve' acting intergovernmentally. Somewhat surprisingly, given their importance, the provisions on the Economic and Monetary Union, including a single currency, form part of the Treaty of Rome.[31] If they come to

29. See T.C. Hartley, 'Constitutional and Legal Aspects of the Maastricht Agreement' (1993) 42 ICLQ, 213–37; D. Wyatt and A. Dashwood, *European Community Law*, 3rd edn (London, Sweet and Maxwell, 1993), pp. 653–73. The UK takes the view that 'overall the institutional balance of the Community is broadly maintained', FCO Memorandum (1992). The ECJ regards institutional balance as an important part of the democratic operation of the EC.

30. See S. Peers, 'The Visa Regulation: Free Movement Blocked Indefinitely' (1996) 21 ELRev, 150–5, for critical comment on the overlapping of visa matters in the EC Treaty and in the third pillar.

31. See also Protocol 10 to the TEU on the transition to the third stage of economic and monetary union.

fruition they would have significant effects on the EU's relationships with the rest of the world community.

In relation to social policy the existing Articles in the EC Treaty
remained in force.[32] However, under Protocol 11 to the TEU on
Social Policy the then twelve member states agreed that eleven of
the twelve (excluding the UK) could have recourse to Community
institutions, procedures and mechanisms, where they wanted to
take action going beyond the provisions of the Treaty of Rome.
Such action would give effect to an Agreement on Social Policy,[33]
which is annexed to the Protocol on Social Policy.[34] Such acts are
not be part of the Community *acquis*, are not applicable in the
UK, and the UK does not bear any financial burden, other than
administrative costs entailed for the institutions.[35] In practice,
subsequent to the TEU, great efforts have been made to keep
measures within the terms of the EC Treaty so as to ensure that
the UK is included.

The TEU inserts 'subsidiarity' into the EC Treaty as a general
principle for the first time.[36] Article 3b sets it out:

> The Community shall act within the limits of the powers conferred
> upon it by this Treaty and of the objectives assigned to it therein. In
> areas which do not fall within its exclusive competence, the
> Community shall take action, in accordance with the principle of
> subsidiarity, only if and in so far as the objectives of the proposed
> action cannot be sufficiently achieved by the Member States and can
> therefore, by reason of the scale or effects of the proposed action, be
> better achieved by the Community. Any action by the Community
> shall not go beyond what is necessary to achieve the objectives of
> this Treaty.[37]

The doctrine is a complex one but essentially the idea is to prevent
unnecessary new Community activity on policies best left to

---

32. Articles 117–22.
33. The Agreement is between the then eleven member states. The three new
member states are also parties to the Agreement. Action has now been taken
under this Agreement. See B. Bercusson, *European Labour Law* (London,
Butterworths, 1996), pp. 35–9, 553–70.
34. See J. Shaw, 'Twin-Track Social Europe – The Inside Track', in O'Keeffe and
Twomey (eds), *Legal Issues of the Maastricht Treaty*.
35. Cf. the problems with the financial distinction under CFSP between
'administrative' and 'operational' expenditure. See ch. 8, pp. 157–8 below.
36. See N. Emiliou, 'Subsidiarity: Panacea or Fig Leaf?' in O'Keeffe and Twomey
(eds), *Legal Issues of the Maastricht Treaty*; J. Steiner, 'Subsidiarity under the
Maastricht Treaty', in O'Keeffe and Twomey (eds), *Legal Issues of the
Maastricht Treaty*; and Article F of the TEU.
37. There are also references to subsidiarity in the Preamble to Article B of the TEU.

member states, and to ensure that where the Community does act it only takes the minimum action necessary. The subsidiarity principle is ultimately justiciable before the ECJ,[38] but more importantly it has had a substantial effect on the practices of the institutions.[39] In the context of the international relations competence of the EC, it is important to note immediately that the principle of subsidiarity simply does not apply where the EC has exclusive competence. Whatever the difficulties of ascertaining when the EC has exclusive competence, this is an important limitation. The matter of exclusive EC competence is considered in Chapter 4, below.

The TEU also made some limited institutional changes. The Commission was largely unchanged, although scrutiny of its actions by the European Parliament have been strengthened. After internal reorganization, external relations are principally delt with by DGI, DGIA and DGIB.[40] The Council remains the main legislative and decision making body of the Community. Its role and procedures were not directly changed. The main changes on its working methods in relation to international relations are:

- the need to take account of subsidiarity when taking decisions;
- new functions (though under different procedures from those under the normal Community system) in the intergovernmental pillars of the Union Treaty (CFSP) and Justice/Home Affairs.

To save confusion, the Council has decided to refer to itself as 'Council of the European Union'. This is simply for ease of reference. To determine the powers of the Council and the relevant voting requirements it will still be necessary to know whether the Council is acting under its EC competence or its intergovernmental competence under the other two pillars of EU activity.

---

38. See A.G. Toth, 'Is Subsidiarity Justiciable?' (1994) 19 ELRev, 268–85; V. Harrison, 'Subsidiarity in Article 3b of the EC Treaty – Gobbledegook or Justiciable Principle' (1996) 45 ICLQ, 431–9. Breach of the principle could be challenged in any applicable procedures, for example, against the Commission or the Council.
39. An inter-institutional agreement 'On procedures for implementing the principle of subsidiarity' was agreed and came into effect with the TEU on 1 November 1993. See also Edinburgh Council, Conclusions of the Presidency, Part A, Annexes 1 and 2 (1992).
40. DGI and DGIB on external economic relations and DGIA on external political relations.

The TEU also extended the range of decisions to be taken by Qualified Majority Voting (QMV),[41] made provision for a new co-decision procedure between the Council and the European Parliament (EP),[42] and extended the range of international agreements requiring the EP's assent.[43]

The current scope of the EC Treaty (as amended by the TEU)

Having explained the development of the EC and the development of its competencies, it is now convenient to set out the structure of the EC Treaty and the current objectives, task and policies of the EC. As will subsequently be explained, a proper understanding of these is essential for the determination of the scope of the EC's international competence.

The EC Treaty is divided into six parts. Part One deals with 'Principles'. Part Two deals with 'Citizenship of the Union'.[44] Part Three deals with 'Community Policies'. This is divided into seventeen different 'Titles'. Many of those Titles are divided into a number of Chapters. As we will see below, this structuring can have an effect on the determination of the EC's international competence.[45] Part Four deals with the 'Association of Overseas Countries and Territories'.[46] Part Five deals with the 'Institutions of the Community'. Finally, Part Six deals with 'General and Final Provisions'. Much of Part Six is of importance for the international relations of the EC and it is considered in Chapter 2, below. Note should also be made of Article 224 on member states taking steps in the event of serious internal disturbances affecting the maintenance of law and order, war, serious international tension constituting a threat of war, or in order to carry out obligations it

41. The fifteen member states exercise 87 votes in total. 61 votes are required for a QMV. Thus, 27 votes are needed to block a decision. Under the 'Ioannina Agreement', as altered to take account of the non-accession of Norway, if member states representing between 23 and 25 votes indicate that they intend to oppose an act, then the Council will do all within its power, within a reasonable time and without prejudice to mandatory time limits, to reach a satisfactory conclusion, See Council Decision of 29 March 1994 [1994] OJ C105/1 as amended by Council Decision of 1 January 1995 [1995] OJ C1/1.
42. Art 189b.　43. See ch. 6 below.　44. See Articles 8–8e.
45. See chs. 3–4 below.
46. These are not dealt with in this book. See Council Decision 91/482/EC, [1991] OJ L263/1 and Cases C-480/93 and 483/93, *Antillean Rice Mills NV and Others v Commission* [1995] ECR nyr, which describes the implementation of the association arrangements between the OCT and the EC as a 'dynamic process'.

has accepted for the purpose of maintaining international peace and security.[47]

Article 2 sets out the 'task' of the EC and what are in effect, although the word is not used, its objectives:

> The Community shall have as its task, by establishing a common market and an economic and monetary union and by implementing the common policies of activities referred to in Articles 3 and 3a, to promote throughout the Community a harmonious and balanced development of economic activities, sustainable and non-inflationary growth respecting the environment, a high degree of convergence of economic performance, a high level of employment and of social protection, the raising of the standard of living and quality of life, and economic and social cohesion and solidarity among Member States.

Article 3 sets out what the 'activities' of the EC shall include for it to achieve the purposes set out in Article 2:

> For the purposes set out in Article 2, the activities of the Community shall include, as provided in the Treaty and in accordance with the timetable set out therein:
>
> a) the elimination, as between Member States, of customs duties and quantitative restrictions on the import and export of goods, and of all other measures having equivalent effect;
>
> b) a common commercial policy;
>
> c) an internal market characterized by the abolition, as between Member States, of obstacles to the free movement of goods, persons, services and capital;
>
> d) measures concerning the entry and movement of persons in the internal market as provided for in Article 100c;
>
> e) a common policy in the sphere of agriculture and fisheries;
>
> f) a common policy in the sphere of transport;
>
> g) a system ensuring that competition in the internal market is not distorted;
>
> h) the approximation of the laws of Member States to the extent required for the functioning of the common market;
>
> i) a policy in the social sphere comprising a European Social Fund;

[47.] See the order of the President of the ECJ refusing interim measures against Greece in Case C-120/94, *Commission v Hellenic Republic* [1994] ECR I-3037. The case was subsequently discontinued at the request of the Commission notwithstanding the request of the Greek Government for the ECJ to rule on the matter, [1996] ECR.

j) the strengthening of economic and social cohesion;

k) a policy in the sphere of the environment;

l) the strengthening of the competitiveness of Community industry;

m) the promotion of research and technological development

n) encouragement for the establishment and development of trans-European networks;

o) a contribution to the attainment of a high level of health protection;

p) a contribution to education and training of quality and to the flowering of the cultures of the Member States;

q) a policy in the sphere of development cooperation;

r) the association of the overseas countries and territories in order to increase trade and promote jointly economic and social development;

s) a contribution to the strengthening of consumer protection;

t) measures in the spheres of energy, civil protection and tourism.

These are very wide-ranging activities, but it is important to note that there are variations between the activities. Notably for our purposes there are a limited number of 'common policies' – the common commercial policy, common agricultural and fisheries policies, and a common transport policy. There are 'policies', but not 'common policies', in the social, environmental and development cooperation spheres. In other areas the scope of competence is limited to measures, systems, encouragement and contributions.

Articles 100 and 100a provide for the harmonization of laws under certain conditions and in accordance with certain procedures. Article 235 provides the EC with a residual legislative power where action is necessary to attain, in the course of the operation of the common market, one of the objectives of the Community and the Treaty has not provided the necessary powers. Article 235 has been widely interpreted by the ECJ, but there are limits to the objectives of the EC.[48]

Article 5 of the Treaty provides that member states shall take all appropriate measures to ensure fulfilment of their obligations arising out of the Treaty or resulting from actions taken by the EC institutions, shall facilitate the achievement of the EC's tasks, and

---

48. See *Opinion 1/91* (First EEA Opinion) [1991] ECR 6079; *Opinion 2/94* (ECHR) [1996] ECR nyr. At the IGC there is a concensus on keeping Article 235 in the Treaty with no changes of procedure, see Progress Report on IGC (1996), Presidency Conclusions, European Council in Florence, 21–22 June 1996, Doc. SN 300/96, Annexes, p. 16.

shall abstain from any measure which could jeopardize the attainment of the objectives of the Treaty. In the 1980s and 1990s the ECJ has given this Article a key constitutional role in the EC legal order.[49]

The European Union

The issue of the international personality of this new entity is considered in Chapter 2, below. Its intergovernmental pillars are considered in Chapters 8 and 9, below.

Citizenship of the Union

The Treaty introduces the concept of citizenship of the Union. Citizenship is automatically enjoyed by nationals of member states. As a matter of both international and community law, member states remain responsible for determining who their nationals shall be. Many rights and duties were already provided for in the existing Treaty of Rome and in secondary legislation, for example, rights of free movement and residence. There are limited additional rights.[50] Citizens of the Union will have the right to consular protection in third countries where their state is not represented.[51] This aspect of citizenship is considered in Chapter 9, below. No further rights can be granted unless there is unanimous agreement in the Council and there is ratification in accordance with national procedures.[52] This is sometimes referred to as a 'double lock'. It clearly puts control of the future content of Union citizenship in the hands of member states.

The 1996 Review Conference

An intergovernmental conference, beginning in 1996, is reviewing a number of areas specified in the Treaty.[53] Further matters have been added since. The European Council in Florence in June 1996 decided to hold a special European Council in Dublin in October 1996 to give fresh momentum to the IGC. A first draft of the revised EU Treaty was considered by the Dublin European Council in December 1996. (See 'General Outline for a draft revision of the

---

[49.] See J. Temple Lang, 'Community Constitutional Law: Article 5 EEC Treaty' (1990) 27 CMLRev, 645–81.

[50.] Articles 8b–8d. [51.] Article 8c. [52.] Article 8e.

[53.] See A. Dashwood, *Reviewing Maastricht: Issues for the 1996 IGC* (London, Sweet and Maxwell/Law Books in Europe, 1996); Asser Instituut Conference Papers (1995).

Treaties', prepared by the Irish Presidency, CONF 2500/96, Brussels, 5 December 1996.) Proposed reforms affecting the international relations law of the EU are considered at the appropriate points in this book.

The legal order of the EC[54]

The new order

One of the difficulties of assessing the development of European Community law is that it is explained by the ECJ as a 'new legal order' of law, with the character of a constitutional law.[55] This has various consequences for the member states, and is of major importance as the intellectual and philosophical foundation of various community law doctrines such as direct effect, supremacy and preemption. However, it does not make sense to consider and analyse a new order without having some understanding of what would be referred to as the 'old legal order'.

The old legal order

The old legal order, in this context, is quite simply the classic international law system, that is, the system of law which principally governs the relations between states.[56] That system has increasingly taken account of the existence and rights of international organizations like the European Community,[57] and also the rights of individuals.[58] In modern times the most common method of creating international law is by Treaty. As well as being based on a Treaty, the EC is a party to numerous Treaties.[59] Under the general international law system, when two or more states become parties to a Treaty, they create a network of international

---

54. On the legal order of international organizations see H.G. Schermers and N.M. Blokker, *International Institutional Law*, 3rd edn (The Hague, Nijhoff, 1995), ch. 8, esp at pp. 707–10.

55. See J. Boulouis, 'Le Droit Des Communautés Européennes Dans Ses Rapports Avec Le Droit International Général' 235 *Recueil Des Cours* (1992–IV), 9–80, pp. 27–50; Wyatt and Dashwood, *European Community Law*, pp. 52–103; Case 294/83, *Les Verts v EP* [1986] ECR 1339; *Opinion 1/91* (First EEA Opinion) [1991] ECR 6079.

56. See R.Y. Jennings and A. Watts (eds), *Oppenheim's International Law*, 9th edn (Harlow, Longman, 1992).

57. See Schermers and Blokker, *International Institutional Law*.

58. See D. McGoldrick, 'A New International Economic Order for Europe?' (1994) 12 YEL 1992, 434–64.

59. See chs. 3–5, 9 below.

obligations owed to the other states parties to the Treaty. If the Treaty creates an international organization, then the states can undertake obligations to that organization in its own right. States cannot be forced or coerced into entering into Treaties. To enter into them is an exercise of their sovereign rights.[60] If a state party acts in breach of the Treaty there are various possible consequences. These principally concern the rights which other states parties to the Treaty have to react to the breach. It became increasingly common for Treaties to set up mechanisms or bodies to ensure implementation of the Treaty. So, for example, under the European Convention on Human Rights (1950) there is a European Commission and a European Court of Human Rights.[61] These institutions can consider applications both from states, non-governmental organizations and individuals. The general approach then is that the consequences of possible breaches of the Treaty are dealt with at the international level, either between states or by bodies established by those states.[62]

In some states there is a further possibility. In those states it is possible for individuals or other bodies to rely on international Treaties before their *own national courts*. Whether this possibility exists depends on the constitutional system of the state concerned. In a number of states the Constitution permits, or has been interpreted to permit, this right of access to national courts. Obviously, not all Treaties are appropriate for implementation in this way and national courts have developed doctrines of 'self-executing Treaties'.[63] Essentially, this is a concept which is used to separate out those Treaties which can be enforced at the national level and those which cannot. A typical example of the require-ments for a Treaty to be self-executing are that the rights it creates are for the benefit of individuals, that the rights created are clear and unambiguous, and that the state concerned does not have to take a series of measures before the right could be effectively invoked. In the UK, individuals cannot rely on international Treaties as a direct source of rights before national courts. An

---

60. See F. Jacobs and S. Roberts (eds), *The Effect of Treaties in Domestic Law* (London, Sweet and Maxwell, 1987): *ex parte Lord Rees Mogg*, n. 22 above. In the UK the exercise of the Treaty power is part of the Royal prerogative.

61. See D.J. Harris, M. O'Boyle and C. Warbrick, *Law of the European Convention on Human Rights* (London, Butterworths, 1995).

62. See R.Y. Jennings and A. Watts (eds), *Oppenheim's International Law*, pp. 1300–3; S. Rosenne, *Breach of Treaty* (Cambridge, CUP, 1985).

63. See J. Jackson, 'Status of Treaties in Domestic Legal Systems: A Policy Analysis' (1992) 86 AJIL, 310–40.

individual can only rely directly on the rights in an international Treaty if they are formally incorporated into UK law.[64]

Does the EC system fit into the old legal order, or does it create a new legal order?

There is no reason in principle why the EC system could not simply have been placed within the classical approach to international law, international institutions and international Treaties, and EC decisions implemented accordingly.[65] However, the ECJ asserted that the founding Treaty of the EC, the Treaty of Rome (1957), had to be understood as creating a *new legal order*, under which states had voluntarily limited their sovereignty.[66] In the famous *Van Gend en Loos* case (1963), it stated that –

> . . . this Treaty is *more* than an agreement creating only mutual obligations between the contracting parties . . . The Community constitutes a *new legal order in International law*, for whose benefit *the States have limited their sovereign rights*, albeit within limited fields . . . Community law therefore not only imposes obligations on individuals but also confers upon them rights which become part of their legal heritage . . .[67]

We must determine precisely what is meant by this new legal order and the concepts and doctrines developed under it. To what extent have states 'limited their sovereign rights'? How are the 'limited fields' to be determined? Can those 'limited fields' be extended? Of what importance is it that this new legal order is 'in international law'? Subsequent cases have dropped this last expression, leaving only the reference to the new legal order. Is EC law still a species of international law or has it grown into a separate and distinct system?[68] If the latter, what are the consequences for international law?[69] What is the ordering framework of the new system? How

64. See *J.H. Rayner (Mincing Lane) Ltd v Dept of Trade and Industry* [1989] Ch. 72; *R v Secretary of State for the Home Department, ex parte Brind* [1990] 1 All ER 469, HL.

65. See. D. Wyatt, 'New Legal Order, or Old?' (1982) 7 ELRev, 147–66.

66. See J.A. Usher, *European Community Law and National Law – the Irreversible Transfer* (London, Allen and Unwin, 1981); J.V. Louis, *The Community Legal Order*, 2nd edn (Brussels, European Commission, 1990).

67. Case 26/62, *NV Algemene Transport-en Expeditie Onderneming van Gend En Loos v Nederlandse Administratie der Belastingen* [1963] ECR 1 (emphasis added). The concept of European citizenship builds on this legal heritage.

68. See J. Boulouis, 'Les Droit Des Communautés Européennes Dans Ses Rapports Avec Le Droit International Général', 235 *Recueil Des Cours* (1992–IV), 9–80.

69. See J. Groux and P. Manin, *The European Communities in the International Order* (Brussels, EC Commission, European Perspective Series, 1985).

can it be reformed, amended and changed? Practice has sometimes been very creative, for example, the internationally binding agreement on Denmark in the context of the TEU.[70] How has the existence of the EC, and now the EU, affected the powers of member states to conduct international relations? How has international law treated the EC?[71] As a state? Simply as an international organization? Or as something between the two? In *Opinion 1/91* (Draft Agreement on European Economic Area) the ECJ stressed how the new legal order of the EC distinguished it from other international organizations.[72] One of the major legal difficulties is that the status of European Community law as a legal order can be viewed from two perspectives:[73] first, from the perspective of the European Community system itself as it looks (some might say down) at the national legal systems of the member states; secondly, from the perspective of those national legal systems as they look at the EC legal system. It is as though two telescopes were laid in a line with a legal space between them. The legal space represents EC law.

Each national legal system sees the EC legal system through its own lens, namely its own constitutional legal order. At the end of the second telescope is the ECJ. It has a vision of its own.[74] It can see through to the national legal systems, but it can see them only through the legal space of the EC legal system. The picture is different. After some degree of unease and opposition it is primarily the EC's perspective which has prevailed in practice.[75] However, there is a substantial extent to which, although the Community's view has prevailed in practice, the views of the national legal systems on the theory of why Community law prevails is different from that of the perspective of the European Community system itself. The end result is the same but the

---

70. See Bull-EC, 12/1992, pp. 25–6; D. Curtin and R. van Ooik, 'Denmark and the Edinburgh Summit: Maastricht Without Tears: A Legal Analysis' in O'Keeffe and Twomey (eds), *Legal Issues of the Maastricht Treaty*.

71. See H.G. Schermers, 'Community Law and International Law' (1975) 12 CMLRev, 77–90; K. Meessen, 'The Application of Rules of Public International Law within Community Law (1976) 13 CMLRev, 485–501.

72. [1991] ECR 6079. See H.G. Schermers, 'Opinion 1/91 of 14 Dec. 1991; Opinion 1/92 of 10 Apr. 1992 with annotation' (1992) 29 CMLRev, 991–1010.

73. See G. Slynn, *Introducing a European Legal Order* (London, Stevens/Sweet and Maxwell, 1992); N. MacCormick, 'Beyond the Sovereign State' (1993) 56 MLR, 1–18.

74. See P. Pescatore, 'The Doctrine of Direct Effect – An Infant Disease of Community Law' (1983) 8 ELRev, 155–77.

75. See A. Oppenheimer, *The Relationship Between EC Law and National Law: The Cases*, (Cambridge, CUP, 1995).

reasoning behind that result is significantly different. The EC justification is concerned with its *new legal order*. The national system response may be more in terms of its own national conception of *sovereignty*.[76] These different perspectives also apply when the international relations of the EC are considered.

[76.] See *Factortame v Secretary of State for Transport* [1991] 1 All ER 70, HL; and the cases in n. 22 above. In *Brunner and Others v European Union Treaty*, n. 22 above, the German Constitutional Court referred to the member states as the 'masters of the Treaty'. The decision imposes limits on the further transfer of powers to the EU without accompanying certainty and accountability.

CHAPTER TWO

The international legal personality of the EC and the EU

Introduction

The original model of public international law (PIL) conceived of it as a purely rule generating, inter-state, normative system. The theoretical structure was composed of a number of autonomously acting spheres of influence/supremacy/jurisdiction called states. The PIL system was simply made up of the accumulation of rules which operate to organize their relations inter se. Modern conceptions of international law are much more sophisticated as to the range of international actors and the values and processes of international law.[1] We need to consider how the EC and the EU are accommodated within the theory and structure of international law.

International organizations

It is undoubtedly accepted that under international law, international organizations can have international personality, that is, rights and duties under the PIL system of law.[2] As there are in excess of 100 intergovernmental organizations, this is of enormous significance to the theory and practice of the system. The leading international law precedent on the international personality of public international law institutions is the *Reparation for injuries suffered in the service of the United Nations case* (1949).[3]

[1.] See R. Higgins, *Problems and Process – International Law and How We Use It* (Oxford, OUP, 1994); A.-M. Slaughter-Burley, 'International Law and International Relations Theory' (1993) 87 AJIL, 205–39.

[2.] See H.G. Schermers and N.M. Blokker, *International Institutional Law*, 3rd edn (The Hague, Nijhoff, 1995), pp. 976–82; N. White, *The Law of International Organisations* (Manchester, Manchester Univ. Press, 1996).

[3.] Advisory Opinion, ICJ Reports, 1949, p. 174.

In September 1948 Count Bernadotte was the Chief United Nations Truce Negotiator in Jerusalem. He was killed, allegedly by a gang of private terrorists. Jerusalem was at the time in Israeli possession. The United Nations General Assembly asked for an advisory opinion from the International Court of Justice (ICJ). It asked, inter alia, whether the United Nations, *as an organization*, had the capacity to bring an international claim against the responsible de jure or de facto government with a view to obtaining reparation due in respect of the damage caused to the UN, and to the victim or to persons entitled through him? The UN Charter contained no express power on international personality or on the bringing of claims.

The ICJ analysed the provisions of the Charter as a whole. It noted in particular that the Charter established organs charged with various tasks, established various obligations for the members in relation to the UN, gave the UN legal capacity and privileges and immunities in the territory of each of its member states, and contained provisions for the conclusion of agreements between the UN and its members which had been acted on in practice. It concluded that the UN was intended to exercise and enjoy functions and rights which could only be explained on the basis of the possession of a large measure of international personality and the capacity to operate upon an international plane. It was not a state, but it was an international person, 'Whereas a State possesses the totality of international rights and duties recognized by international law, the rights and duties of an entity such as the organization must depend upon its purposes and functions as specified in its constituent documents and developed in practice'.[4] The UN therefore possessed a right of functional protection in respect of its agents.

The ICJ was not asked to express an opinion on whether Israel was in fact responsible for the killing, but a second question that was addressed arose from the fact that Israel was not at the relevant time a member of the United Nations.[5] The ICJ could have stated that the United Nations existed as an international person in respect of the member states of the UN only, that is, 'subjective international personality'. This would have been consistent with a view that the member states of the UN had, by becoming parties to the United Nations Charter, consented to the functional degree of international personality necessary for the international organization which they created to exercise its functions. However, the ICJ went further:

4. Ibid., p. 180. 5. It joined in May 1949.

> 50 States, representing the vast majority of the members of the International Community, had the power, in conformity with international law, to bring into being an entity possessing *objective international personality* and not merely personality recognized by them alone, together with capacity to bring international claims . . .

This international law principle of 'objective legal personality' is of enormous practical and theoretical significance. It means that entities can exist within a system even in relation to other entities which have not consented to their existence within that system. There is, therefore, an objective element to the functioning and existence of the system which cannot be denied by other actors within that system.

The precedent of the *Reparations Case* could have been limited in that the opinion related to an organization created by a number of states which represented the 'vast majority of members of the International Community' at that time. Subsequently, however, practice has reduced the strict requirements that could have been drawn from that statement. There is now little doubt that international organizations can have objective international personality even when brought into existence by only a limited number of states. So, as is often the case, a limited breakthrough has very much opened the floodgates in the development of theory and practice. There are now many major international organizations, like the EC, which clearly have international personality. They may have an objective existence in the international system even as regards states which do not recognize them. Until 1988 the EC was not recognized as an international organization by COMECON.[6] This position was rectified only shortly before COMECON itself was dissolved.

The international legal personality of the EC: the EC Treaty[7]

Consideration of this issue requires an examination of the provisions of the EC Treaty which are relevant to the EC's

---

6. See Council Decision 88/345, [1988] OJ L157/34; W. Morawiecki, 'Actors and Interests in the Process of Negotiations between the CMEA and the EEC', 1989/2 LIEI, 1–38.
7. See I. Macleod, I. Hendry and S. Hyett, *The External Relations of the European Communities: A Manual of Law and Practice* (Oxford, OUP, 1996), ch. 2; A.G. Toth, *Oxford Encyclopedia of European Community Law* (Oxford, OUP, 1990),

international relations. These are mainly contained in Part Six of the Treaty, Articles 210–48.[8] On any analysis of those provisions the EC would clearly satisfy the functionalist test of the ICJ in the *Reparations Case*, even more so than the UN. Moreover, this is strongly supported by the EC's extensive international practice.[9]

Article 210 appears clear and precise, 'The Community shall have legal personality'. This is an assertion of personality in international law and not just personality in each of the member states. This is made clearer by Article 211, which provides that the Community shall also 'enjoy the most extensive legal capacity accorded to legal persons' in each of the member states. In relation to that capacity, the EC is represented by the Commission.[10] A Protocol (1965) to the Merger Treaty (1957) makes provision for the privileges and immunities of the EC in the member states.[11]

Powers to enter into international agreements[12]

A number of Articles of the Treaty make express provision for the EC to enter into international agreements. The principal ones relate to the common commercial policy (Article 113); what have become known generically as 'association agreements' (Article 238); the environment (Article 130r(4)); and development cooperation (Article 130y). There are more limited and specific powers relating to monetary or foreign exchange regime matters

---

7. *(continued)* pp. 351–8; J. Boulouis, 'Le Droit Des Communautés Européennes Dans Ses Rapports Avec Le Droit International Général, 235 *Recueil Des Cours* (1992–IV), 9–80, pp. 51–64.

8. See H. Smit and P. Herzog, *The Law of the European Economic Community* (New York, Bender, 1976); J. Megret *et al.* (eds), *Le droit de la Communauté économique européenne, vol. xii: relations extérieures* (Brussels, Editions de l'Université de Bruxelles, 1980).

9. See Macleod, Hendry and Hyett, *The External Relations of the European Communities*; P. Pescatore, 'External Relations in the Case Law of the Court of Justice of the European Communities' (1979) 16 CMLRev, 615–45, pp. 641–3; J. Groux and P. Manin, *The European Communities in the International Order* (Brussels, EC Commission, European Perspective Series, 1985).

10. See e.g. Case T-451/93, *San Marco Impex Italiana SA v Commission* [1994] ECR II-1061; Case C-257/90, *Italsolar SpA v Commission* [1990] ECR I-3841.

11. [1967] OJ 152. For a recent decision on the Protocol see Case C-88/92, *van Rosendaal v Staatssecretaris van Financien* [1993] ECR I-3315. Note also the amendments made by Protocol 7 to the TEU. See also Case 241/87, *Maclaine Watson & Co. Ltd v Council and Commission*, Opinion of AG Darmon, [1990] ECR I-1797.

12. See A.G. Toth, *Oxford Encyclopedia of European Community Law* (Oxford, OUP, 1990), pp. 521–31.

(Articles 109(3)); education, vocational training and youth (Articles 126(3) and 127(3)); culture (Article 128(3)); public health (Article 129(3); and the EC's multiannual framework programme on research and technological development (Article 130m(2)). Moreover, as we will consider below, the ECJ has also established that the EC has a Treaty making capacity that goes much wider than these express powers.[13]

Article 228 makes provision for the procedures to be followed for the 'conclusion of agreements between the Community and one or more States or international organizations'.[14] The Commission negotiates on the basis of authorization by the Council. The Council concludes the agreements. As we will observe in subsequent chapters, the EC has developed a very substantial international treaty practice on this basis. It is solely party to some Treaties, while for others it is a party alongside some or all of the member states. In some circumstances, although only member states may be parties to a Treaty, they are effectively acting as trustees for the EC. This arises when the EC has competence over certain matters but it cannot be a member of a particular organization because membership is limited to states. The International Labour Organization is an example.[15]

Other international agreements foreseen in the EC Treaty

Article 220 provides for the member states to enter into negotiations with each other with a view to securing the certain benefit of their nationals.[16] One of these concerns the 'simplification of formalities governing the reciprocal recognition and enforcement of judgments of courts or tribunals and of arbitration awards'. In 1968 the member states concluded the Convention on Jurisdiction and the Enforcement of Judgments in Civil and Commercial Matters (the Brussels Convention). A Protocol of 1971 gives jurisdiction to the ECJ to give preliminary rulings on the Convention. All member states are parties to the Convention and the Protocol and this is now expected of all new members. The EC is not a party to this Convention. An Article

---

13. See ch. 3 below.   14. See ch. 7 below.
15. See *Opinion 2/91* (ILO Convention) [1993] ECR I-1061.
16. See S. Weatherill and P. Beaumont, *EC Law*, 2nd edn (London, Penguin, 1995), pp. 330–4.

220 Convention on the mutual recognition of companies and legal persons (1968) has never entered into force.[17] There is a Draft Article 220 Convention on insolvency proceedings[18] and a Convention on the private international law aspects of family law is under consideration.[19]

After the TEU, member states may have a choice between an Article 220 Convention and one under the third pillar of the TEU.[20] In the latter case there is the possibility that member states may stipulate that the ECJ has jurisdiction to interpret their provisions and to rule on any disputes regarding its application.[21] This has become a major political issue.

It is also possible for a Convention to accord jurisdiction to the ECJ even though it has no origin in the EC or EU legal orders.[22]

Sanctions

Under Article 228a economic sanctions may be taken by the EC following a common position or joint action relating to CFSP.[23]

Relations with international organizations and institutions[24]

The EC Treaty provides for the Commission to ensure the maintenance of all appropriate relations with the UN, its Specialized Agencies, the GATT, and all international organisations.[25] This relates to arrangements at the administrative level.

---

17. See also the Convention on Company Taxation, [1990] OJ L225/10.
18. See Bull-EU, 9-1995, point 1.5.7.
19. See P. Beaumont and G. Moir, 'Brussels Convention II: A New Private International Law Instrument in Family Matters for the European Union or the European Community' (1995) 20 ELRev, 268–88.
20. Article K(2)(c) of the TEU. See Beaumont and Moir, 'Brussels Convention II'. For JHA Conventions see ch. 9 below.
21. Article K(2)(c) of the TEU.
22. See the Rome Convention on the Law Applicable to Contractual Obligations and its two Protocols, [1980] OJ L266, [1989] OJ L48/1–4, 17–18.
23. See ch. 8 below.
24. See Macleod, Hendry and Hyett, *The External Relations of the European Communities,* ch. 7; Commission, *Relations between the European Community and International Organizations* (Luxembourg, Office for the Official Publications of the European Communities, 1989).
25. Article 229. See also section (5), pr. 5 of the Luxembourg Accords of 1966, Bull-EC, 1966/3, p. 9.

Two other international organizations are singled out, though with reference to the Community rather than the Commission. The Community is to establish 'all appropriate forms of cooperation with the Council of Europe',[26] and 'close cooperation with the Organisation for Economic Cooperation and Development'.[27]

Membership of, or participation in, international organizations[28]

The Treaty contains no express authority for EC membership of other international organizations. None the less, in *Opinion 1/76* the ECJ clearly recognized that the EC has the competence to participate in the establishment of international organizations and to be a member of such organizations.[29] After the TEU, Article 228(3) now refers to the conclusion by the EC of 'agreements establishing a specific institutional framework by organizing cooperation procedures'.[30]

In practice, the EC has had to fight a series of battles with member states and with international organizations in order to gain recognition, or partial recognition, of its role and so be able to obtain membership or participation.[31] These conflicts with member states, and with third parties, partly explain the substantial variations in the rights of the EC, and the different modes of representation, found in the different organizations. Although EC accession to the major international institutions is going to be increasingly on the international agenda, as of 1 July 1996 the EC is a member of only three international organizations or institutions. These are the UN Food and Agriculture Organization (FAO),[32] the European Bank for Reconstruction and

---

26. Article 230.   27. Article 231.
28. See Schermers and Blokker, *International Institutional Law*, pp. 55–9; Toth, *Oxford Encyclopedia of European Community Law*, pp. 259–63.
29. *Opinion 1/76*, [1977] ECR 741, 756.
30. See ch. 6 below.
31. See J. Sack, 'The European Community's Membership of International Organisations' (1995) 32 CMLRev 1227–56; E. Denza, 'The Community as a Member of International Organizations', in N. Emiliou and D. O'Keeffe (eds), *The European Union and World Trade Law – After the GATT Uruguay Round* (Chichester, Wiley, 1996).
32. See R. Frid, 'The EEC: A Member of a Specialized Agency of the UN' (1993) 4 EJIL, 239–55.

Development (EBRD),[33] and the World Trade Organization (WTO).[34] The terms of membership vary enormously between the three institutions.[35] Membership of the FAO was a major breakthrough in political and legal terms. Possibilities for future membership are the International Labour Organization, the International Civil Aviation Authority and, particularly if a single currency comes to fruition, the International Monetary Fund.

The EC is also a member of over 60 international organizations which have been created under the terms of an international Treaty to deal with a specific matter. Such organizations are sometimes referred to as 'Treaty organs' to distinguish them from the more general international organizations. They mainly concern fisheries, environmental protection and commodity agreements under UNCTAD.[36] Some of them can be of major importance. An important one for the near future will be the International Sea Bed Authority, established under the UN Convention on the Law of the Sea (1982).[37]

The EC has sometimes been treated, in terms of membership or participation, simply as any other international organization would be.[38] Increasingly, however, it has been treated in a unique way by a specific provision on the EC,[39] or by a reference to 'regional economic integration organizations'.[40] Although this appears as a general formulation, it is defined in such a way as to cover only the EC. This formulation acknowledges that the EC is a unique entity in terms of its competence. Some Treaties have required the EC, and sometimes member states, to make 'Declarations' of competence, and to update them.[41] The EC is also an observer at a significant number of international organizations, including the United Nations' General Assembly,[42] its the

---

33. See D. McGoldrick, 'A New International Economic Order for Europe?' (1994) 12 YEL 1992, pp. 434–64, at pp. 448–56.
34. See A. Qureshi, *The World Trade Organization* (Manchester, Manchester University Press, 1996), pp. 164–91.
35. See Sack (1995) 32 CMLRev 1227–56, pp. 1243–9.
36. The 'Group of 77', representing the developing countries in the UN, supported EC participation in commodity agreements.
37. 21 ILM (1982), p. 1261.
38. See Article 305(1)(f) and Annex IX of the LOSC; K.R. Simmonds, 'The Communities Declaration Upon Signature of the U.N. Convention on the Law of the Sea' (1986) 23 CMLRev, 521–44.
39. As in the WTO Agreement.
40. See the UN Framework Convention on Biological Deversity.
41. See, for example, Article II(4) of the FAO Constitution, as amended.
42. See GA Resolution 3208 (XXIX) of 11 October 1974. The same resolution also governs the status of the EC at UN conferences, the number and

Economic and Social Council,[43] and most of its Specialized Agencies, including the ILO, the WHO, and UNESCO.[44] The more active role of the UN in the 1990s has enhanced the importance of these links.[45] So too with the OSCE, where the EC is also an observer. The EC has close cooperation with, but not the formal status of observer at, the Council of Europe.[46]

Diplomatic recognition[47]

Diplomatic recognition is also an important indicator of the recognition of the international personality of an international entity.[48] As of June 1996, 168 states and territories were accredited to the EC.[49] After the TEU, many of them have adopted the designation of 'Mission to the EU' to reflect the wider scope of the EU's activities, but this does not have legal significance. Nineteen international organizations or international entities have established 'bureaux de liaison' in Brussels.[50] The EC has a

42. (continued) importance of which is rising. For the UN Conference on Environment and Development in 1992 the GA granted the EC the enhanced role of 'full participant status', GA Resn 6/470 of 12 April 1992. In practical conference of representation, participation in committees and working groups, debating and submitting amendments, this took the EC close to the status of participating states except that it could not vote or submit procedural motions. The EC assumed a leadership and mediation role at different times in the conference. See L.J. Brinkhorst, 'The European Community at UNCED: Lessons to be Drawn for the Future', in D. Curtin and T. Heukels (eds) *Institutional Dynamics of European Integration: Essays in Honour of H.G. Schermers*, vol. II (Dordrecht, Nijhoff, 1994). The EC now often seeks such a status.

43. This extends to its Regional and Functional Commissions. The latter include the Commission on Human Rights and the Comission on Sustainable Development. On the latter see GA Resolution 47/191 of 23 January 1993 providing for the full participation of the EC within its areas of competence but without the right to vote; Bull-EC, 6-1992 on the principle governing the EC's participation. See also Article J.5(4) of the TEU on the Security Council.

44. For full details see Macleod, Hendry and Hyett, *The Exernal Relations of the European Communities*, pp. 195–207.

45. An exchange of letters regulates day to day contacts with the UN Secretariat.

46. In the context of *Opinion 2/94*, on EC accession to the European Convention on Human Rights, the EC did not propose to join the Council of Europe. See pr. 6 of the Opinion. The EC is seeking to strengthen its cooperation with the Council of Europe.

47. See Toth, *Oxford Encyclopedia of European Community Law*, pp. 263–5.

48. See Macleod, Hendry and Hyett, *The External Relations of the European Communities*, ch. 8.

49. Commission, *Corps Diplomatique accrédité auprès des Communautés européennes et représentations auprès de la Commission* (Brussels, June 1996).

50. Ibid.; see Macleod, Hendry and Hyett, *The External Relations of the European Communities*, p. 220, n. 85.

massive and growing diplomatic presence around the world.[51] It maintains 104 delegations, two representations and ten offices in third states or territories. Technically these are 'Commission delegations', based on the Commissions's powers to establish its own departments,[52] rather than EC delegations, based on international diplomatic law. This is because it is not yet accepted that international organizations can send and receive diplomats.[53] In practice, however, the EC maintains the equivalent of a world-wide diplomatic presence. That presence operates in close cooperation with the missions of member states to third countries and international organizations and with the Presidency, which also plays a significant role.[54] It also plays an important role in ensuring compliance with and implementation of CFSP.[55] Commission delegations have also been established to a number of international organizations.[56] All Heads of Delegation of the Commission who are accredited to states or other international organizations have ambassadorial status, with the exception of the Head of the EC Delegation to the UN.

International responsibility[57]

If the EC has international personality, then it can both bring international claims and have claims brought against it.[58] Some international Treaties make specific provision for the EC, e.g., the WTO Agreement.[59] The EC may bear joint or separate

---

51. By contrast, some member states are reducing their diplomatic representation around the world as a cost-saving exercise.
52. See the Opinion of Advocate-General Tesauro in Case C-327/91, *France v Commission*, [1994] ECR I-3641, pr. 28.
53. See Macleod, Hendry and Hyett, *The External Relations of the European Communities*, pp. 208–9.
54. See B.R. Bot, 'Cooperation in the Missions of the EC in Third Countries: European Diplomacy in the making' (1984) I LIEI, 149–69; L.J. Brinkhorst, 'Permanent Missions of the EC in Third Countries: European Diplomacy in the Making' (1984) I LIEI 22–33; Article 8c of EC Treaty.
55. See Article J.6 of the TEU.
56. UN, FAO, UNESCO, OECD, IAEA, and UNIDO.
57. See Toth, *Oxford Encyclopedia of European Community Law*, pp. 265–9.
58. See Groux and Manin, *The European Communities in the International Order*, pp. 141–7.
59. See M. Hilf, 'The ECJ's Opinion on the WTO – No Surprise, but Wise?' (1995) 6 EJIL, 245–59; Qureshi, *The World Trade Organization*. About half of the GATT Panel Reports have concerned the EC.

responsibility with the member states.[60] The ECJ has accepted that the EC is subject to customary international law[61] and that the ECJ itself can be bound by a decision of an international tribunal under the terms of an international agreement to which the EC is a party.[62] A particular problem for the EC is where the practical exercise of its international personality is limited because the relevant procedure or system does not permit the EC to have recourse to it. For example, the EC cannot be a member of the UN because this is limited to states. For the same reason, the EC could not be a party to contentious proceedings before the ICJ.[63] The system under the European Convention on Human Rights does not apply directly to the EC because it is not a party.[64] Indeed, it could not become a party unless the ECHR was amended to permit this. In *Opinion 2/94* the ECJ concluded that, 'As Community law now stands, the Community has no competence to accede to the ECHR'.[65]

The EC is, then, something less than a state but something much more than an international organization. Hence it is often, though not necessarily very helpfully, described as *sui generis*.

The international legal personality of the EU

As we noted above, this new entity embraces both the Treaty of Rome and the two pillars of inter-governmental activity – CFSP

[60.] See Case C-316/91, *Re European Development Fund: EP v Council*, [1994] ECR I-625, pr. 29 on the joint liability of the EC and the member states under the Lome IV Convention. See also Case C-327/91, *France v Commission* [1994] ECR I-3641; Macleod, Hendry and Hyett, *The External Relations of the European Community*, pp. 158–9.

[61.] See Case C-286/90, *Anklagemyndigheden v Poulsen and Diva Navigation* [1992] ECR 6019; Case C-432/92, *R v Ministry of Agriculture, Fisheries and Food, ex p Anastasiou* [1994] ECR I-3087.

[62.] *Opinion 1/91* (First EEA Opinion) [1991] ECR 6079, prs. 39–40.

[63.] Article 34 of the Statute of the ICJ. Nor, under Article 96 of the Statute, could the EC be authorized by the UN to request an advisory opinion.

[64.] See D.J. Harris, M. O'Boyle and C. Warbrick, *Law of the European Convention on Human Rights* (London, Butterworths, 1995), pp. 27–8; *M and Co v FRG*, Appn. No. 13258/67, 64 Decisions and Reports of the European Commission on Human Rights (1990), p. 138; *Human Rights Reexamined*, House of Lords Select Committee on the European Communities, Session 1992–93, 3rd Report, HL Paper 10, (1992). Cf Case T-201/95, *Zanone v Council of Europe and Others*. On the EU and international human rights see ch. 9 below.

[65.] *Opinion 2/94* (ECHR) [1996] ECR nyr. See F. Jacobs, *Human Rights in the European Union* (Durham, Durham Law Institute, 1994).

and Justice/Home Affairs. On the basis of the functional approach of the ICJ, considered above, it is submitted that the EU could have international personality. However, it has been strongly asserted, and seemingly accepted, that the EU does not have international personality. M.R. Eaton sets out the reasoning and it is helpful to consider each point in turn.[66]

> (1) There is no provision in the Treaty on European Union similar to Article 210 of the Treaty of Rome, which expressly says that the Community shall have legal personality.

This is correct but is not conclusive. International personality could be inherent or potential in the EU on a functional basis, applying the approach of the ICJ in the *Reparations Case*.[67]

> (2) Various functions that you would expect the Union to exercise, if it did have such personality, are in fact exercised by the Community, e.g. all the provisions on concluding external Treaties are in the Community Treaty and provide for the Community to conclude such Treaties. There are no such powers given to the Union, in CFSP or elsewhere. Similarly, citizenship is in the Community section.

It is correct that it is only the Community that has in fact concluded international agreements, either alone or alongside some or all of the member states (mixed agreements).[68] However, the point is: what would be the position if the Union sought to make, or be a party to, international agreements, under the EC pillar or as part of the CFSP, or relating to Justice and Home Affairs?[69] If in fact it did so, and was accepted by other international actors, then it would have been recognized as being capable of possessing international personality. Secondly, although citizenship is in the Community part of the Treaty, it is citizenship of the Union, not of the Community.[70] Moreover, there are international aspects to that citizenship.[71]

[66.] M.R. Eaton, 'Common Foreign and Security Policy', in D. O'Keeffe and P. Twomey (eds), *Legal Issues of the Maastricht Treaty* (Chichester, Wiley Chancery, 1994), p. 224. In evidence to the HL Select Committee on the European Communities Eaton stated that, '. . . we do not believe that the Union will constitute an international organization with a separate international legal personality. It would be better characterized as an association of Member States which, for certain purposes described in the Treaty, act in common', n. 64 above, pr. 129.

[67.] See pp. 26–8 above.   [68.] See chs. 3–5 below.   [69.] See chs. 8–9 below on practice to date.   [70.] See ch. 9 below.   [71.] See ch. 9 below.

(3) The evidence of the (unpublished) *travaux préparatoires*: there was a clear intention during negotiations *not* to confer legal personality. The question was raised, and the Dutch Presidency said firmly that the Union would not have legal personality. They were supported by the Director General of the Council Legal Service. The Director General of the Commission Legal Service has taken the same view in evidence to the European Parliament.

This ultimately seems to be the most convincing explanation. The clear intention of the member states for the Union not to have such international personality would seem to negative any implied or inherent basis for it. The UK takes the view that the Union will not have international legal personality.[72] In its submissions to the 1996 IGC, the EP called for the Union to be given international personality.[73] This would suggest that the EP accepts that the EU does not have it at present. The Commission also appears to accept this view.[74]

The question of the EU's international personality was discussed in the Reflection Group for the 1996 IGC. Its final report records that:

> A majority of members points to the advantage of **international legal personality** for the Union so that it can conclude international agreements on the subject-matter of Titles V and VI concerning the CFSP and the external dimension of justice and home affairs. For them, the fact that the Union does not legally exist is a source of confusion outside and diminishes its external role. Others consider that the creation of international legal personality for the Union could risk confusion with the legal prerogatives of member states.[75]

Given the broad objectives of the EU stated in Article B of the TEU, if the EU did have international personality then it would be very wide ranging, though still not plenary. Indeed, it would come very close to having all of the international personality of a state. That is no doubt an important factor for those states that oppose international personality for the EU. However, it should be possible for provisions to be drafted that would allow the EU, rather than the EC, to be party to international agreements without altering the principles on competence in the EC pillar.[76] It

---

72. See the Memorandum from the Foreign and Commonwealth Office in *Europe After Maastricht*, House of Commons, Foreign Affairs Committee (1992).
73. EP's Report to the IGC, pr. 14(ii).
74. See Commission's Report to the IGC, p. 64.
75. RG2, p. 40.   76. See Progress Report on IGC, Presidency Conclusions, European Council in Florence, 21–22 June 1996, Doc. SN300/96, Annexes, p. 36 at 2(a).

would then be no more than a name change. For the EU to be a party to international agreements concerning the inter-governmental pillars could also be useful as long as clear provision was made to deal with questions of competence and the relationship with the powers of the member states.[77]

The 'General Outline for a draft revision of the Treaties' suggests (i) endowing the Union with legal personality; (ii) setting out a procedure for the Presidency to negotiate agreements on behalf of the Union subject to unanimous authorization and negotiating directives issued by the Council. The resulting agreements would be concluded by the Council by unanimity.[78]

[77] Ibid., at 2(b).
[78] Conf 2500/96, ch. 13 (Brussels, 5 December 1996).

CHAPTER THREE

EC competence in international relations

What does 'competence' mean?

In international law the principal actors are states.[1] Once an entity satisfies the international law requirements for being a state, it is, in normal circumstances, accepted as a member of the international community of states and entitled to sovereign equality with other states. It is accepted as having various rights and being subject to various obligations.[2] As a state, it is also recognized as having various powers which flow from its status. This bundle of rights, obligations and associated powers can be described as expressions of the sovereignty of the state. If the EU underwent a sufficient metamorphosis and became a single, federal state, it would then be treated as a state rather than as a *sui generis* international organization.[3]

While international law uses the language of 'power' or 'jurisdiction', EC law has generally used the term 'competence'. So when the question is asked whether the EC has 'competence' to do something, it could equally be rephrased to ask whether the EC has the power or the jurisdiction to do that thing.[4] This chapter

---

[1.] See R.Y. Jennings and A. Watts (eds) *Oppenheim's International Law*, 9th edn (Harlow, Longman, 1992), pp. 117–329.

[2.] Ibid., pp. 330–554.   [3.] See ch. 1, pp. 21–3 above.

[4.] Although they can be distinguished, the ECJ has used the expressions 'competence' and 'powers' interchangeably. See T. Tridimas and P. Eeckhout, 'The External Competence of the Community and the Case-Law of the Court of Justice: Principle versus Pragmatism' (1995) 14 YEL 1994, 143–77, p. 144; N. Neuwahl, 'Joint Participation in International Treaties and the exercise of power by the EEC and its Member States: Mixed Agreements' (1991) 28 CMLRev, 717–40, p. 718; I. Macleod, I. Hendry and S. Hyett, *The External Relations of the European Communities: A Manual of Law and Practice* (Oxford, OUP, 1996), pp. 38–9. On the powers of international organizations see H.G. Schermers and N.M. Blokker, *International Institutional Law*, 3rd edn (The Hague, Nijhoff, 1995), ch. 3.

concentrates on the competence to take legislative measures and engage in certain international activities. Other important aspects of competence include its temporal scope, its geographical extent and its extra-territorial effect. These issues are not within the scope of this book.[5]

How can the EC acquire competence?[6]

There are two elements to this. First, we have already noted that the very establishment of an international institution by states can create something which has a separate international personality.[7] As well as express powers, such an international person may have inherent and implied powers as a matter of international law.[8] Second, as a matter of Community law, the ECJ has taken the view that, in establishing the EC, the member states have permanently 'transferred' some of their powers to it, so limiting their sovereignty.[9] This transfer means that certain competencies (or powers) are now held by the EC – they have been 'conferred' on it, or 'attributed' to it by the member states.[10] Article 3b of the

5. See Macleod, Hendry and Hyett, *The External Relations of the European Communities*, pp. 67–74; A. Bleckmann, 'The Personal Jurisdiction of the European Community' (1980) 17 CMLRev, 467–85. The EU is also on the receiving end of extra-territorial jurisdiction claims. For example, the EU has been engaged in a number of disputes with the US concerning the extra-territorial application of US legislation. The most recent concerns the US Helms-Burton Act on Cuba. For the EU's response, see p. 159 below.

6. See generally P.J.G. Kapteyn and P. Verloren Van Themaat, *Introduction to the Law of the European Communities*, 2nd edn (Deventer, Kluwer, 1990), pp. 769–88; 51 *Halsbury's Laws of England*, 4th edn, 'External Relations' (London, Butterworth, 1984), pp. 477–98; G.A. Bermann, R.J. Goebel, W.J. Davey and E.M. Fox, *Cases and Materials on European Community Law* (St Paul, Minnesota, West, 1993), pp. 891–927; House of Lords Select Committee on the European Communities (1984–85), *External Competence of the European Communities*, 16th Report, HL 236; P. Mengozzi, *EC Law* (London, Graham and Trotman/Kluwer, 1992), pp. 251–66; Macleod, Hendry and Hyett, *The External Relations of the European Communities*, pp. 37–55; A. Dashwood 'The Limits of European Community Powers' (1996) 21 ELRev, 113–28.

7. See ch. 2 above.

8. See N. White, *The Law of International Organisations* (Manchester, Manchester University Press, 1996), ch. 4. This analysis can be applied to the EU. The EU has the inherent potential to be an international legal person if the member states wish to use that potential.

9. Case 6/64 *Costa v ENEL* [1964] ECR 585 at 593–4. Not all member states necessarily accept this theory of the ECJ. The English courts prefer to maintain that EC law is given legal effect because the UK Parliament has legislated for that to be the case.

10. See A. Dashwood, 'The Limits of European Community Powers' (1996) 21 ELRev, 113–28 for a very helpful analysis of competence. Schermers and

EC Treaty refers to the powers 'conferred' upon the EC by the Treaty.[11] The EC has only those specific powers which have been conferred upon it. Thus, the presumption of competence lies with the member states.[12] In *Opinion 2/94* (ECHR) the ECJ clearly stated that, 'That principle of conferred powers must be respected in both the internal action and the international action of the Community'.[13]

As a general theory this is simple and ingenious. Much more difficult is to determine which of the competencies of states have been so transferred. Can the transfer be only on the basis of an express provision? Or can there be a transfer by implication? Are there other possible modes of transfer? More specifically, what is the relationship between internal competence and external competence? Would transfer of internal competence have any consequences for external competencies? Can competence be shared between the EC and the member states? Who decides all of these questions? As we shall see, the processes of competence are complex, dynamic and evolutionary.[14] We also need to consider how third states and international organizations have reacted to these developments. Are their views of any legal or practical relevance?

How to approach the question of competence

General statements on approach will tend to be misleading. It is often said that the EC has competence in relation to certain general areas. Such statements are broadly correct in their substance, but they betray a misunderstanding of how questions of competence should be approached. The question to ask is:

> whether one of the objectives of the Treaties would be obtained by the measures proposed, and whether adoption of such measures would be consistent with the procedures envisaged in the Treaty, in

---

10. (*continued*) Blokker comment that 'Attribution of powers is the normal system for international organizations. It is the fundamental difference between States and international organizations', *International Institutional Law*, pp. 141–2.

11. Note also Article 4, which provides that, 'Each institution shall act within the limits of the powers conferred upon it by this Treaty'.

12. See Tridimas and Eeckhout (1995) 14 YEL 1994, 143–77, p. 154; E. Freeman, 'The Division of Powers Between the European Communities and the Member States' (1977) 30 Current Legal Problems, 159–73.

13. *Opinion 2/94* (ECHR), pr. 24.   14. See chs. 3–4.

conformity with any conditions imposed by the Treaties on the exercise of the power in question and with other principles of Community law.[15]

Once the correct approach is understood, it will be clear why it is not possible, and would indeed be misleading, to provide a listing by subject of matters for which the EC is competent.[16] It will also become apparent that the role of the ECJ in interpreting EC law has been of crucial importance.[17]

1. Identify the subject matter

The first point is to identify the subject matter at issue. In the nature of things this will be a particular aspect of a general subject matter. Identification is not just a formality. The EC institutions and the member states may differ on exactly what is at issue. The power of the ECJ to determine the level of precision or abstraction used in the identification is an important one.

2. Does the subject matter come within an 'express' external relations competence of the EC?

In respect of any subject matter it is necessary to examine the express terms of the EC Treaties and Acts of Accession.[18] Those terms may give authority for the EC to enter into international agreements or to cooperate with international organizations. The number of these express provisions has been significantly expanded as the Community has been given additional

---

[15.] See Macleod, Hendry and Hyett, *The External Relations of the European Communities*, p. 38.

[16.] Cf. Similarly, in relation to requests for listings of matters in which the EC has exclusive competence. The Reflection Group was not in favour of incorporating a catalogue of the Union's powers in the Treaty. It preferred to maintain the present system. See Reflection Group's Progress Report, Doc. SN509/1/95, Rev. 1 (Reflex 10) (Brussels, 1 September 1995), p. 36; Reflection Group's Final Report, Doc. SN520/95 (Brussels, 5 December 1995), p. 125.

[17.] See A. Barav, 'The Division of External Relations Powers between the European Community and the Member States in the Case-law of the Court of Justice', in Timmermans and Völker (eds) *Division of Powers between the European Communities and their Member States in the Field of External Relations*, (Deventer, Kluwer, 1981) pp. 29–64.

[18.] See the listing in s. 2 of European Communities Act 1972, as amended. On Community Treaties and Accession Treaties up to 1990 see A.G. Toth, *Oxford Encyclopedia of European Community Law* (Oxford, OUP, 1990), pp. 3–9, 103–13.

competencies.[19] The most important[20] of the express author-
izations to enter into international agreements relate to:

(a) the common commercial policy (Article 113);
(b) cooperation on environmental matters (Article 130r(4));
(c) cooperation on development policy (Article 130y);[21]
(d) what have come to be known generically as 'association
     agreements' (Article 238).[22]

It is crucial to comprehend that, at this stage, the focus of analysis
in a question regarding express powers will be on the interpretation of these Articles. Their scope varies widely and it is that
scope which determines the extent of the external relations power.
This task of interpretation may fall to the ECJ and, indeed, there is
substantial jurisprudence on some of the relevant Articles.[23] In
general terms, the ECJ has adopted the same kind of purposive,
teleological interpretation of the Treaty and Acts as in other
fields.[24] So, for example, the concept of the common commercial
policy (CCP) has been widely interpreted. However, for long
periods the scope of the CCP was the subject of intense political
and academic debate.[25] Major controversies have concerned the

19. See F. Dehousse and G. Katelyne, 'Le Traité De Maastricht et les Relations
    Extérieures de la Communauté Européenne' (1994) 5 EJIL, 151–72; ch. 1, pp.
    10–20 above.
20. Other provisions deal with monetary or foreign exchange regimes (Article
    109(3)), implementation of multiannual framework programmes for
    cooperation in research, etc (Article 130m).
21. Before this provision was added by the TEU, development cooperation had to
    be based on Articles 113 and 235 unless it fell within an association agreement.
    See the very important decision in n. 34 below.
22. As replaced by the TEU.
23. See F. Jacobs, 'Judicial Review of Commercial Policy Measures After the
    Uruguay Round', in Emiliou and O'Keeffe (eds), *The European Union and
    World Trade Law – After the GATT Uruguay Round*, 329–42 (1996).
24. See J. Bengoetxea, *The Legal Reasoning of the European Court of Justice:
    Towards a European Jurisprudence* (Oxford, OUP, 1993).
25. See C.-D. Ehlermann, 'The Scope of Article 113 of the EEC Treaty', in
    Mélanges Offerts à Pierre-Henri Teitgen (Paris, Pedone, 1984), 148–69;
    J. Bourgeois, 'The Common Commercial Policy: Scope and Nature of the Powers',
    in E.L.M. Völker (ed.) *Protectionism and the European Community*, 2nd edn
    (Deventer, Kluwer, 1986); M. Cremona, 'The Completion of the Internal Market
    and the Incomplete Commercial Policy of the European Community' (1990) 15
    ELRev, 283–97; M. Maresceau (ed.), *The European Community's Commercial
    Policy after 1992: The Legal Dimension* (Dordrecht, Nijhoff, 1993); P. Eeckhout,
    The European Internal Market and International Trade (Oxford, Clarendon Press,
    1994); D. Chalmers, 'Legal Basis and External Relations of the European
    Community', in N. Emiliou and D. O'Keeffe (eds), *The European Union and
    World Trade Law – After the GATT Uruguay Round* (Chichester, Wiley, 1996);
    P.S.R.F. Mathijsen, *A Guide to European Union Law*, 6th edn (London, Sweet
    and Maxwell, 1995), pp. 366–89.

different forms of provision of services,[26] intellectual property,[27] air transport,[28] and maritime transport.[29] The scope of the 'common commercial policy' was at the heart of *Opinion 1/94* on the World Trade Organization Agreements (WTO).[30]

There have been a number of cases concerning an 'association agreement'.[31] In the *European Development Fund*[32] case the scope of 'development aid' was in issue. In the *Bangladesh* case [33] the issue was that of 'humanitarian aid'.[34] As well as the express wording of each Article, the whole context and scheme of the Treaty is important.[35] We outlined this scheme in Chapter 1.[36] The relationship between different Articles and different objectives of the EC is important. So, in *Opinion 1/94* (WTO), the ECJ drew attention to the distinction in Article 3 between 'common commercial policy' and 'measures concerning the treatment of

26. See P. Mengozzi, 'Trade in Services and Commercial Policy' in Maresceau (ed.), *The European Community's Commercial Policy after 1992*, pp. 223–47.

27. See I. Govaere, 'Intellectual Property Protection and Commercial Policy', in Maresceau (ed.), *The European Community's Commercial Policy after 1992*, pp. 197–222; P. Demiray, 'Intellectual Property and the External Power of the European Community: The New Dimension' (1994) 16 Mich.JIL, 187–239.

28. See J. Balfour, 'Freedom to Provide Air Transport Services in the EEC' (1989) 14 ELRev, 30–46; G. Close, 'External Relations in the Air Transport Sector: Air Transport Policy or the Common Commercial Policy?' (1990) 27 CMLRev, 108–27; P. Haanappel, 'The External Aviation Relations of the European Economic Community and of EEC Member States into the Twenty-First Century' (1989) 14 Air Law, 122–46; *Conduct of the Community's External Aviation Relations*, House of Lords Select Committee on the European Communities, 9th Report 1990–91, HL39.

29. See D. Charles Le Bihan and J. Lebullenger, 'Common Maritime Transport Policy: Bilateral Agreements and the Freedom to Provide Services' (1990) 9 YEL 1989, 209–23.

30. [1994] ECR I-5267. See M. Hilf, 'The ECJ's Opinion on the WTO – No Surprise, but Wise? (1995) 6 EJIL, 245–59; P.J. Kuijper, 'The Conclusion and Implementation of the Uruguay Round Results by the EC' (1995) 6 EJIL, 222–44; A. Arnull, 'The Scope of the Common Commercial Policy: A Coda on Opinion 1/94', in Emiliou and O'Keeffe (eds) *The European Union and World Trade Law – After the GATT Uruguay Round*, pp. 343–60; A. Appella, 'Constitutional Aspects of Opinion 1/94 of the ECJ Concerning the WTO Agreement, (1996) 45 ICLQ, 440–62.

31. See especially Case 12/86, *Demirel v Stadt Schwäbisch Gmund* [1987] ECR 3719. On the range of Association Agreements see ch. 10 below.

32. Case C-316/91, *Parliament v Council* [1994] ECR I-625.

33. Cases C-181/91 and C-248/91, *Parliament v Council and Commission* [1993] ECR I-3885.

34. See also Case C-268/94, *Portugal v Council*, 'mere inclusion of provisions for cooperation in a specific field does not therefore necessarily imply a general power such as to lay down the basis of a competence to undertake any kind of cooperation in that field', pr. 47.

35. See also the Joined Cases 3, 4 and 6/76, *Kramer and Others* [1976] ECR 1279 (hereinafter *Kramer Case*), prs. 19–20.

36. See ch. 1, pp. 17–20 above.

nationals of non-member countries'.[37] Similarly, the existence of different 'Titles' in the Treaty is relevant:[38]

> More generally, the existence in the Treaty of specific chapters on the free movement of natural and legal persons shows that these matters do not fall within the common commercial policy.[39] . . . Turning next to the particular services comprised in transport, these are the subject of a specific title (Title IV) of the Treaty, distinct from Title VII on the common commercial policy.[40]

The substantive content of EC legislation and the legislative practice of the EC is also relevant to interpretation, but they need to be examined in context. In *Opinion 1/94* (WTO) both the Commission and the member states sought to rely on the legislative practice on application of embargoes, which were based on Article 113, to support their arguments as to whether international agreements of a commercial nature in relation to transport fell within the CCP. The ECJ ruled that –

> since the embargoes related primarily to the export and import of products, they could not have been effective if it had not been decided at the same time to suspend transport services. Such suspension is to be seen as a necessary adjunct to the principal measure. Consequently, the precedents are not relevant to the question whether the Community has exclusive competence pursuant to Article 113 to conclude international agreements in the field of transport.[41]

The ECJ went on to note that, in any event, '[A] mere practice [of the Council][42] cannot derogate from the rules laid down in the Treaty and cannot, therefore, create a precedent binding on Community institutions with regard to the correct legal basis'.[43]

---

37. *Opinion 1/94* (WTO), pr. 46. For criticisms of this approach to the determination of competence see Tridimas and Eeckhout (1995) 14 YEL 1994, 143–77; N. Neuwahl, 'The WTO Opinion and The Implied External Powers of the Community – A Hidden Agenda? (1996, unpublished).
38. See ch. 1, pp. 17–20 above on the structure of the EC Treaty.
39. Ibid.   40. *Opinion 1/94* (WTO), pr. 48.
41. *Opinion 1/94* (WTO), pr. 51.
42. Or, presumably, of any other EC institution.
43. WTO, pr. 52. See also prs. 61–71 in the context of TRIPs. 'Institutional practice in relation to autonomous measures or external agreements cannot alter this conclusion', pr. 61; Case 68/86, *UK v Council* [1988] ECR 855, pr. 24. See also Case C-292/89, *R v Immigration Appeal Tribunal, ex p Antonissen* [1991] ECR I-745 on the legal significance of a declaration in the Council minutes. In international law such institutional practice is given greater weight, see Article 31 VCLT (1969).

In addition, the concept of 'institutional balance' may be a factor.[44] In *Opinion 1/94* (WTO) the ECJ looked at the competence of the EC in relation to internal legislation on harmonization in the field of intellectual property. Measures were subject to different voting rules and different rules of procedure (consultation or joint-decision making with the EP) from those under the common commercial policy (Article 113). The ECJ stated that, if the EC had exclusive competence to enter into agreements with non-member countries to harmonize the protection of intellectual property and, at the same time, to achieve harmonization at Community level, the Community institutions would be able 'to escape the internal constraints to which they are subject in relation to procedures and to rules on voting'.[45]

3. Other international activities for which there is express provision

In the areas of education, vocational training and youth,[46] culture[47] and public health[48] there are no express references to international agreements. However, there is a more limited power for the Community and the member states to 'foster cooperation' with third countries and international organizations. It would seem that there is a power to enter into international agreements within that limited scope.[49]

4. Cooperation with international organizations

A number of Treaty Articles make provision for this. For ease of analysis, and to keep the focus on competence to enter into international agreements, these were considered in Chapter 2, above.

---

44. See ch. 1, p. 14, n. 29 above; Case C-327/91, *France v Commission* [1994] ECR I-3641, prs. 28 and 41.
45. *Opinion 1/94* (WTO), prs. 59–60.
46. Articles 126(3), 127(3).
47. Article 128(3).
48. Article 129(3).
49. See Macleod, Hendry and Hyett, *The External Relations of the European Communites*, pp. 47–8. Analogous reasoning can be applied to Article 129c(3) on cooperation to promote projects of mutual interest and to ensure the interoperability of trans-European networks in the areas of transport, telecommunications and energy infrastructures.

5. Is the competence of the EC to enter into international agreements restricted to the express provisions considered above?

Such a restriction would appear to be logical. If a Treaty contains a very limited number of express powers, the intention of the authors of that Treaty might well be thought to have been to preclude any assertion of more extensive powers.[50] This conclusion is reinforced when the parties only gradually extend the number of express powers. In the Treaty of Rome (1958), apart from the provisions on cooperation with international organizations, there were only express powers to enter into international agreements in relation to the CCP (Article 113) and association agreements (Article 238). In line with the perfectly defensible reasoning indicated above, the member states, the Council, and the Advocate-General in the leading case (ERTA),[51] took the view that the EC's powers were so limited. Some respectable academic opinion was in support.[52] However, this view did not prevail. It was eventually overwhelmed by the jurisprudential weight of the *doctrine of parallelism*.

6. The doctrine of parallelism

The essence of this doctrine is not sophisticated.[53] It asserts that the competence of the EC to enter into international agreements should run in 'parallel' with the development of its internal competence – *in interno in foro externo*. As the internal competence develops, so the external competence automatically develops. The doctrine expressly appears in Article 101(1) of the Euratom Treaty: 'The Community may, within the limits of its powers and jurisdiction, enter into obligations by concluding agreements or contracts with a third State, an international organization or a national of a third State.'[54] That a similar provision does not appear in the Treaty of Rome, negotiated and signed at the same time, was a strong argument for it not being applicable.

---

50. Particularly when compared with Article 101 of Euratom, see text to n. 54 below.
51. See *ERTA Case*, Case 22/70, *Commission v Council* [1971] ECR 263 at pp. 265–72, 284–95.
52. See P. Pescatore, 'Les Relations Extèrieures des Communautés Européennes 103 *Recueil Des Cours*, (1961–II) 1–244.
53. See J. Groux, 'Le parallèlisme des compétences internes et externes de la Communanté économique européenne' (1978) Cahiers de droit européenne, 3–32.
54. On the ECSC and Euratom see Macleod, Hendry and Hyett, *The External Relations of the European Communities*, pp. 42–4.

The logic of the doctrine runs as follows. If the EC has an internal law making power it should also be able to conclude international agreements in that field. The basis of this argument is said to lie in the theory of implied powers.[55] This is more of an assertion than a reason. More convincing, perhaps, is the argument that if the EC has adopted internal rules in a given area, then a member state should not be able to undermine those rules by entering into an international agreement with a third state or with an international organization. Taking account of the EC's contemporary jurisprudence, a member state would also arguably be in breach of Article 5 in such a situation.[56] On the principle of parallel competence, Dashwood helpfully comments that:

> I am not sure whether, after all, it is right to treat this as a recognition of implied Community powers, although that is how the Court itself seems to regard the matter. To my mind, the logic of implied powers is that they relate to matters which, it is assumed, would have been specifically mentioned in the text, if draftsmen were infinitely wise and prescient. Here, I suggest, the logic is different. The failure to mention external powers in the Treaty provisions on agriculture or transport, say, is not because the matter slipped the draftsman's mind: it is because to confer powers in these policy areas that stopped short at the Community's frontiers would simply not have made any sense. In other words, a text that is silent on its external application should not be interpreted as one that expressly confers internal powers only: the natural way of interpreting an express grant of powers is that they are to apply as needed, internally or externally, in furtherance of the objectives specified in the relevant Treaty Articles.[57]

The leading case on the doctrine of parallelism, and indeed on the whole field of external relations, is the *ERTA Case*.[58] Its importance merits separate analysis. It is important to bear in mind, though, that the implied powers basis of the ERTA doctrine of external competence does not mean that it is irrelevant whether or not express powers are conferred. On the contrary, the doctrine requires close examination of the express terms of the Treaty. Express limitations on internal powers are thus reflected in a

[55]. See T.C. Hartley, *The Foundations of European Community Law*, 3rd edn (Oxford, Clarendon Press, 1994), pp. 110–11; Dashwood (1996) 21 ELRev, pp. 124–6.
[56]. See J. Temple Lang, 'Community Constitutional Law: Article 5 EEC Treaty' (1990) 27 CMLRev, 645–81.
[57]. Dashwood (1996) 21 ELRev, p. 125.
[58]. Case 22/70, *Commission v Council* [1971] ECR 263.

limitation on implied external powers, for example, by ruling out the possibility of harmonization, or by expressly providing for member states to have continuing competence.

The ERTA Case (1970): Case 22/70, Commission v Council[59]

Although the principles established in this case are now accepted by the member states,[60] it is helpful to bear in mind that, at the time, it was regarded as one of the ECJ's most startling and controversial decisions. The judgment 'produced shockwaves among national bureaucrats and politicians'.[61] The case concerned the negotiations for an international Treaty, the European Road Transport Agreement (ERTA), which would harmonize certain social provisions relating to road transport. In particular, these related to travel and rest periods for drivers. Negotiations had taken place since 1962 and an agreement had been reached and signed,[62] but it did not attract sufficient participation to come into force. Negotiations for a revised ERTA began in 1967. Both sets of negotiations were conducted solely by the member states. In 1969, while the negotiations were continuing, the EC adopted an internal measure, Regulation 543/69,[63] concerning the harmonization of certain social provisions in the field of road transport. The Commission then took the view that it should have the right to negotiate the ERTA on behalf of the EC. It therefore challenged a 'Resolution' adopted in the Council to the effect that the member states would continue as negotiators.[64] Essentially, the *ERTA Case* could then have been limited to the significance for the conduct of external relations when an internal measure has been adopted.[65]

---

59. Ibid.
60. See the Declarations to the SEA and the TEU that particular provisions of the EC Treaty were not to be understood as undermining the application of the ERTA principles.
61. See E. Stein, 'External Relations of the European Community: Structure and Process', Academy of European Law, European University Institute, Florence, 1990, vol I, 115–88, p. 160. See also J.H. Weiler, 'The Transformation of Europe' (1991) 101 Yale LJ, p. 2416.
62. More precisely, five of the then six member states had signed it.
63. L77/49, [1969] I OJ Special Edition p. 170.
64. The ECJ treated the resolution as an act *sui generis* and so capable of annulment.
65. It could have been even more limited as the internal measure itself made provisions for the EC to reach international agreements in the field and therefore could have been dealt with simply as an express power, see above.

As so often, though, the ECJ stated principles of more general and radical application.

The ECJ began by considering the situation where there was an 'absence of specific provisions of the Treaty' relating to Treaty making power in the area concerned – in this case, transport policy. In such a situation:

[12] . . . one must turn to the general system of Community law in the sphere of relations with third countries.

[13] Article 210 provides that 'The Community shall have legal personality'.

[14] This provision, placed at the head of Part Six of the Treaty, devoted to 'General and Final Provisions', means that in its external relations the Community enjoys the capacity to establish contractual links with third countries over the whole field of objectives defined in Part One of the Treaty, which Part Six supplements.

To pause here, this is purposive, teleological interpretation at its finest. It is building a legal edifice on straw. In the Treaty there was no 'general system of Community law in the sphere of relations with third countries'.[66] There were merely a small number of express provisions. This would suggest that there was no intention to create a general system for such relations.[67] Even if this is true, given the ECJ's approach to interpretation, the determination of this intention is not so crucial.[68] Moreover, that the EC has 'legal personality' is a completely separate issue from the extent of the field over which it has 'capacity' to enter into international agreements. It certainly does not 'mean' that the EC has an extensive external relations capacity. The ECJ considered Article 210 'as being not only a statement on the civil capacity of the Community, but also a claim to international personality'.[69] What the ECJ did was what the drafters of the EC Treaty had not done, that is, given the EC an external relations competence that ran in *parallel* with its internal competence.[70] The ECJ had accepted the arguments of the Commission over those of the

---

66. The ECJ again used this expression in the *Kramer Case*, pr. 16.
67. See pp. 43–7 above on 'express provisions'.
68. See P. Craig and G. De Burca, *EC Law – Text, Cases and Materials* (Oxford, OUP, 1995), pp. 79–88. The travaux préparatoires to the Treaties were deliberately never published.
69. See P. Pescatore, 'External Relations in the Case Law of the Court of Justice of the European Communities' (1979) 16 CMLRev, 615–45, p. 641.
70. See pp. 48–50 above.

member states, the Council and the Advocate-General in the *ERTA Case*.

The ECJ continued:

> [15] To determine in a particular case the Community's authority to enter into international agreements, regard must be had to the whole scheme of the Treaty no less than its substantive provisions.

A distinction is drawn here between the EC's 'capacity', which covers the whole field of objectives in Part One of the Treaty, and its 'authority' to enter into international agreements. The latter must be a limitation on the former. The scope and nature of any particular agreement must be examined to determine whether the EC has authority to enter into it.

This 'authority', the ECJ continued:

> [16] . . . arises not only from an express conferment by the Treaty – as is the case with Articles 113 and 114 for tariff and trade agreements and with Article 238 for association agreements – but may equally flow from other provisions of the Treaty and from measures adopted – within the framework of those provisions, by the Community institutions.

Express conferment of authority has been considered above.[71] The ERTA judgment gives two other sources of authority.

'Other provisions of the Treaty'

First, 'other provisions of the Treaty'. In effect, these can imply authority to enter international agreements. In subsequent cases the word 'implicitly' is added after 'flow', and the Acts of Accession are added as other sources from which this authority can implicitly flow.[72] This 'implied' source of authority is significant in that it is not dependent on internal EC measures having been taken.[73] However, as we will see below, in subsequent cases the ECJ has significantly restricted the possibility of using an implied external competence in the absence of internal measures.[74]

---

71. See pp. 43–7 above.
72. *Kramer Case*, prs. 19–20; *Opinion 2/91* (ILO), pr. 7. There have been three such 'acts of accession' – 1972, 1986 and 1994.
73. See pp. 58–61 below.
74. See pp. 58–61 below on *Opinion 1/76* (Rhine Navigation Case) and *Opinion 1/94* (WTO).

In the *Kramer Case*, considered below, the ECJ reviewed the Treaty texts and the measures adopted. However, it also made a more general statement:

> The only way to ensure the conservation of the biological resources of the sea both effectively and equitably is through a system of rules binding on all the states concerned, including non-member countries. In these circumstances it follows from the very duties and powers which Community law has established and assigned to the institutions of the Community on the internal level that the Community has the authority to enter into international commitments for the conservation of the resources of the sea.[75]

This general statement referring to duties and powers under EC law, rather than measures taken, can be read to mean that there would have been an EC Treaty making competence even in the absence of any internal measures, justified principally by the need to make the conservation policy effective.[76] However, the practical significance of this independent, implied source of authority is limited because of the fact that there are EC measures over such a massive range of activities. Implied authority could conceivably be of importance when the EC receives new competencies, for example, as under the SEA and the TEU.[77] However, these new competencies commonly reflect existing EC practices developed using Article 235 alone or in conjunction with other Articles. So there are often already EC internal measures when these new competencies are expressly added. Moreover, it is rare for the EC to seek to proceed first by way of international agreement rather than by internal measures.[78]

---

75. *Kramer Case*, prs. 30–3. On the facts of the *Kramer Case* the ECJ achieved a pragmatic outcome by upholding the national conservation measures which had been taken.

76. Macleod, Hendry and Hyett, *The External Relations of the European Communities*, suggest that the same argument could be made for the EC's powers to regulate competition, 'the nature of the Community's internal power as regulator precludes the exercise of Member State competence externally on matters which fall within the Community's competition jurisdiction', p. 53. See *Opinion 1/92* (Second EEA Opinion) [1992] ECR I-2821, prs. 40–1 on EC's power to enter into agreements on competition matters; Case C-327/91, *France v Commission* [1994] ECR I-3641 on the US-EC Competition Agreement.

77. See ch. 1, pp. 11–20 above.

78. But note that the EC had Fisheries Agreements with Norway and other Scandinavian countries before it had a Common Fisheries Policy. See Macleod, Hendry and Hyett, *The External Relations of the European Communities*, pp. 241–52.

'Measures adopted – within the framework of those provisions, by the Community institutions'

Secondly, authority can flow from 'other measures adopted' by EC institutions within the framework of those other provisions of the Treaty. 'Measures', in this context, means legislative measures, that is, Regulations or Directives. In the *ERTA Case*, after referring to this source of authority, the ECJ continued:

> [17] In particular, each time the Community, with a view to implementing a common policy envisaged by the Treaty, adopts provisions laying down common rules, whatever form these might take, the Member States no longer have the right, acting individually or even collectively, to undertake obligations with third countries which affect those rules.
> [18] As and when such common rules come into being, the Community alone is in a position to assume and carry out contractual obligations towards third countries affecting the whole sphere of application of the Community legal system.
> [19] With regard to the implementation of the provisions of the Treaty the system of internal Community measures may not therefore be separated from that of external relations.

Applying this approach in the *ERTA Case*, the ECJ referred to a number of Treaty Articles. In particular, Article 74, according to which the objectives of the Treaty in relation to transport shall be pursued 'within the framework of a common transport policy'. Also to Article 75, which directs the Council, inter alia, to lay down 'common rules applicable to international transport to or from the territory of a Member State or passing across the territory of one or more Member States', and 'any other appropriate provisions'. It continued:

> [26] This provision is equally concerned with transport from or to third countries, as regards that part of the journey which takes place on Community territory.
> [27] It thus assumes that the powers of the Community extend to relationships arising from international law, and hence involve the need in the sphere in question for agreements with the third countries concerned.
> [28] Although it is true that Articles 74 and 75 do not expressly confer on the Community authority to enter into international agreements, nevertheless the bringing into force, on 25 March 1969,

of Regulation No. 543/69 of the Council on the harmonization of certain social legislation relating to road transport . . . necessarily vested in the Community power to enter into any agreements with third countries relating to the subject-matter governed by that regulation.

Since the subject matter of the ERTA fell within that of Regulation 543/69, the competence to negotiate and conclude the ERTA passed to the Community when that Regulation entered into force. Even though it lost the case on the merits, and for practical reasons the member states were allowed to complete the negotiations,[79] the Commission's argument about the external relations competence of the Community had been successful. We must then consider exactly what principle the ERTA Case established, particularly in the light of subsequent ECJ rulings and subsequent EC practice.[80] We will observe that, although the principles of ERTA are accepted, member states have used a number of legal strategies to mitigate its application.[81]

We now need to analyse the principles articulated by the ECJ in paragraphs 17–19 of the *ERTA Case*. Those principles are another expression of the doctrine of parallelism. In some cases the internal measure 'expressly recognizes' the EC's power to negotiate with third countries for the purpose of implementing the internal measure.[82] This, indeed, was the situation in the *ERTA Case* itself, where Article 3 of Regulation 543/69 recognized this power.[83] It is crucially important, however, to note that this is merely a *recognition* of competence. It is not a *conferment* of it. An express provision on competence within an internal measure is obviously helpful in terms of clarity, but the competence would arise even in its absence.[84] In ERTA the competence appeared to arise from the passing of the internal measure. This 'necessarily vested' in the EC the external competence. However, as we consider below, subsequent decisions have shown that, in some circumstances, external competence may arise even without the passing of an internal measure.[85]

79. Another pragmatic outcome to a crucial judgment on principle.
80. See the declarations referred to in n. 60 above.
81. See Stein, op. cit., p. 160.
82. See *Opinion 1/94* (WTO), prs. 94–5, giving examples. Such a measure must not conflict with the EC Treaty.
83. ERTA, pr. 29.
84. See ERTA, *Opinion 2/91* (ILO) and *Opinion 1/94* (WTO).
85. See pp. 58–61 below.

In ERTA the ECJ referred to 'provisions laying down common rules' adopted by the EC with a view to 'implementing a common policy' envisaged by the Treaty. As we will see below, the nature of the internal measures adopted or capable of being adopted, i.e., whether they are 'common rules' or set 'minimum standards', is relevant to whether the competence of the EC is exclusive or not. It is not relevant to the conferring of competence in the EC.

One of the supposedly clear cases on implied powers is the *Kramer Case*.[86] A number of Dutch fishermen were subject to criminal proceedings for infringing national fishing quotas. Those quotas had been adopted on the basis of the provisions of a Fisheries Convention.[87] The questions referred to the ECJ included that of whether the member states had retained the power to adopt such national rules. In reply, the ECJ referred to the Treaty provision on the adoption of a common agricultural policy as an objective of the EC (Article 3(d)); the specific Articles on that policy (Articles 39–46); two internal measures on fisheries policy (Regulation 2141/70 laying down a common structural policy for the fishing industry and Regulation 2142/70 on the common organization of the market in fisheries products); and Article 102 of the Act of Accession 1972, which provided for the Council to determine conditions for fishing with a view to ensuring protection of the fishing grounds and conservation of the biological resources of the sea. These provisions, taken as a whole, gave the EC the power at the *internal level* to take any measure for the conservation of the biological resources of the sea. The ECJ then stated that it was 'clear' that it followed from Article 102 of the Act of Accession, from Article 1 of Regulation 2141/70 and 'moreover from the very nature of things', that the rule making authority of the Community *ratione materiae* also extends – in so far as the member states have similar authority under public international law – to fishing on the high seas.

The ECJ continued with the quotation cited above.[88] From the 'whole scheme' of Community law relating to the subject matter it found that the EC has external competence. However, which of the components of that scheme of law are decisive? Would it be enough if there was an EC objective but no specific Treaty Articles

86. Joined Cases 3, 4 and 6/76, *Kramer and Others* [1976] ECR 1279. See A.W. Koers, 'The External Authority of the EEC in Regard to Marine Fisheries' (1977) 14 CMLRev, 269–301.
87. The North East Atlantic Fisheries Convention (1959).
88. See p. 54 above.

on that objective?[89] Is it the existence of specific Treaty Articles that is crucial?[90] Is it the taking of internal measures, the Regulations in this case, which is crucial? The judgment in ERTA seemed to suggest that this was the case. Or is it 'the very nature of things', which is not explained, but may be a reference to the ECJ's view that 'a system of rules binding on all states' was the only way to 'effectively and equitably' ensure the conservation of the biological resources of the sea? As a general statement this is undoubtedly true. However, it does not necessarily follow that the EC must therefore have competence to commit itself and the member states to those binding rules. The member states could equally have competence to commit themselves. If the member states exercised such a competence, a system of binding conservation rules could be established. The ECJ could have said that some limited external competence was actually necessary for the EC effectively to support its common fisheries policy. Such an argument would be defensible. However, its assertion of a much more general external competence over the whole field of fisheries conservation anywhere in the world is more difficult to support in principle. The ECJ gave an example of the necessity for exclusive EC competence to be given in *Opinion 1/94* (WTO). It referred to the need, in the context of effective conservation, to be able to apply restrictions to 'vessels flying the flag of a non-member country *bordering on the same seas*'.[91] This makes evident sense, but why should the principle necessarily be extended to relations with states whose waters do not border the same seas?

Macleod, Hendry and Hyett suggest that *Kramer* can be read to mean that there would have been an EC Treaty making competence, even in the absence of any internal measures, flowing simply from the power to establish a common fisheries policy. Effective control of Community fishing stocks necessitated such a power.[92] They also suggest that the same is 'probably true' in relation to the EC's power to regulate competition.[93]

89. This is the case for one of the competencies added by the TEU.
90. That is, the Articles of the EC or those of the Acts of Accession.
91. *Opinion 1/94* (WTO), pr. 85 (emphasis added).
92. Macleod, Hendry and Hyett, *The External Relations of the European Communities*, p. 53.
93. Ibid., pp. 53, 75. See n. 76 above. The argument here is the *Opinion 1/76* (Rhine Navigation Case) doctrine turned the other way. It is now the Community's participation in the international system which is necessary for the particular EC policy to be effective. The reasoning in *Opinion 1/94* (WTO), considered at pp. 59–61 below, would suggest a strict approach to this kind of thinking.

Some of these issues are raised by considering the situation where the EC has powers to pass internal measures but these have not been exercised. If there are no EC internal measures, can the EC still have external competence? If the answer is 'yes', this suggests that it is the existence of specific Treaty Articles which is crucial. If the answer is 'no', then it is the passing of internal measures which is crucial. In its *Opinion 1/76* (Rhine Navigation Case)[94] the ECJ clearly stated that external relations competence can be implied in certain circumstances even when no internal measures have been taken. *Opinion 1/76* concerned a draft international agreement which would have established a 'European Laying-Up Fund For Inland Waterway Vessels', which used the Rhine and Moselle rivers. The international agreement was concerned with a scheme to eliminate over-capacity on certain inland waterways. As well as six of the then nine member states, Switzerland had to be involved in the negotiations as its vessels were users of the relevant waterways. The EC had competence under the EC Treaty provisions on transport to pass an internal measure. However, this alone would have had no application to Switzerland and so was inappropriate to dealing with the problem. According to the ECJ, this absence of any internal measure did not prevent the EC from having competence to conclude the agreement:

> Although the internal Community measures are only adopted when the international agreement is concluded and made enforceable, as is envisaged in the present case by the proposal for a regulation to be submitted to the Council by the Commission, the power to bind the Community *vis-à-vis* third countries nevertheless flows by implication from the provisions of the Treaty creating the internal power and in so far as participation of the Community in the international agreement is, as here, necessary for the attainment of one of the objectives of the Community.[95]

So the implication flows simply from the existence of the internal power. Some uncertainly was, however, raised by the possibility that the concluding words of this paragraph put a limitation on this implied competence. Was the external competence implied only when its exercise would allow the Community to participate in an international agreement that was 'necessary for the

[94]. *Opinion 1/76* (Rhine Navigation Case) [1977] ECR 741. See M. Hardy, 'Opinion 1/76 of the Court of Justice' (1977) 14 CMLRev, 561–600.
[95]. *Opinion 1/76* (Rhine Navigation Case), pr. 4.

attainment of one of the objectives of the Community'? In the agreement at issue in *Opinion 1/76* (Rhine Navigation Case), such participation was necessary because of the need to bring Switzerland into the proposed scheme. The possibility of this being the correct interpretation was heightened by the terms of *Opinion 2/91* (ILO), in which the implied power of external competence was stated to arise, 'whenever Community law created for the institutions of the Community powers within its internal system for the purpose of obtaining a *specific objective* . . .'.[96] The addition of the word 'specific' made this a slightly narrower formulation of the justification for EC participation given in *Opinion 1/76* (Rhine Navigation Case).[97] Participation by the EC would now only be justified if it was 'necessary' to attain a 'specific objective' of the EC.

The correct interpretation of the *Opinion 1/76* doctrine (Rhine Navigation Case) was partly clarified by the ECJ in *Opinion 1/94* (WTO). In relation to the General Agreement on Trade in Services (GATS), the Commission argued for *exclusive* Community competence on the basis of a number of possible sources. One of these was based on the reasoning in *Opinion 1/76* (Rhine Navigation Case). The Community's participation in the GATS was argued to be, 'necessary for the attainment of one of the objectives of the Community'.[98] Without such participation, the 'coherence of the internal market would be impaired'. In addition, at the external level the EC 'could not allow itself to remain inactive at the international stage'. The need for a WTO agreement reflecting a global approach to international trade was indisputable.[99]

The ECJ rejected this interpretation of *Opinion 1/76* doctrine (Rhine Navigation Case). Participation in the agreement concerned in that case was required because of the position of Switzerland. Common internal rules alone would not have achieved the objective of eliminating short-term over-capacity on the waterways. The ECJ gave another example of where this reasoning would apply –

---

96. *Opinion 2/91* (ILO), pr. 7 (emphasis added).
97. See above.
98. *Opinion 1/94* (WTO), pr. 82.
99. Ibid., pr. 83. None of the governments which submitted observations, nor the Council, made any observations on the need for external action on the part of the EC, prs. 249–50.

in the context of conservation of the resources of the seas, the restriction, by means of internal legislative measures, of fishing on the high seas by vessels flying the same flag of a Member State would hardly be effective if the same restrictions were not to apply to vessels flying the flag of a non-member country bordering on the same seas.[100]

In such situations, external powers could be exercised (and become exclusive) without any internal legislation having been first adopted. However, in the sphere of services this was not the situation because –

> attainment of freedom of establishment and freedom to apply services for nationals of Member States is not inextricably linked to the treatment to be afforded in the Community to nationals of non-member countries or in non-member countries to nationals of Member States of the Community.[101]

The Commission made similar arguments, relying on the *Opinion 1/76* doctrine (Rhine Navigation Case), in relation to the Agreement on Trade Related Intellectual Property Rights (TRIPs).[102] Again, the ECJ rejected the application of the *Opinion 1/76* (Rhine Navigation Case) doctrine to that Agreement because –

> unification or harmonization of intellectual property rights in the Community context does not necessarily have to be accompanied by agreements with non-member countries in order to be effective.[103]

This interpretation of the '*Opinion 1/76* doctrine' (Rhine Navigation Case) makes it crucial to identify what 'Community objectives' are. This can be very difficult, and, indeed, they may appear to conflict. In *Opinion 1/94* (WTO) the ECJ had to consider and explain the scope and objectives of various EC policies and what their objectives were. This obviously leaves considerable room for judicial discretion and the tendency will be for the ECJ to state Community objectives in fairly wide terms. A point of importance here is that the ECJ can be examining the scope of Community objectives that are principally related to the establishment of the common market or the internal market. So, for example, in relation to services, the ECJ took the view that the objective of the various Treaty provisions was 'the attainment of freedom of establishment and freedom to apply services for

---

100. *Opinion 1/94* (WTO), pr. 85.   101. Ibid., pr. 86.
102. Ibid., prs. 83, 99.   103. Ibid., pr. 100.

nationals of Member States'.[104] The objective of the Treaty provisions and legislation on intellectual property was 'unification or harmonization of intellectual property rights in the Community context'.[105] Essentially, then, the ECJ is distinguishing between some situations in which the EC has external objectives which require the participation of third states (use of resources which third states also use, conservation), and internal objectives which can be achieved within the community context without the participation of third states (freedom of establishment and freedom to apply services for nationals of member states, internal harmonization of intellectual property rights). Obviously, the EC also has broader external relations objectives of achieving global agreement on these latter objectives. This is exactly what the GATS and TRIPS tried to do. The distinction which the ECJ draws is that it can achieve its internal objectives in these areas without third party participation. Only if participation of a third state is necessary to achieve that 'objective' will the EC have *exclusive* competence. Does this mean that the *Opinion 1/76* (Rhine Navigation Case) doctrine has been limited to such a situation? If so, this would be a substantial limitation. An alternative reading is that the necessity of third state participation is relevant only to the question of *exclusive* EC competence – this is what the Commission was arguing for in *Opinion 1/94* (WTO).[106] If this is correct, and a number of member states supported it in their submissions in *Opinion 1/94* (WTO),[107] then the general *Opinion 1/76* (Rhine Navigation Case) doctrine remains. The EC has competence to conclude international agreements, even in the absence of internal measures, if EC participation is necessary for the attainment of one of the specific objectives of the Community. However, this competence is not exclusive.[108] Until the competence is exercised, the member states remain competent to enter into international agreements.

---

104. Ibid., prs. 81–6.
105. Ibid., pr. 100.
106. See N. Neuwahl, 'The WTO Opinion and the Implied External Powers of the Community' (unpublished, 1996).
107. *Opinion 1/94* (WTO), s. XII.
108. It could become exclusive by the adoption of internal measures of a certain nature, see pp. 71–5 below.

Competence based on general provisions: Articles 235, 100 or 100a[109]

Article 235 provides that:

> If action by the Community should prove necessary to attain, in the course of operation of the common market, one of the objectives of the Community and this Treaty has not provided the necessary powers, the Council shall . . . take the appropriate measures.

This is clearly a broad power and it has been used extensively and imaginatively by the Council, for example, in developing EC environmental law before Treaty amendments added environmental provisions.[110] The member states are in a powerful position under Article 235, as it requires unanimity in the Council and merely the consultation of the Parliament. Member states have sometimes sought to take advantage of Article 235 and take measures based on it that could properly have been taken under other Articles of the Treaty.[111] So the ECJ has had to exercise a restraining influence.[112]

Article 235 is not limited to internal measures. Measures can be taken in the field of external relations if they satisfy the terms of the Article.[113] Early EC participation in international environmental Treaties was based on Article 235.[114] A more contemporary example is the use of Article 235 for the Agreement establishing the European Bank for Reconstruction and Development.[115] External measures taken under Article 235 should not

---

109. On Article 235 see Macleod, Hendry and Hyett op. cit., pp. 53–5; Dashwood (1996) 21 ELRev, pp. 123–4. See also the discussion in Case C-268/94, *Portugal v Council* [1996] ECR nyr.
110. The SEA and the TEU extended the competencies of the EC. See L. Kramer, *EC Treaty and Environmental Law*, 2nd edn (London, Sweet and Maxwell, 1994). If measures fall within those new powers there should be no resort to Article 235 because the Treaty does now provide the 'necessary powers'. See the Opinion of A-G La Pergola in Case C-271/91, *Parliament v Council* (22 November 1995).
111. See G. Close, 'Harmonisation of Laws: Use or Abuse of the Powers under the EEC Treaty?' (1978) 3 ELRev, 461–81; Hartley, *The Foundations of European Community Law*, 3rd edn, pp. 111–19.
112. See Case 45/86, *Commission v Council* [1987] ECR 1493; Case 165/87, *Commission v Council* [1988] ECR 5545.
113. See Case 22/70, ERTA, pr. 95; *Opinion 1/94* (WTO); *Opinion 2/94* (ECHR), considered below.
114. See, for example, Decision 81/462 approving the conclusion of the Bonn Convention on the Conservation of Migratory Species of Wild Animals, [1981] OJ L171/11.
115. Decision 90/674, [1990] OJ L372/1.

conflict with express terms of the Treaty which prohibit harmonization[116] or specify that certain matter fall within the responsibility of member states.[117]

In *Opinion 2/94* (ECHR) the opinion was concerned with whether accession by the EC to the European Convention on Human Rights would be compatible with the EC Treaty.[118] There was a consensus among the institutions and the member states that the only possible legal basis was Article 235.[119] However, the ECJ took the view that:

> That provision, being an integral part of an institutional system based on the principle of conferred powers, cannot serve as a basis for widening the scope of Community powers beyond the general framework created by the provisions of the Treaty as a whole and, in particular, by those that define the tasks and the activities of the Community. On any view, Article 235 cannot be used as a basis for the adoption of provisions whose effect would, in substance be to amend the Treaty without following the procedure which it provides for that purpose.[120]

The ECJ referred to various declarations of the member states and of the Community institutions on the importance of respect for human rights, references to human rights in the EC Treaty, the SEA and the TEU, and to its own jurisprudence on fundamental rights forming an integral part of the general principles of law whose observance the ECJ ensures.[121] It concluded that:

> Respect for human rights is therefore a precondition of the lawfulness of Community acts. Accession to the Convention would, however, entail a substantial change in the present Community system for the protection of human rights in that it would entail the entry of the Community into a distinct international institutional system as well as integration of all of the provisions of the Convention into the Community legal order.
>
> Such a modification of the system for the protection of human rights in the Community, with equally fundamental institutional implications for the Community and for the Member States, would

116. See, for example, Articles 128(5) and 129(4) excluding harmonization in relation to culture and public health requirements.
117. See Article 126 on education. Member states are responsible for the content of teaching and the organization of education systems, and their cultural and linguistic diversity.
118. *Opinion 2/94* (ECHR) [1996] ECR nyr (28 March 1996).
119. Ibid., p. 7.
120. Ibid., pr. 30.
121. Ibid., prs. 32–3.

be of constitutional significance and would therefore be such as to go beyond the scope of Article 235. It could be brought about only by way of Treaty amendment.

It must therefore be held that, as community law now stands, the Community has no competence to accede to the Convention.[122]

Whether human rights provisions should be inserted into the EC Treaty is one of the issues being considered by the IGC.[123] If they are inserted then they will bring some degree of external competence in accordance with the approach to specific provisions considered above.

The Treaty also provides for specific powers concerning harmonization in the context of the common market (Article 100) and the single market (Article 100a).

How does exercise of these internal powers affect external relations?

If measures taken under any of these articles establish common rules, then the EC has exclusive external competence in accordance with the 'ERTA principle'.[124] If the rules were 'minimum rules', rather than 'common rules',[125] then member states could retain an external relations competence. More controversial is the situation where no internal measures have been taken under Articles 235, 100 or 100a. Under the general principle in *Opinion 1/76* (Rhine Navigation Case) the EC could exercise an external relations power based on Articles 235, 100 or 100a, if the participation of the Community in the international agreement is 'necessary for the attainment of one of the objectives of the Community'.[126] In *Opinion 1/94* (WTO) the ECJ drew a distinction between those objectives of the EC that could be achieved by internal measures alone, and those which would require international measures. Freedom of establishment and freedom to provide services for nationals of the member states was not 'inextricably linked' to the treatment to be afforded in the Community to nationals of

---

122. Ibid., prs. 34–6.
123. See Reflection Groups Progress Report (1995), pp. 18–22; Reflection Group's Final Report (1995), pp. 11–15.
124. See pp. 71–5 below.
125. On the distinction see ch. 4, pp. 75–7 below.
126. This makes it important to determine what the objectives of the EC are, see ch. 1, pp. 18–19 above.

non-member countries or in non-member countries to nationals of member states of the Community.[127] The internal objective could be achieved by internal measures alone. Similarly, in the context of intellectual property, 'unification or harmonization of intellectual property rights in the Community context does not necessarily have to be accompanied by agreements with non-member countries in order to be effective'.[128] This is quite a high threshold of 'necessity'. That wider international protection of intellectual property rights is widely agreed to be in the interests of the EC is not sufficient to give the EC exclusive external competence. The terms of Articles 100 and 100a make it more likely, but no more than that, that measures relating to the common market and the internal market respectively could be achieved by internal measures alone. However, Article 235 clearly goes wider and there is a stronger argument for being able to use it as a basis for Community action which is necessary to achieve a Community objective notwithstanding the absence of internal rules.[129] In *Opinion 2/94* (ECHR) the ECJ's opinion that the EC had no competence to accede to the ECHR using Article 235 was based on such accession being of constitutional significance and therefore beyond the scope of Article 235. The opinion is not based on the absence of internal EC rules on human rights.[130]

If Community participation is not 'necessary for the attainment of one of the objectives of the Community', as required by the *Opinion 1/76* (Rhine Navigation Case) doctrine, can these Articles provide a basis for exclusive competence in the absence of internal measures? In *Opinion 1/94* (WTO) the ECJ answered this question in the negative. As regards Article 100a, the ECJ stated that where harmonization powers have been exercised, the measures adopted could limit, or even remove, the freedom of member states to negotiate with non-member countries. However –

> an internal power to harmonize which has not been exercised in a specific field cannot confer exclusive competence in that field on the Community.[131]

---

127. *Opinion 1/94* (WTO), pr. 86.   128. Ibid., pr. 100.
129. Remembering that this must be 'in the course of the operation of the common market'.
130. Of course, certain rights in the EC system also have a human rights quality to them. Macleod, Hendry and Hyett, op. cit., p. 55, note that *Opinion 1/94* (WTO) can be read to exclude only exclusive competence arising from the use of Article 235 in the absence of internal measures.
131. *Opinion 1/94* (WTO), pr. 88.

Similarly, Article 235 'cannot in itself vest exclusive competence in the Community at the international level'.[132] It seems clear, then, that internal competence on the basis of Articles 100, 100a and 235 can only give rise to external competence when they are exercised. That competence will only be exclusive if the internal measures constitute common rules. The rationale is presumably that the scope of these Articles is potentially very wide and, unless restricted by necessity or a pre-condition of internal measures, they would generate a wide-ranging external competence of unknown scope. On this point *Opinion 1/94* (WTO) accepted the views of the Council and a number of member states.

The ECJ reaffirmed its views on Articles 100a and 235 in *Opinion 2/92* concerning the 'Third Revised Decision on National Treatment of the Council of the OECD'.[133] The ECJ also stressed that recourse to Article 235 was justified only where no other provision of the Treaty gives the Community institutions the power to adopt the measure in question.

132. Ibid., pr. 89.
133. [1995] ECR I-525.

CHAPTER FOUR

The nature of EC competence in international relations

Introduction

That the EC may exercise a wide-ranging external relations competence on the basis of its express and implied powers is now well established and is accepted by the member states.[1] The debate has really moved on. The central concern for the member states is the 'nature' of the EC's competence. Is it exclusive or is it shared in some way with the member states?[2]

If the EC's competence is 'exclusive', then this drastically affects the powers of the member states to act unilaterally or collectively. They must seek to maintain their interests through the Community institutions and processes.[3] In particular, this means in the Council. As the Council is the institution in which the power of the member states is most evident, then it could appear that this is a formality. In practice, this is not the case. Voting requirements, the extensive involvement of the Commission, the role of the European Parliament, and control by the ECJ, all change the perspective and influence the power of the member states. A Community discipline operates. If the competence of the EC in

---

1. See ch. 3 above.
2. See C.W.A. Timmermans and E.L.M. Völker (eds), *Division of Powers between the European Communities and their Member States in the Field of External Relations* (Deventer, Kluwer, 1981); M. Hilf, 'The ECJ's Opinion on the WTO – No Surprise, but Wise?' (1995) 6 EJIL, 245–59; T. Tridimas and P. Eeckhout, 'The External Competence of the Community and the Case-Law of the Court of Justice: Principle versus Pragmatism' (1995) 14 YEL 1994, 143–77; N. Emiliou, 'The Allocation of Competence Between the EC and its Member States in the Sphere of External Relations', in N. Emiliou and D. O'Keeffe (eds) *The European Union and World Trade Law – After the GATT Uruguay Round* (Chichester, Wiley, 1996), pp. 31–45.
3. Similarly, it affects where economic and political interest groups need to direct their efforts at lobbying.

relation to a particular agreement is shared with the member states, then the member states may retain some power to act. There need to be mechanisms for the EC and the member states to cooperate, and a form of Agreement that can reflect this shared competence.[4] In *Commission v Council* (FAO Fishery Agreement) the ECJ found the Council to be in breach of the arrangement between the Commission and the Council on preparation for FAO meetings, voting and statements.[5] There is an internal code of conduct on questions relating to services in the WTO which was agreed in 1994. The Commission has proposed a general code of conduct.[6] If the agreement is one in relation to which the EC has no competence, e.g. defence, then only the member states would be able to conclude the agreement. We consider all these practical matters below.

First, we must determine in what circumstances the EC will have exclusive competence.

Exclusive competence

The process of analysis here broadly follows that concerning the existence of EC competence in the first place.[7] Indeed, in many of the leading cases the ECJ has examined both questions at the same time.[8] The presumption, linked to the principle of attributed powers,[9] is that there is shared competence.[10] We must, therefore, examine the various means by which the presumption is departed from and, thus, exclusive competence can arise.

Exclusive competence may be based on: (i) express provisions of the Treaty or the Acts of Accession; or (ii) express provisions in

---

4. See J. Sack, 'The European Community's Membership of International Organisations' (1995) 32 CMLRev, pp. 1252–6. On the duty of cooperation in these circumstances see *Opinion 1/94* (WTO), prs. 106–9; *Opinion 2/91* (ILO), prs. 26, 36–8.
5. Case C-25/94, [1996] ECR nyr (19 March 1996).
6. See Bull-EU, 5-1995, point 1.4.16.
7. See ch. 3, above.
8. 'It is obvious that in practice these two aspects are very much two sides of the same coin', J. Bourgeois, 'Some Comments on the Practice', in Timmermans and Völker (eds), *Division of Powers*, p. 97. See also J.A. Usher, 'The Scope of Community Competence – Its Recognition and Enforcement' (1985) 24 JCMS, 121–36.
9. On attributed powers see ch. 3, pp. 41–2 above.
10. See the Opinion of A-G Jacobs in Case C-316/91, *Parliament v Council* [1994] ECR I-625; J. De La Rochere Duthiel, 'L'ère des compétences partagées a propos de l'entendue des compétences extérieures de la Communauté européenne' (1995) RMC, 461–70.

internal measures; or (iii) it may be based on the scope of internal measures adopted by Community institutions. Finally, (iv) there can be exclusive competence if, in the particular circumstances, internal powers could only be effectively exercised at the same time as external powers. We consider each source of exclusive competence in turn.

Competence derived from express provisions

Provisions of the Treaty or Acts of Accession
There is clear judicial authority that there is exclusive competence in relation to the 'common commercial policy',[11] and 'the conservation of fisheries'.[12] There is judicial support, but no direct judicial authority, for the view that there must also be exclusive EC competence in relation to competition matters within the scope of Articles 85–90 of the Treaty and the internal measures adopted under those Articles.[13] However, these general statements must be immediately qualified. The scope of these fields or areas as a matter of Community law is subject to the interpretation of the ECJ. Consistent with its general jurisprudential approach, the ECJ has taken a very expansive interpretation of the scope of EC competencies. The interpretation of the subject matter in issue and the scope of the EC fields of competence are therefore crucial. For example, in *Opinion 1/94* (WTO), one of the central arguments was directed to whether the provision of various kinds of 'services' (the subject matter) came within the scope of the 'common commercial policy' (a field of EC competence). If any did, then the EC had exclusive competence in relation to them. If any did not, then competence in relation to them could remain shared with the member states. A similar analysis was made in *Opinion 2/92*[14] as to whether the Third Revised Decision on National Treatment of the Council of the OECD fell within the exclusive competence of

---

11. See *Opinion 1/75* (OECD Local Cost Standard) [1975] ECR 1355; *Opinion 1/94* (WTO); I. Macleod, I. Hendry and S. Hyett, *The External Relations of the European Communities: A Manual of Law and Practice* (Oxford, OUP, 1996), pp. 266–95.

12. See Case 804/79, *Commission v UK* [1981] ECR 1045; Macleod, Hendry and Hyett, op. cit., pp. 241–52; C. Noirfalisse, 'The Community System of Fisheries Management and the *Factortame* Case' (1994) 12 YEL 1992, 325–51.

13. See *Opinion 1/92* (Second EEA Opinion) [1992] ECR I-2821, prs. 40–1. On international competition agreements see A.D. Ham, 'International Cooperation in the Anti-Trust Field and in particular between the United States of America and the Commission of the European Communities' (1993) 30 CMLRev, 571–98.

14. [1995] ECR I-525.

the EC under Article 113. The ECJ rejected this view.

How has exclusive competence in these areas been justified?

In *Opinion 1/75* (OECD Local Cost Standard) the ECJ explained that the CCP in Article 113 is conceived, 'in the context of the operation of the Common Market, for the defence of the common interests of the Community, within which the particular interests of the Member States must endeavour to adapt to each other'.[15] It is not necessarily apparent why it was only exclusive EC competence that could defend that commonality of interest. According to the ECJ, if member states could adopt, in relations with third states, different positions from those which the Community intended to adopt, this would also 'distort the institutional framework' and, 'call into question the mutual trust within the Community'. Neither of these grounds is very persuasive. The institutional framework in a particular area is determined by whether competence lies with the EC or with member states. To argue that it is distorted if member states can take action is to presume that the fact that the EC has exclusive competence is the norm. Reference to 'mutual trust' does not advance the argument.[16] It again presumes that the question of competence has been decided in a particular way when that is the very question to be decided. In any event, the ECJ regarded the provisions of Articles 113 and 114 on the conclusion of international agreements as clearly showing that the exercise of concurrent power by the member states and the EC was impossible. The CCP covers both internal and external measures and is obviously intended to defend the common interests of the Community against the rest of the world.[17] In a sense, it represents the EC at the height of its legal powers, control, and supremacy over the member states.

In relation to fishing, the decisive factor seemed to be that the nature of conservation measures was such that equitable and effective measures were only possible at the international level.[18] The position in relation to competition is not so certain, but would be grounded on the EC having exclusive competence to regulate matters within the scope of Articles 85–90.[19]

15. [1975] ECR 1355.
16. A more contemporary analysis might consider Article 5 to be important.
17. See *Opinion 1/75* (OECD Local Cost Standard) [1975] ECR 1355.
18. See Case 804/79, *Commission v UK* [1981] ECR 1045, prs. 17–18.

Express provisions in internal measures

As we noted above, competence for the EC to enter into agreements with third countries can also be expressly provided for in internal measures, and, indeed, this is quite common in some areas.[20] Such competence will normally be interpreted as being exclusive, but could not override any express provisions in the Treaty on competence.[21] Exclusive competence is justified as reflecting the clear intention of the internal measure. Presumably, however, it could be possible for such an internal measure to be challenged as contrary to the terms of the treaty.

Competence derived from the scope of internal measures which do not include express provisions on the EC entering into agreements with third countries

We considered above the concept of EC competence arising from the adoption of internal measures.[22] Whether that competence is exclusive or not is very much the contemporary battleground between the EC and the member states. It is necessary to recall the statement of principle in ERTA that:

> [17] In particular, each time the Community, with a view to implementing a common policy envisaged by the Treaty, adopts provisions laying down common rules, whatever form these might take, the Member States no longer have the right, acting individually or even collectively, to undertake obligations with third countries which affect those rules.
> [18] As and when such common rules come into being, the Community alone is in a position to assume and carry out contractual obligations towards third countries affecting the whole sphere of application of the Community legal system.

The essence of this principle is not difficult to comprehend. If the EC has adopted 'common rules' then it would obviously be

---

19. See Macleod, Hendry and Hyett, op. cit., p. 57.
20. *Opinion 1/94* (WTO), pr. 95.
21. For example, harmonization may be excluded. Similarly, Treaty provisions can clearly state that member state competence to negotiate in international bodies and conclude international agreements is not prejudiced. See Article 130s and 130y.
22. See ch. 3, p. 54 et seq. above.

nonsensical if these could be undermined by later agreements between member states and third states.[23] If that were the case, then the concept of supremacy of EC law over national law would be overridden. So it is crucial for member states to understand clearly that if they agree to the EC adopting common rules, then the practical effect will be to accord the EC exclusive external relations competence within the scope of those common rules. If they want to avoid this effect, then they must not adopt common rules. Indeed, as we will see below, they must not even adopt common rules which cover an area to a 'large extent'.[24]

The ERTA effect of adopting common rules is presumably reversed if the relevant internal measure is repealed.[25] The introduction of the subsidiarity principle by the TEU has led to more EC legislation being repealed.

Are common rules limited to measures taken within the framework of a common policy?

The ERTA principle appeared to be limited to common rules adopted 'with a view to implementing a common policy'.[26] However, in *Opinion 2/91* (ILO) the ECJ stated that the authority of the ERTA decision –

> cannot be restricted to instances where the Community has adopted community rules within the framework of a common policy. In all the areas corresponding to the objectives of the Treaty, Article 5 EEC requires Member-States to facilitate the achievement of the Community's tasks and to abstain from any measure which could jeopardize the attainment of the objectives of the Treaty.[27]

So an EC measure in any area could, prima facie, constitute a common rule unless the Treaty itself forbids harmonization in the area concerned.

What are 'common rules'?

Interestingly, the expression 'common rules' does not appear in EC Treaty law, though it regularly appears in secondary legislation.

[23] On pre-existing international obligations see pp. 123–4 below.
[24] See p. 74 below.
[25] See A. Dashwood, 'The Limits of European Community Powers' (1996) 21 ELRev, 113–28, p. 215, n. 7.
[26] On the EC's common policies see ch. 1, above.
[27] *Opinion 2/91* (ILO), pr. 10. Limiting the ERTA principle to the context of common policies had been contended for by Germany, Spain and Ireland.

Under Article 189 there are powers for the EC institutions to take various kinds of internal measures, 'In order to carry out their task and in accordance with the provisions of this Treaty'. A number of specific Treaty Articles provide for various measures to be taken. Article 100 provides for directives, and Article 100a for measures, to be taken for the approximation of laws, regulations or administrative provisions in certain circumstances. We have considered above Article 235, which also provides for measures to be taken in certain circumstances.[28]

It might have been expected that an EC measure taken under any of these provisions would constitute a 'common rule', in the *formal* sense that it applies to all of the member states. It would provide 'rules' which are 'common' to them all. However, this is not the sense in which 'common rules' referred to in the ERTA case have been understood. Rather, they have been given a *substantive* meaning.

EC rules will be treated as common rules in a number of circumstances. The first of these is arguably a logical extension of the principle of pre-emption that applies to internal EC law.[29] According to this principle, if the internal EC measures which have been adopted exhaustively cover a particular field, then the member states are pre-empted from taking any further legislative action in that particular field. This is sometimes picturesquely described as the EC 'occupying the field' concerned.[30] This internal pre-emption is then parallelled at the external level. The exhaustive internal measures generate an exclusive external relations competence for the EC.[31]

Applying this approach, how the field is defined becomes crucial. This requires close analysis of the preamble and the express provisions of the measure concerned. The same approach is then applied to the international agreement concerned. This may

---

[28.] See ch. 3, pp. 62–6 above.

[29.] See E.D. Cross, 'Pre-Emption of Member State Law in the European Community: A Framework for Analysis' (1992) 29 CMLRev, 447–72; S. Weatherill, 'Beyond Pre-Emption? Shared Competence and Constitutional Change in the European Community', in D. O'Keeffe and P. Twomey (eds), *Legal Issues of the Maastricht Treaty* (Chichester, Wiley Chancery, 1994).

[30.] Cf. Bourgeois, op. cit., who considered that for ERTA-type situations to be considered as an occupation of the field and that the whole field is preempted, 'would probably be inappropriate', p. 104.

[31.] See C.W.A. Timmermans, 'Division of External Powers between Community and Member States in the Fields of Harmonization of National Law: A Case Study', in Timmermans and Völker (eds), *Division of Powers*.

be difficult at an early stage of proposals and negotiations. The respective fields are then analysed side by side. To the extent that the internal measures exhaustively regulate a particular field, or part of a field, then the EC has exclusive competence to that extent. For example, in *Opinion 2/92* (OECD National Treatment Instrument) internal measures had been taken under Articles 57(2), 75, 84 and 100a. However, it was undisputed that those measures did not cover all the fields of activity to which the OECD decision at issue related. Thus, although the EC was competent to participate in the OECD decision, in the fields in which internal measures had not been taken, its competence was shared with that of the member states. This kind of analysis means that much of the argument in cases before the ECJ is directed to how the particular fields in issue are to be characterized for the purposes of this analysis.

In *Opinion 2/91* (ILO) the ECJ pushed the concept of the occupied field a little further.[32] It effectively reduced the requirement that a field or area be exhaustively regulated, to one that it be, 'covered to a large extent by Community rules adopted ... with a view to achieving an ever greater degree of harmonization'.[33] This formulation may give rise to great uncertainty as to when an area has become covered by EC rules to a sufficiently 'large extent' that the EC's competence becomes exclusive.

Affecting common rules or altering their scope

The scope of the ERTA principle could also have been limited by interpreting it as only prohibiting member states from assuming 'obligations which might *affect* those rules or *alter* their scope'.[34] In *Opinion 2/91* (ILO) the ECJ specifically stated that there was 'no contradiction' between certain provisions of the ILO Convention and those of the relevant EC Directives which did establish 'common rules'. None the less, it still took the view that the commitments in Part II of the ILO Convention fell within the

---

[32.] For comment on *Opinion 2/91* (ILO) see N. Emiliou, 'Towards a clearer demarcation line? The Division of external relations power between the Community and Member States' (1994) 18 ELRev, 76–86; N. Neuwahl, 'Comment on Opinion 2/91' (1993) 30 CMLRev, 1185–95.

[33.] *Opinion 2/91* (ILO), pr. 25.

[34.] *ERTA*, pr. 22 (emphasis added). See J. Temple Lang, 'The Ozone Layer Convention: A New Solution to the Question of Community Participation in "Mixed" International Agreements' (1986) 23 CMLRev, 157–76; F. Burrows, 'The effects of the main cases of the Court of Justice in the field of the external competences on the conduct of member states', in Timmermans and Völker (eds), *Division of Powers*, pp. 111–25.

area covered by a number of EC Directives and, 'were of such a kind as to affect the Community rules'.[35] Consequently, the EC had exclusive competence for that part of the ILO Convention. This still leaves open for argument that the international commitments at issue do not affect or alter the scope of the common rules. An example would be where member states purported to extend the territorial application of the EC rules. Or if the international obligations assumed by them would affect the common rules in a beneficial way.[36]

Common rules and minimum rules

After *Opinion 2/91* (ILO), in particular, it is the distinction between 'common rules' and 'minimum rules' that is going to be of greatest significance. This is because of the EC policy of harmonization on the basis of minimum standards but, sometimes, with discretion for states to apply higher standards.[37] ILO Convention 170 concerned safety in the use of chemicals at work. Under Article 19(8) of the ILO Constitution, the adoption of conventions is regarded as establishing only minimum standards. They are not to be deemed to have affected any laws which ensure more favourable conditions for workers.[38] After considering the preamble and the substantive obligations of Convention 170 the ECJ took the view that the 'field' covered by it fell within the 'social provisions' of the EC Treaty. Under Article 118a the Council has the power to adopt 'minimum requirements', relating to health and safety of workers, by means of Directives. In accordance with Article 118(3), the adoption of such measures 'shall not prevent any Member State from maintaining or introducing more stringent requirements for the protection of working conditions compatible with this Treaty'.

Crucial for the outcome on the issue of exclusive competence was the ECJ's view that, in relation to the health and safety of workers, 'the provisions of Convention 170 are not of such a kind as to affect rules adopted pursuant to Article 118a'.[39]

The reasoning behind this was as follows. If the EC adopted *less*

---

35. *ERTA*, pr. 26.
36. Burrows (1981) op. cit., gave the example of international commitments which would have the effect of maintaining or improving the quality of bathing water in the EC. This would not be a problem given the terms of Article 130t, introduced by the SEA and amended by the TEU.
37. The most notable example being Article 100a.
38. ILO Constitution, Article 19(8), cited in *Opinion 2/91* (ILO), pr. 12.
39. *Opinion 2/91* (ILO), pr. 18.

stringent rules than those in the ILO Convention, the member states could rely on Article 118(3) as justifying their introduction of *more* 'stringent requirements'. If the EC adopted *more* stringent rules than those in the ILO Convention, there was nothing to prevent the 'full application' of these by member states, because Article 19(8) of the ILO Constitution expressly provides for national laws that are more favourable to workers to exceed the standards of ILO Conventions.

Opinion 2/91 (ILO) was unusual in that both the internal measures and the international convention essentially provided that they established minimum standards only. States were free to establish more stringent standards. If the international agreement concerned did not expressly state that it established only minimum standards, would the obligations under it then 'affect' common rules?

The Commission argued that it was sometimes difficult to determine whether a specific provision was more favourable to workers than another. This in turn could lead to a reticence by member states to adopt EC measures for fear of being in breach of an ILO Convention. This would happen if that EC measure was subsequently considered by the ILO to be below its convention standard. To the extent that such an attitude would risk impairing the development of Community law, the EC should have exclusive jurisdiction.[40] This is a curious argument. Caution by member states to avoid their being in breach of international conventions is surely to be commended. The ECJ summarily dismissed the Commission's argument:

> Difficulties, such as those referred to by the Commission, which might arise for the legislative function of the Community cannot constitute the basis for exclusive Community competence.

> Nor, for the same reasons, can exclusive competence be founded on the Community provisions adopted on the basis of Article 100 EEC, such as, in particular, Council Directive 80/117 on the protection of workers from the risks related to exposure to chemical, physical and biological agents at work and individual directives adopted pursuant to Article 8 of directive 80/1107, all of which law down minimum requirements.[41]

In policy terms, the distinction between common rules and minimum rules in the ECJ's jurisprudence is a neat solution. If common EC rules are established which are higher than minimum

---

40. Ibid., pr. 19.   41. Ibid., prs. 20–1.

rules then they should not be undermined. If agreement can only be reached on establishing minimum rules, then the member states remain free to apply higher standards. The overall effect is that rules should get pushed higher, rather than lower. This will not happen if the EC legislative process produces common rules that represent the lowest common denominator of agreement rather than minimum ones.[42]

Exclusive competence if, in the particular circumstances, internal powers could only be effectively exercised at the same time as external powers

We considered this matter in the discussion of *Opinion 1/76* (Rhine Navigation Case) and the *Kramer Case* in Chapter 3.

---

42. Some specific EC provisions are an attempt to guard against this, e.g. Article 100a(4) on the Commission's harmonization proposals under Article 100a concerning health, safety, environmental protection and consumer protection taking as a base a 'higher level of protection'.

CHAPTER FIVE

Mixed agreements

Introduction

Mixed agreements are of enormous legal significance for the international relations of the EC.[1] They are used in a number of different circumstances[2] and dominate in the Treaty practice of the EC. For example, environment Treaties, most commodity agreements, and virtually all of the range of association agreements, are mixed. An agreement can be regarded as mixed if the EC and one or more of the member states are parties to it. These are considered in section 1 below. An agreement can also be regarded as mixed if the EC and the member states share competence in relation to it, even if only member states can be parties. These are considered in section 2 below. Finally, an agreement can be in a mixed form because of requirements relating to its financing or relating to its provisions on voting. These are considered in section 3 below.

Each international agreement will require consideration of its subject matter to determine the allocation of competence between

---

[1.] See C.W.A. Timmermans and E.L.M. Völker (eds), *Division of Powers between the European Communities and their Member States in The Field of External Relations* (Deventer, Kluwer, 1981); D. O'Keeffe and H.G. Schermers (eds), *Mixed Agreements* (Dordrecht, Nijhoff, 1983); J.F.M. Dolmans, *Problems of Mixed Agreements* (Hague, Asser Instituut, 1985); E. Stein, 'External Relations of the European Community: Structure and Process', Academy of European Law, European University Institute, Florence (1990) vol. I, 115–88; A.G. Toth, *Oxford Encyclopedia of European Community Law* (Oxford, OUP, 1990), pp. 370–9; N. Neuwahl, 'Joint Participation in International Treaties and the exercise of power by the EEC and its Member States: Mixed Agreements' (1991) 28 CMLRev, 717–40; N. Neuwahl, 'Shared powers or combined incompetence? More on mixity' (1966) 33 CMLRev, 667–87; I. Macleod, I. Hendry and S. Hyett, *The External Relations of the European Communities: A Manual of Law and Practice* (Oxford, OUP, 1996), pp. 142–64.

[2.] See H.G. Schermers, 'A Typology of Mixed Agreements', in O'Keeffe and Schermers (eds), *Mixed Agreements*.

the EC and the member states, and the nature of that competence.[3] It is also important to bear in mind that the allocation of competence can evolve over the lifetime of an agreement[4] or series of agreements. This has been the case with the GATT.[5]

I. Mixed agreements in the sense of shared competence

If competence in the subject matter of a Treaty lies partly with the EC and partly with the member states, then the agreement is described as a mixed one. If the EC has exclusive competence over parts of the agreement, the expression is misleading to the extent that it suggests that the EC's competence is somehow 'mixed' with that of the member states. This is not the case. Similarly, when parts of an agreement may be solely within the competence of the member states.

The expression 'mixed agreement' more accurately describes agreements where the EC and the member states genuinely share competence. A number of particular Treaty provisions expressly provide for shared competence.[6] They state that 'within their respective spheres of competence', the EC and the member states shall cooperate with third countries and with competent international organizations. Examples of this are Articles 130r(4) (environment) and 130y (development cooperation). In Case C-268/94, *Portugal v Council*, Portugal unsuccessfully argued that the agreement in issue should have been a mixed agreement. Another possibility is that the powers of the EC and the member states run in parallel.[7] Finally, there can be a situation in which the EC has potentially exclusive competence over the whole of an agreement but, in the meantime, there is residual competence for the member states to act.[8]

The compatibility with EC law of the phenomena of mixed agreements has been questioned by writers.[9] Their 'increased use

---

3. See chs. 3–4 above.
4. Even during the drafting of an agreement, see Case C-24/95, *Commission v UK* (FAO Fisheries Agreement) [1996] ECR nyr.
5. See E.-U. Petersmann, 'Participation of the European Communities in the GATT: International Law and Community Law Aspects', in O'Keeffe and Schermers, *Mixed Agreements*; ch. 7 pp. 118, 121 below.
6. Cf. the general provision in Article 102 Euratom.
7. For example, in respect of intellectual property, see *Opinion 1/94* (WTO), prs. 54–71; P. Demiray, 'Intellectual Property and the External Power of the European Community: The New Dimension' (1994) 16 Mich.JIL, 187–239.
8. See ch. 4, p. 68 et seq. above.
9. See P. Pescatore, 'Les Relations Extèrieures des Communautes Européennes', 103 *Recueil Des Cours* (1961-II) 1–244, p. 104; J.J. Costonis, 'The Treaty Making Power of the EEC: The Perception of a Decade' (1967–68) 5 CMLRev, 421–57, p. 450; Neuwahl, op. cit. (1991), pp. 720–3.

must undermine the practical effectiveness of the doctrine of exclusivity if not its theoretical basis'.[10] They are open to abuse by member states who can seek to include provisions in an agreement for the purpose of making it a mixed one.[11] They distort the concept of the EC acting as a single international actor. They can undermine the role and position of the Commission as the representative of the international personality of the EC.[12] Moreover, they do not necessarily reflect the division of competence between the EC and the member states in relation to the subject matter concerned, they raise serious legal and practical problems, and they generate considerable uncertainty.[13] However, unless and until the EC is accorded exclusive competence in relation to all matters within the scope of the Treaty, it ultimately seems difficult to dispute the legality of mixed agreements in EC law. 'Mixed agreements are not as such ruled out by the Treaty.'[14] If competence is shared between the EC and the member states, then a mixed agreement is an accurate reflection of the distribution of the legal rights and responsibilities of the EC and the member state.[15] A party, whether the EC or the member state, should only undertake to implement obligations if it has the competence to do so.[16] From a strictly legal perspective, in relation to an agreement over which competence is shared, neither the EC nor the member

10. See M. Cremona, 'The Doctrine of Exclusivity and the Position of Mixed Agreements in the External Relations of the European Community' (1982) 2 OJLS, 393–428, p. 428.

11. 'Agreements are made "mixed" whenever the smallest ground can be found for that. Only rarely do the Member States not succeed in finding some elements in an international agreement which are outside the exclusive competence of the Community', O'Keeffe and Schermers, *Mixed Agreements*, p. ix.

12. See Case C-24/95, *Commission v UK* (FAO Fisheries Agreement) [1996] ECR nyr, on practical difficulties concerning voting.

13. See Cremona (1982) 2 OJLS, 393–428; C.-D. Ehlermann, 'Mixed Agreements: A List of Problems', in O'Keeffe and Schermers, *Mixed Agreements*; A. Bleckmann, 'The Mixed Agreements of the EEC in Public International Law', in O'Keeffe and Schermers, op. cit.; Neuwahl (1991) 28 CMLRev, 717–40.

14. See Ehlermann, op. cit., p. 4.

15. See C. Tomuschat, 'Liability for Mixed Agreements', in O'Keeffe and Schermers, *Mixed Agreements*; G. Gaja, 'The European Community's Rights and Obligations under Mixed Agreements', in O'Keeffe and Schermers, op. cit.; W.H. Balekjian 'Mixed Agreements: Complementary and Concurrent Competencies', in O'Keeffe and Schermers, op. cit.

16. 'In those circumstances, it must be considered that the commitments arising from Part III of the Convention, falling within the area covered by the directives cited in paragraph 22, are of such a kind as to affect the Community rules laid down in the directives and consequently member-States cannot undertake such commitments outside the framework of Community institutions', *Opinion 2/91*

state should become a party without the other. Neither of them in isolation is capable of fulfilling all of the obligations under the agreement. In practice the EC normally only ratifies an agreement after the member states concerned (which may not necessarily be all of them). This requirement for national ratification may delay the entry into force of the agreement for a number of years.[17] We consider how such agreements have been dealt with in practice in section 2 below.

Moreover, in its jurisprudence, the ECJ has clearly accepted the concept of mixed agreements.[18] In relation to the scope of its opinions under Article 228, it has accepted that one of the uses of such an opinion can be to determine the powers of the EC institutions to negotiate and conclude international instruments.[19] In its conclusion in *Opinion 2/91* (ILO) it stated that the 'conclusion of' an agreement, 'is a matter which falls within the joint competence of the member states and the Community'.[20] Thus, according to its content, a mixed agreement is required.

However, under ILO Conventions, only member states can become parties. If the 'conclusion' of the convention is a matter of 'joint competence', then the decision to conclude it must be taken by the EC and the member states jointly.[21] Such an approach would be consistent with the view that if the EC and the member state share competence, and can both become parties, neither can do so without the other. They could arguably do so if it was possible for either the EC or the member state to make reservations to those parts of the agreement for which it did not have competence. Similarly, if the agreement permitted participation to the extent of a parties competence only.

Given that shared competence is the norm, so too are mixed agreements. Moreover, Weiler has argued that a positive assessment of mixed agreements is defensible –

[17.] Hence the recourse to interim agreements concerning the trade parts of such agreements which can be entered into by the EC alone.

[18.] See *Ruling 1/78* (Nuclear Material Case) [1978] ECR 2151, *Opinion 1/78* (Natural Rubber) [1979] ECR 2871, *Opinion 2/91* (ILO) [1993] ECR I-1061, and *Opinion 1/94* (WTO) [1994] ECR I-5267. See also the analysis of A-G Jacobs in Case 316/91, *Parliament v Council* [1994] ECR I-625.

[19.] See *Ruling 1/78* (Nuclear Material Case); K.P.E. Lasok, *The European Court of Justice* (London, Butterworths, 1994), pp. 588–92; Rules of Procedure – ECJ, Article 107(2).

[20.] *Opinion 2/91* (ILO), pr. 39; see N. Neuwahl, 'Comment on Opinion 2/91' (1993) 30 CMLRev, 1185–95, pp. 1192–3.

[21.] See. Neuwahl 'Comment on Opinion 2/91', 30 CMLRev, 1185–95, p. 1193.

... despite the dangers of abuse, on many occasions mixed agreements may be regarded as beneficial to the Community process and as a faithful image of the federal/international character of the EC ... [22] Mixed agreements offend the purist but they do after all bring and tie together the main actors of European integration – Community and Member States. In my view, mixed agreements though not resulting in a further exclusive building of the *centre* may – by virtue of their capacity to eliminate tensions and by constituting a growing network whereby Community and Member States gain in international strength simultaneously and become among themselves even further inextricably linked – be regarded as a contribution to the strengthening of the overall *framework* of European integration.[23]

The doctrine of subsidiarity in Article 3b may well provide further legal support for the continuation of mixed agreements, though this has not yet appeared in the jurisprudence of the ECJ.[24]

2. Agreements to which only member states can become parties

In some circumstances, however, the EC cannot become a party to an agreement and this has effectively left some or all of the member states as the parties. This can be because of objections to the recognition of the EC per se, as was the case with the COMECON countries.[25] Or it can be because the Treaty is only open to states, and the other states parties are not willing to amend it to allow the EC to become a participant. A current example is with the ILO. Whatever the reason, such an agreement is obviously not 'mixed' in the sense of both EC and member state participation. It is, however, mixed in the sense of EC and member states sharing competence. An example is ILO Convention 170, considered by the ECJ in *Opinion 2/91* (ILO).[26] Another possibility is that EC participation may not be possible even though its competence is exclusive. Again, in such cases member

---

22. J. Weiler, 'The External Relations of Non-Unitary Actors: Mixity and the Federal Principle', in O'Keeffe and Schermers, *Mixed Agreements*, p. 39.
23. Ibid., p. 85.   24. See ch. 1, pp. 15–16 above.
25. See ch. 2 above.
26. See N. Emiliou, 'Subsidiarity: Panacea or Fig Leaf?', in D. O'Keeffe and P. Twomey (eds), *Legal Issues of the Maastricht Treaty* (Chichester, Wiley Chancery, 1994); J. Auvret-Finck, 'L'Avis Relatifs A La Convention No. 170 De L'OIT' (1995) 31 CDE, 443–60.

states have, in practice, become parties. What is important, however, is that in relation to matters of EC competence the member states are effectively acting as trustees for the EC. In *Opinion 2/91* (ILO) the ECJ stated that the external competence of the EC 'may, if necessary, be exercised through the medium of the member-states acting jointly in the Community's interest'.[27]

If member states alone are parties, then, in relation to matters of EC competence, they must exercise their voting rights in accordance with any common position reached in what is known as 'Community co-ordination'.[28] Otherwise, the concept of EC competence would be undermined. If a common position cannot be reached on a matter over which the EC has exclusive competence, it is probable that the member states cannot act in accordance with their own views. Their actions are limited to defending the essential interests of the Community.[29] This may be a difficult line to draw if the EC is faced with proposals that are to be put to a vote. The member states will either have to vote for, against, or abstain. Member states may take different views about which of these best defends the essential interests of the Community. If a common position cannot be reached on a matter over which competence is shared, there is a stronger argument for saying that, ultimately, the member states retain the right to take a separate national view.[30] Otherwise, their national competence is effectively undermined.

The jurisdiction of the ECJ under Article 228 extends to agreements over which only member states can become parties, so that the underlying issues of competence can be determined. Again, *Opinion 2/91* (ILO) on the ILO Convention was an example of this.

3. Mixed agreements required for voting purposes[31]

If the EC has exclusive competence and is a party to an agreement to the exclusion of member states, its general policy is to secure the same number of votes, or weighted votes, as if the member states

27. *Opinion 2/91* (ILO), pr. 5. See also the *ERTA Case*, pr. 90, on member states acting in the interest and on behalf of the Community in accordance with their obligations under Article 5 of the Treaty; Case 804/79, *Commission v UK* [1981] ECR 1045, on member states as trustees of the common interest.
28. See Macleod, Hendry and Hyett, *The External Relations of the European Communities*, pp. 171–3.
29. Joined Cases 3, 4 and 6/76, *Kramer*; Case C-804/79, *Commission v UK*.
30. See Macleod, Hendry and Hyett, op. cit., pp. 148–50.
31. See J.J. Feenstra, 'A Survey of the Mixed Agreements and their Participation Clauses', in O'Keeffe and Schermers, *Mixed Agreements* (1983), pp. 234–9.

were parties.[32] Otherwise a relative weakening of the international power of the member states has occurred vis-à-vis third states. Its economic and political power mean that the EC can sometimes secure its objective.[33] However, the EC may be forced to accept the concept of 'one member, one vote'. Examples are the Antarctic Convention 1959[34] and the North Atlantic Fisheries Organization.[35] As the number of member states in the EC has increased so the loss of voting rights in such circumstances has become more dramatic. If exclusive Community participation will result in loss of voting rights, then a mixed agreement may actually be in the interest of the EC so as to preserve its voting power.

There are a number of examples of international organizations in which the votes of the EC as a member are calculated by reference to the number of member states of the EC who are also members.[36] Participation by the member states is then required to allow the EC to be a more effective participant in the organization. This can give the member states some political leverage over the Commission.

In relation to a mixed agreement, the member states vote on matters of national competence and the EC votes on matters of EC competence.

We have considered above the situation where the EC is not a party.[37]

4. Mixed agreements required for financing purposes

In *Opinion 1/78* (Natural Rubber) the ECJ held that the CCP covered an agreement establishing a buffer stock as part of the regulation of the world trade in natural rubber. As we have seen, the CCP is a field in which the EC has exclusive competence.[38]

---

32. In recent decades the trend in international law has been to reach decisions by consensus rather than by voting. The question of the single vote is particularly important in the context of the World Trade Agreement.
33. See. J. Sack, 'The European Community's Membership of International Organisations' (1995) 32 CMLRev, 1227–56.
34. See Article 12.
35. See P. Davies, 'The EC/Canadian Fisheries Dispute in the Northwest Atlantic' (1995) 44 ICLQ, 927–39 on an EC defeat in NAFO by a 6:5 vote with EC only having one vote.
36. See, e.g., Article 31(2) of the UN Convention on Biological Diversity.
37. See pp. 82–3 above.
38. See ch. 3, pp. 69–70 above.

However, the ECJ held that there was shared competence in relation to the agreement because the financing of the buffer stock was done by the member states.[39] This role of the member states was seen as a central element because the agreement was viewed as establishing a 'financial instrument', which was crucially important to its operation. The ECJ took this view notwithstanding that the logic of its decision on competence would have suggested that financing should have come from the EC.[40] Instead, the ECJ worked back from the agreement itself to establish competence. It was thus the nature of the agreement, rather than the fact of member state financing, which was crucial.

In *Opinion 1/94* (WTO) the ECJ narrowed the scope of *Opinion 1/78* (Natural Rubber) as a precedent. It dismissed arguments based on member state financing:

> Given that the WTO is an international organization which will have only an operating budget and not a financial policy instrument, the fact that the Member States will bear some of its expenses cannot, on any view, of itself justify participation of the Member States in the conclusion of the WTO Agreement.[41]

How is the division of competence in relation to a mixed agreement determined?

An EC declaration is determined by the Council on the basis of the same provisions which are used for the conclusion of the agreement.[42] This will also determine whether the declaration has to be adopted by unanimity or by qualified majority. If the agreement provides that a declaration of competence also has to be made by member states of a participating organization, then for the member states of the EC, this needs to be coordinated in the Council.[43]

---

39. *Opinion 1/78* (Natural Rubber) [1979] ECR 2871, prs. 52–60.
40. See the criticisms of Cremona (1982) 2 OJLS, 393–428, pp. 417–20; J. Weiler op. cit., n. 22, p. 82; T. Tridimas and P. Eeckhout, 'The External Competence of the Community and the Case-Law of the Court of Justice: Principle versus Pragmatism' (1995) 14 YEL 1994, 143–77, p. 157.
41. *Opinion 1/94* (WTO) [1994] ECR I-5267, pr. 21.
42. See Temple Lang, 'The ERTA Judgement and the Court's Case-Law on Competence and Conflict' (1987), 6 YEL 1986, 183–218.
43. See, e.g., Article 5 of Annex IX of UNCLOS (1982) on 'Participation by International Organizations'.

What are the practical effects of mixed agreements on the negotiation, conclusion and implementation of agreements?

The EC institutions and the member states are under a legal duty to cooperate on the negotiation, conclusion and implementation of mixed agreements. This duty results from the, 'requirement of unity in the international representation of the Community'.[44] Such cooperation is 'all the more necessary' if the EC cannot become party to the agreement, as with ILO Convention 170.[45] The duty to cooperate was 'all the more imperative in the case agreements such as those annexed to the WTO Agreement, which are inextricably linked, and in view of the cross retaliation measures established by the Dispute Settlement Understanding'.[46] When the Commission represents the EC in negotiations, it usually does so under a formal mandate from the Council. The absence of a formal mandate may reflect uncertainties as to competence or a negotiating tactic. For example, there was no formal mandate for the WTO negotiations. The mandate may or may not specify the likely legal basis of the eventual agreement. It may be easier to determine the legal basis when the text of the agreement is finalized, which can be a considerable time after any mandate is agreed. Moreover, it may not even be clear from any mandate whether the agreement will be concluded as a mixed agreement. This can occur when the contents of the agreement are uncertain or may evolve substantially over time, and when there may be a dispute between the EC and the member states concerning competence.[47] Mandates will usually cover, inter alia, the need for an EC participation clause, the regime for voting rights, financial contributions and declarations of competence. There are various complicated sets of possibilities for the composition of delegations negotiating mixed agreements.[48]

[44.] *Ruling 1/78* (Natural Rubber), prs. 34–6; *Opinion 2/91* (ILO), pr. 36; *Opinion 1/94* (WTO), pr. 108. On cooperation obligations see Article 5 EC and Article C of the TEU.

[45.] *Opinion 2/91* (ILO), pr. 37.

[46.] *Opinion 1/94* (WTO), pr. 109, and the anonymous editorial comment, 'The Aftermath of *Opinion 1/94* or 'How to Ensure Unity of Representation for Joint Competences', in (1995) 32 CMLRev, 385–90. On the DSU see ch. 7, pp. 131–2 below.

[47.] For a case where the content did change over time with a dramatic effect on competence see Case C-25/94, *Commission v Council* (FAO Fishery Agreement) [1996] ECR nyr, where provisions on reflagging were not included in the final agreement.

[48.] See J. Groux, 'Mixed Negotiations', in O'Keeffe and Schermers, *Mixed*

If the EC shares competence in relation to an agreement, the member states are under a duty to seek to negotiate a participation clause that would permit EC membership.[49] In some agreements, such a clause has been included even before it has been established that the EC has competence. This latter option carries greater risks for the member states because it is likely to be seen by the EC as an invitation to assert competence in relation to the subject matter of the agreement or part of it. The ability to obtain the agreement of third states to an EC participation clause depends in part on the negotiating strength of the member states and the EC. Such clauses became increasingly common, although the diversity of their terms remains striking.[50] They often refer in general terms to 'regional international economic organization', but these in fact only cover the EC. They may provide that the EC can become a party only if one or more of the member states have become parties. These are known as 'subordination clauses'.[51] A leading example is Article 3 of Annex IX to the Law of the Sea Convention (1982), which provides that the EC may become a party only if a majority of the member states ratify or accede.[52] Subordination clauses simply reflect the negotiating demands of third states. They are not intended to, and do not, alter competence in any way. They may, though, effectively give the member states the power to delay Community ratification by delaying their own ratification. Coordination of member state ratification is obviously desirable, and there has been considerable progress in this direction.[53] Article

48. *(continued)* *Agreements;* Macleod, Hendry and Hyett, *The External Relations of the European Communities,* pp. 151–3.

49. See Joined Cases 3, 4 and 6/76, *Kramer and Others* [1976] ECR 1279. If the EC has exclusive competence it can result in the EC becoming bound by the provisions of that agreement in substitution for the member states. This, at least according to the ECJ, was the case with the GATT, see Cases 21–24/72, *International Fruit Company* [1972] ECR 1219.

50. See P. Allott, 'Adherence To and Withdrawal From Mixed Agreements', in O'Keeffe and Schermers, *Mixed Agreements,* pp. 102–5; Feenstra, op. cit.

51. See G. Close, 'Subordination Clauses in Mixed Agreements' (1985) 34 ICLQ, 382–91.

52. See K.R. Simmonds, 'The Communities Declaration Upon Signature of the U.N. Convention on the Law of the Sea' (1986) 23 CMLRev, 521–44. The LOSC entered into force on 16 November 1994. However, an 'agreement' on Part IX of the LOSC has meant that there is a much greater likelihood that more member states will ratify. Ratification of the LOSC by the EC is under active consideration. A delay in ratification announced by the UK in May 1996 may delay EC ratification.

53. See Ehlermann, op. cit, pp. 16–17; G. Close, 'Subordination Clauses in Mixed Agreements' (1985) 34 ICLQ, 382–91.

116 was used to coordinate signature of international agreements, but it was deleted by the TEU.[54]

The implementation of mixed agreements is a sophisticated process. It may be achieved by the direct effect of the agreement or of decisions taken by institutions establishing it, or by implementation at the EC level, or by implementation at member state level, or a combination of these.[55] The jurisdiction of the ECJ to interpret the provisions of a mixed agreement which are within the jurisdiction of member states is unclear.[56]

---

54. See Macleod, Hendry and Hyett, op. cit., p. 268.
55. See Macleod, Hendry and Hyett, op. cit., pp. 155–62; Stein, op. cit., pp. 164–79; Allott, op. cit; Balekjian, op. cit; Gaja, op. cit; Tomuschat, op. cit.
56. See the discussion of the *Demirel Case* in ch. 7, p. 122 below.

CHAPTER SIX

Practice and policy on EC competence

Introduction

We have considered the principles which govern competence and the use of mixed agreements in Chapters 3–5 above. This chapter begins by explaining the procedures for, and the role of the institutions in, the conclusion of international agreements by the EC.[1] It examines the practical exercise of the EC's competence, both exclusive and shared.[2] It then considers, from a policy perspective, the range of strategies and approaches open to the member states, the EC institutions, third states and interest groups.

The conclusion of international agreements – the roles of the institutions

This is provided for in Article 228.[3] It sets out a general procedure but also specifies a significant number of exceptions to it. When an

---

[1.] See I. Macleod, I. Hendry and S. Hyett, *The External Relations of the European Communities: A Manual of Law and Practice* (Oxford, OUP, 1996), pp. 75–122.

[2.] See J. Bourgeois, 'Some Comments on the Practice', in C.W.A. Timmermans and E.C.M. Völker (eds), *Division of Powers between the European Communities and their Member States in the Field of External Relations* (Deventer, Kluwer, 1981); F. Burrows, 'The effects of the main cases of the Court of Justice in the field of the external competences on the conduct of member states', in Timmermans and Völker (eds), *Division of Powers*, pp. 111–25; P. Pescatore, 'Treaty-making by the European Communities', in F. Jacobs and S. Roberts (eds), *The Effect of Treaties in Domestic Law* (London, Sweet and Maxwell, 1987).

[3.] As amended by Article G(80) of the TEU. See also Articles 109(1) and (2); Baroness Elles, 'The Role of EU Institutions in External Trade Policy', in N. Emiliou and D. O'Keeffe (eds) *The European Union and World Trade Law – After the GATT Uruguay Round* (Chichester, Wiley, 1996).

agreement has been concluded in accordance with one of the procedures in Article 228 it is 'binding on the institutions of the Community and on Member States' (Article 228(7)). The word 'agreement' is used in Article 228 in a general sense to cover any undertaking entered into by entities subject to international law which has binding force, whatever its formal designation.[4] The acts of the Council concerning international agreements usually take the form of a 'decision sui generis', though some acts concluding international agreements have been in the form of a Regulation. In terms of possible direct effect it is the substance rather than the form which will be crucial. Whatever form of act is chosen to conclude the agreement it must specify its legal basis.[5] The effect of Article 228 after its amendment by the TEU is that acts concluding an international agreement have to specify a double legal basis. First, the substantive basis of competence, for example, Articles 113, 238, or the legal basis for internal rules in the area concerned. The scope of the agreement may require that a number of Articles be specified. Second, the particular procedural basis under Article 228 which is relevant for the agreement concerned. As we will see below, Article 228 sets out a series of different procedures so the legal basis must be to a specific paragraph or subparagraph of Article 228. An example may be helpful. The 'sui generis decision' of the Council concluding the WTO Agreement was based on Articles 43, 54, 57, 66, 84(2), 99, 100, 100a, 113 and 235 in conjunction with the second subparagraph of Article 228(3).[6]

The general procedure: negotiation

Article 228(1) provides:

> Where this Treaty provides for the conclusion of agreements between the Community and one or more States or international organisations, the Commission shall make recommendations to the

---

4. Case C-327/91, *France v Commission* [1994] ECR I-3641, pr. 27. See also Article 2 of the VCLT (1969).
5. Case 45/86, *Commission v Council* [1987] ECR 1493; Case C-187/93, *Parliament v Council* [1994] ECR I-2875. Early acts of the Council, e.g., on a negotiating mandate may not specify any legal base due to uncertainty as to the ultimate scope of an agreement. Also on legal basis see *Opinion 2/92* (OECD National Treatment Instrument, [1995] ECR I-521; K. Bradley, 'The European Court and the Legal Basis of Community Legislation' (1988) 13 ELRev, 379–402; D. Chalmers, 'Legal Basis and External Relations of the European Community', in Emiliou and O'Keeffe, *The European Union and World Trade Law*.
6. Council Decision 94/800, [1994] OJ L336/1.

Council, which shall authorize the Commission to open the necessary negotiations. The Commission shall conduct these negotiations in consultation with the special committees appointed by the Council to assist it in this task and within the framework of such directives as the Council may issue to it. In exercising the powers conferred upon it by this paragraph, the Council shall act by qualified majority, except in the cases provided for in the second sentence of paragraph 2, for which it shall act unanimously.

The process thus begins with a Commission recommendation.[7] Its right of initiative is thus important, but it is weaker than under the EC legislative system because the Council does not need to be unanimous to amend the recommendation.[8] Only the Council can authorize negotiations.[9] The Commission has the dominant negotiating role but it must act within the framework of the Council's directives. Even when the envisaged agreement is likely to be a mixed one the Commission will normally be the negotiator if extensive community competence is involved. The special committees which the Council can appoint have a consultative rather than a directive role but, of course, they can be crucial in ensuring that the agreement reached will be acceptable to the member states. The special committees operate as working groups of the Council. Article 113 makes specific provision for the negotiation and conclusion of agreements within the CCP on the same lines as the Article 228 procedure. The accompanying 'Article 113 Committee' is considered to be particularly influential.

The general procedure: conclusion

The general rule is that the Council concludes international agreements acting by QMV on the basis of a proposal from the Commission and after having consulted the EP (Article 228(2) and (3)). In accordance with the normal rule, the Commission's proposal can only be amended if the Council is unanimous.[10] Although Article 228(2) on the conclusion of international agreements begins with the words 'Subject to the powers of the

---

7. These take the form of a 'Communication' to the Council. It could concern a single bilateral agreement, a series of agreements or a multilateral agreement.
8. The Council could use its right under Article 152 to request proposals from the Commission. The EP's power under Article 138b would not appear to extend this far as it may only request proposals for a Community act.
9. See B.R. Bot, 'Negotiating Community Agreements: Procedure and Practice' (1970) 7 CMLRev, 286–310.
10. Article 189a(1).

Commission in this field . . . ', the Commission cannot, as a matter of Community law, conclude international agreements binding the EC.[11] In *France v Commission*[12] the ECJ was not willing to accept any of the Commission's arguments that it had such a competence.[13] However, it was careful not to suggest that the international agreement itself was invalid.[14]

The EP's opinion shall be delivered within a time limit which the Council may lay down according to the urgency of the matter (Article 228(3)). If the EP does not act within the time limit the Council may act. This deprives the EP of the possibility of using delay as a means of negotiating concessions from the Council.

The exceptions to the general procedures

As to voting

There are two specified exceptions in which the Council must act unanimously both in respect of the authorization of negotiations and the conclusion of agreements (Article 228(2)). These are (i) when the agreement covers a field[15] for which unanimity is required for the adoption of internal rules, and (ii) what are generally known as association agreements.[16]

As to the powers of the EP[17]

The EP does *not* have to be consulted in relation to the conclusion of international agreements based on Article 113(3) (Common

11. Case C-327/91, *France v Commission* [1994] ECR I-3641. See J. Kingston, 'External Relations of the European Community – External Capacity Versus Internal Competence' (1995) 44 ICLQ, 659–70. Under Article 7 of the Protocol on the Privileges and Immunities of the EC (1965), 'The Commission may conclude agreements for these laissez-passer to be recognized as valid travel documents within the territories of third countries', [1967] OJ L152.
12. Ibid. 13. Ibid., prs. 28–43.
14. Following the ECJ's decision the Council concluded the agreement in Council and Commission Decision 95/145/EC/ECSC [1995] OJ L95/45. The legal basis in the EC Treaty were Articles 87 and 235 in conjunction with the first sub-paragraph of Article 228 (3).
15. This is flexibly interpreted and follows the approach to legal base of identifying the main aim and content of a provision. See Macleod, Hendry and Hyett, *The External Relations of the European Communities*, p. 97.
16. See ch. 10 below.
17. See R. Corbett, F. Jacobs and M. Shackleton, *The European Parliament*, 3rd edn (London, Cartermill, 1995), pp. 212–17; N. Neuwahl, 'The European Parliament and Association Council Decision 1/95 of the EC/Turkey Association Council' (1996) 33 CMLRev, 51–68.

Commercial Policy).[18] The EP is pressing for reform of this.[19] The justification given for this exclusion is the need to be able to act speedily.[20] In practice, the EP is normally consulted.[21]

More positive, from the perspective of the EP, is that a number of classes of agreements require the *assent* of the EP.[22] The classes of agreement are: (i) association agreements;[23] (ii) other agreements establishing a specific institutional framework by organizing cooperation procedures; (iii) agreements having important budgetary implications for the Community; and (iv) agreements entailing amendment of an act adopted under the co-decision procedure in Article 189b. Categories (ii) and (iii) are potentially wide and generous extensions of the assent power of the EP.[24] EP assent to the agreements relating to the GATT/WTO was sought on the basis of class (ii) rather than class (iii).

In an 'urgent situation' the Council and the EP may agree upon a time limit for the assent. The EP is in a stronger position here, as it must agree to the time limit in the first place. However, even if a time limit is breached, it would not seem to be possible for an international agreement within the specified classes to be concluded in the absence of assent by the EP.

Delegation of powers to the Commission

The Council may, when concluding an agreement, 'authorize the Commission to approve modifications on behalf of the

18. Article 228(3). An interesting institutional result of this is that those member states which seek to limit the interpretation of Article 113 are supported by the EP. See R. Gosalbo Bono 'The International Powers of the European Parliament, The Democratic Deficit and the Treaty on European Union' (1994) 12 YEL 1992, 85–138, pp. 106–23.
19. See EP's Report to the IGC, 19 May 1995, EP Doc. A4-0102/95, pp. 14–15.
20. This justification is unconvincing in relation to major commercial agreements or instruments, rather than day to day implementation measures.
21. See M. Westlake, *A Modern Guide to the European Parliament* (London, Pinter, 1994), p. 40. In Case C-65/93, *Parliament v Council* [1995] ECR I-643, the ECJ found the Parliament to have failed in its duty of genuine cooperation in relation to the adoption of a GSP package.
22. Assent requires an absolute majority of the votes cast, Article 141.
23. On the EP and Decisions by Association Councils see Neuwahl (1996) 33 CMLRev, 51–68.
24. Dashwood suggests that the drafting of (ii) and (iii) is too wide, 'The Limits of European Community Powers' (1996) 21 ELRev, 113–28. At the IGC it has been suggested that the assent procedure should cover certain international agreements, accession treaties, decisions on own resources (excluding legislative acts), Article 235 and revision of the treaties, Progress Report on IGC, Presidency Conclusions, European Council in Florence, 21–22 June 1996, Doc. SN 300/96, Annexes, p. 21.

Community where the agreement provides for them to be adopted by a simplified procedure or by a body set up by the agreement' (Article 228(4)). The Council may attach specific conditions to such authorization. This power is increasingly important as the number of agreements providing for such modification are growing, for example, in the sphere of international environmental law.

Agreements amending the EC Treaty

If an envisaged agreement requires the amendment of the EC Treaty, then those amendments must first be adopted in accordance with the procedures in Article N of the TEU (Article 228(5)).[25]

Requesting an opinion from the ECJ on an international agreement[26]

Article 228(6) provides for the possibility of the Council, the Commission or a member state, requesting an opinion from the ECJ on whether an envisaged agreement is compatible with the EC Treaty.[27] Most of the Article 228 opinions have been sought by the Commission.[28] The EP cannot seek an opinion, but the ECJ has permitted it to submit observations and has made specific reference to these in its opinions.[29] An interesting procedural point is that all of the Advocate-Generals give their views to the ECJ.[30] Those views are not published and are not referred to by the ECJ in its opinions. The total number of Article 228 opinions is small, ten in total. Notably, seven of that ten have been sought in the 1990s.

The purpose of an Article 228(6) opinion is to 'forestall complications which would result from legal disputes concerning

25. See *Opinion 2/94* (ECHR), 28 March 1996.
26. See L. Neville-Brown and T. Kennedy, *The Court of Justice of the European Communities*, 4th edn (London, Sweet and Maxwell, 1994), pp. 227–43; T. Tridimas and P. Eeckhout, 'The External Competence of the Community and the Case-Law of the Court of Justice: Principle versus Pragmatism' (1995) 14 YEL 1994, 143–77, pp. 146–8.
27. See K.P.E. Lasok, *The European Court of Justice* (London, Butterworths, 1994), pp. 588–92.
28. The exceptions are *Opinion 2/92* (National Treatment Instrument) sought by Belgium, *Opinion 3/94* (Bananas Agreement) sought by Germany and *Opinion 2/94* (ECHR), sought by the Council.
29. See *Opinion 1/94* (WTO); *Opinion 2/94* (ECHR). Thus, in effect, the EP may be able to protect its prerogatives but only when an opinion has been requested.
30. For example, *Opinion 2/94* (ECHR) was an opinion of a Court of fifteen judges given after hearing the views of nine Advocate-Generals.

the compatibility with the Treaty of international agreements binding upon the Community'.[31] Those complications may be external as well as internal:

> A Decision by the ECJ to the effect that such an agreement is, by reason either of its content or of the procedure adopted for its conclusion, incompatible with the provisions of the Treaty could not fail to provoke, not only in a Community context but also in that of international relations. serious difficulties and might give rise to adverse consequences for all interested parties, including third countries.[32]

In *Opinion 2/94* (ECHR) the ECJ described the Article 228(6) procedure as –

> a special procedure of collaboration between the Court of Justice on the one hand and the other Community institutions on the other whereby, at a stage prior to the conclusion of an agreement which is capable of giving rise to a dispute concerning the legality of a Community act which concludes, implements or applies it, the Court is called upon to ensure, in accordance with Article 164 of the Treaty, that in the interpretation and application of the Treaty the law is observed.

The ECJ will state an opinion under Article 228(6) 'at any time before the Community's consent to be bound by the agreement is finally expressed'.[33] The ECJ has been very robust in dismissing submissions that a request for an opinion is inadmissible, premature or too late. It has only once refused a request for an opinion.[34] Commonly in international law, and particularly for important agreements, there is a two-stage process – signature, followed by ratification.[35] The latter represents the expression of

---

31. *Opinion 3/94* (Bananas Agreement), [1995] ECR I-4577, pr. 16.
32. Ibid., pr. 17.
33. *Opinion 1/94* (WTO), pr, 12. The final expression of consent, usually by ratification or accession, is as a matter of international law rather than of EC law. See Macleod, Hendry and Hyett, *The External Relations of the European Communities*, pp. 116–19.
34. *Opinion 3/94* (Bananas Agreement) [1995] ECR I-4577. The ECJ regarded the request as devoid of purpose because the Framework Agreement on Bananas had already been concluded. It noted that the member states or community institution which had requested the opinion could bring an action for annulment of the Council's decision to conclude the agreement and may in that context apply for interim relief.
35. Agreements which are binding on signature alone are legally permissible in international law and are increasingly used.

consent to be bound, so signature of an agreement does not preclude an opinion for the ECJ. *Opinion 1/94* concerned the WTO Agreement, which had been signed.[36]

Opinion 2/94 on the ECHR concerned the possible accession of the EC to an international Treaty dating from 1952. There was no draft Treaty on EC accession. Indeed, there had been no negotiations and none was envisaged before the ECJ's opinion. Moreover, according to the Council, no decision on the principle of opening negotiations could be undertaken until the ECJ had considered whether the proposed accession was compatible with the EC Treaty. The Council, the Commission, the EP and five member states submitted that the request was admissible. The Council stressed that it was confronted with fundamental issues concerning legal and institutional order. The ECHR was well known and the legal issues surrounding accession were sufficiently clear. Four member states submitted that the request was inadmissible or premature. The UK also argued that there was no agreement 'envisaged' within the meaning of Article 228(6). The ECJ identified the two main problems raised by the request. The first concerned the competence of the Community to conclude such an agreement. The ECJ considered that the general purpose and subject matter of the ECHR and the institutional significance of accession were perfectly well known. There had been various Commission studies and proposals and the issue was on the Council's agenda. The Council had a 'legitimate concern to know the exact extent of its powers before taking any decision on the opening of negotiations'.[37] Finally, for the Article 228(6) procedure to be effective it had to be possible to refer a question of competence to the ECJ before negotiations had formally begun.[38] As far as it concerned competence the request was therefore admissible.[39]

The second problem identified by the ECJ was compatibility of an envisaged agreement with the provisions of the EC Treaty, in particular, those relating to the jurisdiction of the ECJ itself. Many of the problems and issues had been addressed in the submissions to the ECJ.[40] However, the ECJ accepted that it had been given no

---

36. *Opinion 1/94* (WTO), prs. 10–12. See P.J. Kuijper, 'The Conclusion and Implementation of the Uruguay Round Results by the EC' (1995) 6 EJIL, 222–44.

37. *Opinion 2/94* (ECHR), pr. 14.   38. Ibid., pr. 16.

39. *Opinion 2/94* (ECHR) concluded that the EC did not have competence to accede to the ECHR.

40. The ECJ's two opinions relating to the EEA Agreement were particularly important. Compatibility with Articles 164 and 219 of the Treaty are among the central issues. See *Opinion 2/94* (ECHR), Part VI.

detailed information as to the solutions that were envisaged to give effect in practice to the submission of the Community to the present and future judicial control machinery of the ECHR. Accordingly, the ECJ was not in a position to give its opinion on the compatibility of Community accession to the ECHR with the rules of the Treaty.[41]

Even when the process of conclusion under Article 228 is completed as a matter of EC law, the international law requirements and formalities as to ratification or accession will have to be complied with.[42]

It is important to be clear on the legal context in which the ECJ gives an opinion. It does not determine the capacity of the EC to enter into agreements as a matter of international law. It determines that capacity solely as a matter of Community law. It will consider all questions of the compatibility of an agreement with the provisions of the EC Treaty. In particular, it will determine the competence of the Community and of the member states within the area of the agreement,[43] and the powers and procedures of the EC institutions.[44] If the ECJ decides that an agreement would be incompatible with the EC Treaty, then the agreement may either not proceed, be revised so as to comply with the opinion of the Court, or the procedure to amend the EC Treaty must be gone through first.[45] For example, the European Economic Area Agreement had to be revised after the first opinion of the ECJ on it.[46] After the second opinion of the ECJ on the revised agreement it was proceeded with.[47] The ECJ's opinion in *Opinion 2/94* (ECHR) that the Community has no competence to accede to the ECHR means that accession could only be brought about by amendment of the EC Treaty.[48]

Once the ECJ has decided on any questions of competence, it is then a matter of international law how other states or international organizations respond to those assertions of competence. Further negotiations may be required so as to permit

---

41. *Opinion 2/94* (ECHR), prs. 19–22.
42. See P. Pescatore, 'Treaty-making by the European Communities' in F. Jacobs and S. Roberts (eds), *The Effect of Treaties in Domestic Law* (London: Sweet and Maxwell, 1987).
43. *Opinion 1/94* (WTO), prs. 3–4. See also Article 107(2) of the ECJ's Rules of Procedure, [1991] OJ L176/7.
44. See *Opinion 1/78* (Natural Rubber), pr. 30.
45. This last possibility has never occurred.
46. *Opinion 1/91* (First EEA Opinion) [1991] ECR 6079.
47. *Opinion 1/92* (Second EEA Opinion) [1992] ECR I-2821.
48. *Opinion 2/94* (ECHR), pr. 35.

the EC to ratify the agreement in place of, or in addition to, the member states. The EC and the member states may need to cooperate to determine how the competence of the EC or shared competence can be given practical effect.[49] A declaration of the respective competencies of the EC and the member states may be required by the other parties. It can even be the case that the competence of the EC has to be exercised 'through the medium of the member states acting jointly in the Community's interest'.[50] For example, this was the case with ILO Convention No. 170 because that Convention was only open to member states. The EC could not, as a matter of international law, become a party to it. Similarly, in operative terms, the EC could not participate in the tripartite system of the ILO – states, employers and employees. In relation to agreements where there is shared competence there is, as matter of EC law, a duty of cooperation, 'to ensure that there is a close association between the institutions of the Community and the member states in the process of negotiation and in the fulfilment of the obligations entered into'.[51] The Community institutions and the member states must take all the measures necessary so as best to ensure such cooperation.[52] This duty of cooperation results from the requirement of unity in the international representation of the Community. This duty has been stressed a number of times by the ECJ.[53]

The same reasoning can apply even if the EC has exclusive competence but it cannot become a party. The competence can be exercised through the medium of the member states acting jointly in the Community's interest. This was the situation in respect of the GATT, where the member states were contracting parties, although the EC, by the end of the transitional period, had acquired exclusive competence.[54]

An international agreement can also be the subject of a proceedings under Articles 169 or 170; a direct challenge before the ECJ under Article 173;[55] a preliminary reference under Article 177; or a claim for damages for non-contractual liability under

---

49. See J. Auvret-Finck, 'L'Avis Relatifs A La Convention No. 170 De L'OIT' (1995), 31 CDE, 443–60, pp. 457–60.
50. Ibid., pr. 5.   51. Ibid., pr. 36.   52. Ibid., pr. 38.
53. See *Ruling 1/78* (Draft Convention on Nuclear Material); *Opinion 2/91* (ILO); *Opinion 1/94* (WTO). See Macleod, Hendry and Hyett, *The External Relations of the European Communities*, pp. 148–50.
54. *International Fruit Company Case.*
55. See, e.g., Case C-327/91, *Re the EC-USA Competition Laws Agreement: France v EC Commission*, [1994] ECR I-3641.

Article 215.[56] As these various proceedings protect different kinds of interests, so the approach and receptivity of the ECJ may vary.[57]

Strategies relating to competence

How do member states approach questions of competence?

We have already noted that the wide external relations capacity of the EC is now accepted by the member states.[58] The central issues for member states now revolve around whether the competence of the EC in a particular field exists at all, and if it does, whether it is exclusive or shared with the member states. In practical terms, questions of competence, and therefore of legal base, are at the forefront when the member states are considering proposed developments in the EC. This partially explains why the Commission's right of initiative and its power to alter its proposals are so important.[59] The Council can only amend Commission proposals by a unanimous vote.[60]

We consider first the range of options open to member states, remembering all the time that member states' views may vary across a wide spectrum.

a) Objecting to any EC competence

At one extreme, a member state may take the view that, even accepting that the EC has a wide external relations capacity, that should not be extended beyond the task, activities and objectives of the EC.[61] So there may be matters which a member state argues

---

56. Many of the cases discussed in ch. 7 below were Article 173 proceedings. For a fascinating Article 215 claim on the responsibility of the Commission and the Council for their acts and omissions relating to EC fishing agreements with Senegal and Guinea, see Case T-572/93, *Odigitria v Council and Commission* [1995] ECR II-2025.

57. See Tridimas and Eeckhout (1995) 14 YEL 1994, pp. 145, 158–9; H.G. Schermers and D. Waelbroeck, *Judicial Protection in the European Communities*, 5th edn (Deventer, Kluwer 1992).

58. See p. 67 above. See also the Declarations to the SEA and the TEU that certain provisions 'do not affect the principles resulting from the judgment' in the ERTA case.

59. Article 189a. See also Article 152 under which the Council can request the Commission to undertake studies and to submit proposals, and the EP's power in Article 138b.

60. Article 189a(1). See also n. 8 above.

61. On the task and activities of the EC see ch. 1. pp. 18–19 above. To determine the 'objectives' of the Treaty for the purposes of Article 235, reference can be made to the Preamble of the Treaty, see Case 43/75, *Defrenne v SABENA* [1976] ECR 455.

should not be dealt with by the EC at all. For example, in *Opinion 2/94* (ECHR) five of the member states argued that the protection of human rights was not an objective of the EC, so that Article 235 could not be a legal basis for accession to the ECHR. Eight of the member states, the Commission and the EP submitted that respect for human rights could be seen as an objective of the EC. The ECJ's opinion was that, 'No Treaty provision confers on the Community institutions any general power to enact rules on human rights or to conclude international conventions in this field',[62] and that the implications of accession to the ECHR went beyond the scope of Article 235.[63] It did not explicitly state whether or not the protection of human rights was an objective of the EC.

Another contemporary example is whether the EC should take measures relating to racial discrimination and xenophobia.[64] The UK and France appears to take the view that these are not within the competence of the EC but should be dealt with under the Third Pillar of the TEU.[65] An alternative view is that such phenomena can be viewed as obstacles to the free movement of workers, to establishment and to the provision of services, and the establishment of the internal market generally. Interestingly, the Commission has expressed the view that the EC Treaty contains no possible basis for regulating racial discrimination.[66] However, it will propose non-discrimination clauses in Community instruments on a case by case basis.[67]

Politically there is great pressure to agree some measures because of the growing incidence of racism in parts of Europe. The European Council in Corfu (1994) agreed that 'steps would be taken to combat these phenomena'.[68] It established a Consultative Committee to report and put forward concrete proposals.[69] In

---

62. *Opinion 2/94* (ECHR), pr. 27.   63. Ibid., prs. 28–36.
64. See D. Curtin and M. Guerts, 'Race Discrimination and the European Union Anno 1996: From Rhetoric to Legal Remedy' (1996) 14/2 Netherlands Quarterly of Human Rights, 147–71.
65. See G. Bindman, 'The Starting Point' (1995) 145 NLJ, 62–3.
66. See Commission's White Paper on European Social Policy, COM (94)333, pr. 25.
67. See Communication from the Commission on Racism, Xenophobia and Anti-Semitism, COM(95)653, at p. 17. See Curtin and Guerts (1996) 14/2 Netherlands Quarterly of Human Rights, 147–71.
68. See Bull-EU, 6-1994, points I.23 and I.29. See also Council Conclusion on an overall strategy to combat racism and xenophobia, Bull-EU, 6-1995, point 1.2.2; and the Conclusions of the Cannes European Council, Bull-EU, 6-1995, point I.23.
69. European Council Consultative Commission on Racism and Xenophobia, Final Report, 12 April 1995, Doc. SN2129/95.

October 1995 the Council and the representatives of the governments of the member states adopted (i) a Resolution on racism and xenophobia in the fields of employment and social affairs, and (ii) a Resolution on the response of educational systems to the problems of racism and xenophobia.[70] Clearly these are limited steps. Whether the EC Treaty should have specific texts is one of the issues being considered at the IGC.[71]

In any event, if any of the forms of measures in Article 189[72] are eventually agreed on, it is then very difficult to argue that the matter does not come within EC competence. This is so even in relation to 'Recommendations' and 'opinions' which, under the terms of Article 189, 'have no binding force'.[73] The various measures that can be taken by the different institutions under Article 189 are expressly limited to those, 'In order to carry out their task and in accordance with the provisions of this Treaty'.

If a member state can secure that only a 'Declaration' or a 'Resolution' is passed then this strengthens the argument that its subject matter is not within the EC's competence.[74] An example might be the Joint Declaration on Fundamental Rights by the European Parliament, the Council and the Commission in 1977.[75] However, it must be borne in mind that the ECJ stresses substance over form in its analysis of acts. It also puts great weight on the duty of cooperation on member states. Thus, in *France v United Kingdom* the ECJ considered a Resolution of the Council, on 'certain external aspects of the creation of a 200 mile fishing zone' (the Hague Resolution). It took the view that the Resolution, 'in the particular field to which it applies, makes specific the duties of cooperation which the Member states assumed under Article 5 of the EEC treaty when they acceded to the Community'.[76] The UK was found to be in breach of its obligations under the Resolution, as well as under the Treaty and secondary legislation.[77]

A member state's argument is stronger again if it can force a

---

70. [1995] OJ C296 and [1995] OJ C312 respectively. See Bull-EU, 10-1995, point 1.2.1–1.2.2.
71. See Progress Report on IGC, p. 4; 'General Outline', ch. 1.
72. I.e. Regulations, Directives, Decisions, Recommendations and Opinions.
73. Article 189. On the legal effect of recommendations see Case C-322/88, *Grimaldi v Fonds des Maladies Professionelles* [1989] ECR 4407.
74. On the ECJ's approach to informal instruments see J. Klabbers, 'Informal Instruments Before the European Court of Justice' (1994) 31 CMLRev, 997–1023.
75. Treaty Series 1995, p. 887.
76. Case 141/78, *France v United Kingdom* [1979] ECR 2923, pr. 8.
77. Ibid., pr. 12.

proposed text to be adopted outside of the Council altogether. For example, the UK's objection to the 'Community Charter of the Fundamental Social Rights of Workers' (1989) was so strong that it would not adopt it. So the Charter was adopted by the Heads of State or Government of the then eleven other member states.[78] Another technique is the adoption of a 'Resolution of the member states meeting within the Council'. This is not a Community act. More problematic is a 'Resolution of the Council and the representatives of Governments meeting within the Council'. These can be used where the substance of the resolution arguably covers matters within the competence of the EC and of the member states and so they do not prejudice the issue of competence.[79]

It as also worth pointing out that national legislatures may be acutely conscious of the issue of EC competence in its own right, and in relation to their own relative power. This is clearly a factor that the member state must take account of.[80] Also, more generally, the policy of a member state in relation to competence must form part of an overall political and legal strategy towards the EC. All strategies have outcomes which cover the essential, the desirable, and the merely preferable. The EC, like any other political community, moves forward on the basis of many compromises and accommodations. It is also important to remember that member states do not always share the same legal views, and even if they agree to the answer on the legal question they may differ in their reasoning.[81]

b) Accept that EC competence can serve national interests

A member state may legitimately take the view that EC competence (and indeed exclusive EC competence) is in its interest because that offers the best possibility of achieving its national objectives. Those objectives may relate to the general political evolution of the EC. More federalist-minded member states are doubtless aware that exclusive competence has a kind of

78. Commission 1990, Luxembourg: Office for Official Publications. See B. Bercusson, *European Labour Law*, 1996, pp. 575–606. See now the Protocol to the TEU on Social Policy.
79. See, e.g., the Resolution on human rights, democracy and development of 28 November 1991, Bull-EC, 11-1991, p. 130, point 2.3.1.
80. See *EC External Competence*, House of Lords Select Committee on the European Communities, 17th Report, 1984–85, HL 236. See Declarations Nos 13 and 14 to the TEU on National Parliaments.
81. See, e.g., the submissions of the member states in *Opinion 1/94* (WTO) and in *Opinion 2/94* (ECHR).

federalising, integrative effect.[82] Or the member state's objectives may relate to a specific area which is under international negotiation. The EC as a single superpower may be able to achieve a better negotiating result. Also, if the EC asserts its exclusive competence, then unilateral action by member states is largely ruled out.[83] Some member states may judge this to be in their long-term interest.

c) Continue to cooperate in practice but reserve the legal position

On one level, issues of competence can sometimes appear as a kind of machiavellian political struggle between the EC and the member state in an area of deep complexity and obscurity. One might even be surprised that any work can progress in the light of these difficulties and uncertainties. In reality, practice has to continue. Even if a member state is willing to accept that the EC has competence, or at least potential competence, it still has various strategies open to it.

Positions are often reserved while progress continues, for example, the Commission acts as the sole negotiator on behalf of the Community and the member states, even though there is a continuing dispute about whether it had competence or exclusive competence in a number of areas. This was the approach taken to the Uruguay Round of the GATT negotiations.[84] In the minutes of the meeting of the Council which decided that the Commission would be the sole negotiator it was stated that that decision did, 'not prejudice the question of the competence on the Community or of the Member States on particular issues'. It is just more practical to operate in this way because it, 'ensures the maximum consistency in the conduct of the negotiations'.[85] The member states retain important influence though the special committees that the Council can appoint to work alongside the Commission while it is negotiating.[86]

[82.] For example, in *Opinion 2/92* (OECD National Treatment Instrument), see n. 5 above (Belgium).

[83.] See G. Close, 'Self-restraint by the EEC in the Exercise of its External Powers' (1982) 1 YEL 1981, 45–68. On the limited possibilities for member states see Macleod, Hendry and Hyett, *The External Relations of the European Communities*, pp. 61–3.

[84.] See Kuijper (1995) 6 EJIL, 222–44.

[85.] *Opinion 1/94* (WTO), pr. 3. Third states may not appreciate the subtlety of this though.

[86.] See p. 91 above.

d) Secure an express statement on competence

Member states can seek to ensure that their position on competence is recorded in the minutes of Council meetings.[87] Such a statement would normally be to the effect that the decision concerned does not imply any extension of EC competence. Although the ECJ has consistently held that a 'mere practice' of the Council cannot derogate from the rules laid down in the Treaty, the minutes of the Council are clearly of evidential weight.[88] This was the case in the *Opinion 1/94* on the WTO. Such a statement on competence can also appear in the negotiating mandate of the Commission.[89] It can also appear in the decision of the Council approving Community participation in the international agreement. In relation to the GATT/WTO negotiations the Council authorized the President of the Council and the relevant Commissioner to sign the Final Act and the WTO Agreement. As the representatives of the member states took the view that those acts 'also covered matters of national competence', they agreed on the same date to proceed to sign the documents. The Commission ensured that the minutes of the Council also recorded its position that 'the Final Act ... and the agreements annexed thereto fall exclusively within the competence of the European Community'.[90] Again, these strategies will only be of evidential weight but they may well be effective in practice.[91]

A parallel technique is for the international agreement itself to expressly provide that it does not imply any extension of EC competence. Such a provision is known as a 'Canada-Clause'. This is a reference to the first use of such a provision in the EC-Canada Agreement of 1976.[92]

There is also an interesting example of practice by the ECSC.

87. See W. Nicoll, 'Note the Hour – and File the Minute' (1993) 31 JCMS, 558–66; Klabbers (1994) 31 CMLRev, 997–1023; J. Monar, 'Interinstitutional Agreements: The Phenomenon and its New Dynamics After Maastricht' (1994) 31 CMLRev, 693–719.
88. *Opinion 1/94* (WTO), pr. 52. On access to the minutes of the Council and of the Commission see the Code of Conduct concerning public access to documents, OJ 1993 L340/43; Council Decision 93/731 on public access to Council Documents; Case T-194/94, *Carvel v Council* [1995] ECR II-2765.
89. See pp. 90–1 above. 90. *Opinion 1/94* (WTO), pr. 5.
91. See above on 'mere practice'. Of course, where both the Council and the Commission's views are recorded in the minutes their evidential weight may cancel each other out. The ECJ's approach to the use of minutes has not been consistent. See Klabbers (1994) 31 CMLRev, 997–1023.
92. [1976] OJ L260/1. See Macleod, Hendry and Hyett, *The External Relations of the European Communities*, pp. 234–5.

This concerned a series of agreements in 1982 with the US on steel products. Whether such products fell within Article 113 was an open question because of the terms of Article 71 of the ECSC Treaty which provided that the powers of the member states in matters of commercial policy shall not be affected by the ECSC Treaty. However, the US wanted the agreements to be with the EC rather than with the member states. The Commission adopted a series of Decisions under Article 95 ECSC Treaty, which broadly parallels Article 235 of the EC Treaty. The Decisions recited that they did not affect the powers of the member states in matters of Commercial policy within Article 71 of the ECSC Treaty. Arguably, such a situation is one where the ECSC was acting as trustee for the member states.[92A]

e) Resist the adoption of 'common rules'

The nature of the Community measures under Article 189 may be of more significance here. As recommendations and opinions are not legally binding, they cannot constitute 'common rules' for the purpose of the ERTA doctrine.[93] According to *Opinion 1/92* (ILO), there can be shared competence if the EC's rules are minimum rules rather than common ones.[94] If the member states want to resist exclusive EC competence they need to avoid the adoption of common rules. There has been a discernable tendency in EC legislation to adopt minimum rules.[95] There is express provision for this in Article 100a concerning internal market measures. The TEU added a number of other provisions in which harmonization is excluded,[96] although the EC is required to be mindful of a 'high level' of protection.[97] If measures were adopted in these fields they would presumably not establish common rules.

We also noted above the importance, in relation to questions of competence, of identifying the subject matter at issue.[98] When the member states are adopting measures in the Council that will constitute common rules, they need to consider the scope of the

---

[92A.] See now *Opinion 1/94* (WTO) [1994] ECR I-5267, prs. 25–7.

[93.] See G. Close, 'Self-restraint by the EEC in the exercise of its external powers', (1982) 1 YEL 1981, 45–68; ch. 4, pp. 71–5 above on common rules. In education and culture EC action is restricted to incentive measures and recommendations, see Articles 126(4) and 128(5).

[94.] Ibid.

[95.] S. Weatherill and P. Beaumont, *EC Law*, 2nd edn, 1995, pp. 23–5; Conclusions of the European Council, Edinburgh, 1992.

[96.] See Articles 126(2), 127(4), 128(5) and 129(4).

[97.] See Articles 126(1), 129(1), 129a(1) and 130(r) 2.   [98.] See p. 43 above.

precedent they are setting. This makes the drafting of the preamble to the measure, and its substantive scope, of considerable importance.[99] If the matter is subsequently litigated the Commission will tend to press for the widest interpretation of any precedent.[100] Again, the adoption of minutes in the Council may be of some assistance.

f) Seek mixed negotiations, mixed agreements, and mixed representation on implementing bodies

The power of the negotiator is a well recognized phenomenon. Member states may seek mixed negotiations and mixed representation on the implementing bodies of the international organizations established by those agreements. As Groux noted – '. . . experience shows that the Council decision to use the mixed procedure in negotiating a draft agreement almost inevitable coincides with the subsequent decision of the Council to give a mixed character to the negotiated agreement'.[101] Ensuring that a particular agreement is in mixed form will set a precedent for any agreement amending it and for similar agreements. Such a precedent is hard to overturn.

If the EC is solely authorized to become a party to an international agreement this will be an acceptance by the member states that it has exclusive competence over the matters in that agreement. It will also imply that the EC has internal competence even if there are no express Treaty provisions or common rules. If there are any doubts about the EC's competence then the member states will press for the use of a mixed agreement. These are effectively a legal and political compromise. Member states often have the political power to successfully secure the negotiation and conclusion of mixed agreements.[102]

---

99. An interesting example is Council Regulation 3381/94 on Dual Purpose Goods, [1994] OJ L367/1 as amended, read along with Council Decision 94/942/CFSP, [1996] OJ L367/8. See I. Govaere and P. Eeckhout, 'On Dual Use Goods and Dualist Case Law: The *Aimé Richardt* Judgment on Export Controls' (1992) 29 CMLRev, 941–66; Case C-70/94, *Fritz-Werner Industrie-Ausrustengen Gmbh v FRG*, [1995] ECR I-3189, on national controls on dual purpose goods based, *inter alia*, on Articles 223 and 224 of the EC Treaty.
100. As it did in Opinion 1/94 (WTO).
101. J. Groux, 'Mixed Negotioations', in D. O'Keeffe and H.G. Schermers (eds), *Mixed Agreements* (Dordrecht, Nijhoff, 1983), p. 90.
102. See ch. 5, above; E. Stein, 'External Relations of the European Community: Structure and Process', Academy of European Law, European University Institute, Florence (1990) vol. I, 115–88, pp. 160–3.

g) Resist declarations of competence

This strategy leaves more room for negotiation with the Commission. It also reflects the point that competence is an evolving phenomenon. Declarations of competence also defeat one of the advantages of mixed agreements which is that they de-emphasize disputes between the Commission and the member states over the precise demarcation of competence. Thus if member states are obliged by third states to make declarations of competence, they make them as general as possible and may refer to its evolutionary nature.[103]

Decisions authorizing the conclusion of association agreements often provide that questions relating to the division of powers between the member states and the EC are to be solved internally before discussion in the Association Council takes place.

h) Resist external competence based on Articles 100, 100a or 235 until that competence is exercised internally

We have considered above the possibility of basing external EC competence on Articles 100 and 235.[104]

i) Seek an opinion of the ECJ under Article 228 on whether an international agreement is compatible with the EC Treaty

This is probably best seen as a strategy of last resort.[105] Any litigation is always unpredictable. The ECJ is institutionally disposed towards the enhancement of the powers of the EC and its institutions rather than preserving those of the member states.[106] Indeed, the ECJ has been in the forefront of the evolution of the law on external relations.[107] Even if a member state wins on the substance, there is the danger than the ECJ will state principles of more general application that the member state would wish to avoid. It is striking to contrast the increasing use of the ECJ to challenge the legal basis of internal measures with the limited number of opinions under Article 228. It is possible to argue that

---

103. See K.R. Simmonds, 'The Communities Declaration Upon Signature of the U.N. Convention on the Law of the Sea' (1986) 23 CMLRev, 521–44.
104. See ch. 3, pp. 62–6 above.
105. Though Belgium sought *Opinion 2/92*, on the OECD National Treatment Instrument, seeking to establish that the EC had exclusive competence.
106. See pp. 94–9 above.
107. See chs. 3–4 above; E. Stein, op. cit., pp. 127–8.

the more recent opinions, on the ILO, the WTO and the OECD, are more in line with the interests of the member states.[108] In *Opinion 1/92* the ECJ found that there was joint competence. Similarly, in *Opinion 1/94* (WTO) in relation to the GATS, TRIMs and TRIPs, and in *Opinion 2/92* (OECD) on an OECD Decision on a National Treatment Instrument. In *Opinion 2/94* (ECHR) the member states were clearly divided. The ECJ opinion favoured the more restrictive view of the minority of member states that the EC did not have competence to accede to the EC Treaty. It is arguable that the greater conservatism evident in the ECJ's more recent opinions and decisions may reflect its sensitivity to the political controversy surrounding the ratification of the TEU, the concerns of the German Constitutional Court in the *Brunner Case*,[109] and even to fears of member states seeking to limit its powers.[110]

Finally, it is interesting to note that, until recently, relatively very few member states made submissions to the ECJ concerning Article 228 opinions. By contrast, in *Opinion 2/94* (ECHR) all of the member states made written or oral submissions.

j) Maintain that member states retain a separate competence in the field concerned

For example, in *Re European Development Fund: EP v Council* the ECJ accepted that in the field of development aid the EC's competence was not exclusive and member states were accordingly entitled to enter into commitment themselves vis-à-vis non-member states, either collectively or individually, or even jointly with the EC.[111] In *Re Aid to Bangladesh: EP v Council and Commission* the ECJ similarly accepted that in the area of humanitarian aid the EC does not have exclusive competence and, therefore, member states are not prevented from exercising collectively their powers in this respect.[112] They could do this inside the Council or outside it. Moreover, the member states may delegate the task to the Commission of supervising the

---

108. See Tridimas and Eeckhout, (1995) 14 YEL 1994, 143–77.
109. *Brunner and Others v the European Union Treaty* [1994] 1 CMLR 57.
110. See the differing views of T.C. Hartley, 'The European Court, Judicial Objectivity and the Constitution of the European Union' (1996) 112 LQR, 95–109 and A. Arnull, 'The European Court and Judicial Objectivity: A Reply to Professor Hartley' (1996) 112 LQR, 411–23.
111. Case C-316/91, [1994] ECR I-625, pr. 26.
112. Cases C-181/91 and C-248/91, [1993] ECR I-3885, pr. 16.

co-ordinating of a collective action undertaken by them, and may use the Community's budgetary rules.

k) Ensure that any new Treaty texts expressly provide for joint competence

The extensions of EC competence in the TEU were very carefully worded in competence terms. It is likely that this pattern will be repeated in the texts from the IGC.

How do the EC institutions approach questions of competence?

We consider the institutions in turn.

The Council

This can be briefly considered because it is the forum in which the member states interests are substantially represented. Many of the strategies open to member states apply equally to the Council. However, it is important to recognize that the practice and voting requirement in the Council mean that compromises must be sought and agreements reached. Many decisions can now be taken by QMV, for example, in relation to internal market measures. Under the ERTA doctrine to the extent that these measures establish common rules, they may generate a parallel exclusive competence.[113] Invocation of the Luxembourg Accord remains a residual possibility but in practice it is of influence more in securing agreement than in its being used.[114] There is no evidence that it has ever been used to block measures establishing internal rules solely because of objections relating to external competence, though of course member states are fully aware of the ERTA effect of their adoption of internal measures. In respect of requests for opinions under Article 228(6) the Council makes separate submissions to the ECJ. It has its own institutional voice in which the Legal Service of the Council plays an important role.

The Commission

The Commission's range of options are often the reverse of those of the member states. As with any other negotiator, the

---

113. See chs. 3–4 above.
114. See T.C. Hartley, *The Foundations of European Community Law*, 3rd edn (Oxford, Clarendon Press, 1994), pp. 21–3.

Commission tends to push its legal and policy arguments to the limit. Some of its legal submissions in *Opinion 1/94* (WTO) were described by the UK as 'extravagant'.[115] It pushes its arguments in the knowledge that this leaves it scope to negotiate an accommodation with the member states and with the Council.

a) Assert the widest interpretation of EC competence

As an institution committed to defending the interests of the Community, the Commission's natural strategy is to assert ever widening EC competence. Its right of proposal is crucial, particularly in the light of the ERTA doctrine. In pursuing this strategy it has found a ready ally in the ECJ.

b) Assert exclusive EC competence

The Commission's strategy is often to seek exclusive EC participation in international agreements. With exclusive competence comes sole external representation by the Commission and, arguably, a more consistent and coherent representation of the Community's interests vis-à-vis the rest of the world. Thus the Commission argues for the widest interpretation of the articles of the Treaty which generate exclusive competence, notably Article 113 on the common commercial policy (CCP). *Opinion 1/94* (WTO) was a good example of this.[116] The Commission argued that the GATS, TRIMS and TRIPS all fell within the scope of the CCP, and so within the exclusive competence of the EC. Similarly the Commission presses for the widest interpretation of internal measures in terms of their ERTA effect of generating external competence. *Opinion 1/94* (WTO) again illustrates this. Finally, the Commission can argue that EC participation is 'necessary' in accordance with the *Opinion 1/76* (Rhine Navigation Case) doctrine.[117] The Commission also stresses the practical difficulties and disadvantages it faces if exclusive competence is denied to the EC.[118]

---

115. *Opinion 1/94* (WTO), [1995] 1 CMLR at p. 242. For a similar view from the Legal Adviser to the Council at the time of *Opinion 1/94* (WTO), see A. Dashwood, 'The Limits of European Community Powers' (1996) 21 ELRev, 113–28, p.126.
116. See the Commission's arguments in that opinion.
117. See ch. 4 above.
118. *Opinion 1/94* (WTO), pr. 106.

c) Accept that shared competence can be in the interests of the EC

The reality of practice is more complex than to allow the Commission to engage in a single-minded pursuit of Community competence. Inter-institutional tension is not conducive to the harmonious and cooperative development of the Community. Thus, notwithstanding the arguments in b) above, the Commission may decide that shared competence can be in the interests of the EC. Mixed agreements have thus rapidly increased as a political and legal accommodation. As the former Directive of the Legal Service of the European Communities has explained, selectivity and self-restraint may be part of a rational strategy –

> Rather than being a sign of weakness, it may . . . be taken as a sign of maturity if the Community recognizes that in the external relations field also a certain selectivity is necessary and that there are cases where self-restraint may be appropriate in the exercise of competence.[119]

This argument may have particular weight if the Commission can trade off a strong position on exclusive competence for an agreed strong position as negotiator on a wide range of international instruments. This happened in relation to commodity agreements under an informal arrangement known as 'PROBA 20'.[120] In exchange for conceding that all commodity agreements would be mixed agreements, the Commission obtained the Council's agreement that they would be Article 113 agreements, and that the Community would be represented by one single delegation for the Community and the member states. The normal spokesman would be the Commission and it would express with 'one voice' the common position established at Community co-ordination meetings. Obtaining common positions can be a time-consuming process and result in a 'Community package' which does not leave much room for negotiation.[121]

---

119. Close, op. cit., n. 93, p. 46.
120. See Groux, op. cit., n. 101; E. Wellenstein, 'Participation of the Community in International Commodity Agreements', in St. John Bates *et al.* (eds), *In Memoriam J.D.B. Mitchell* (London, Sweet and Maxwell, 1983), 65–73; J. Sack, 'The European Community's Membership of International Organisations' (1995) 32 CMLRev, 1227–56, pp. 1253–4. The arrangement is based on the understanding that all legal and institutional questions are set aside.
121. M. Cremona, 'The Doctrine of Exclusivity and the Position of Mixed Agreements in the External Relations of the European Community' (1982) 2 OJLS, 393–428, p. 423.

Accepting mixed agreements can allow the Commission to devote its energies to obtaining terms of agreement which are in the Community's best interest and will be acceptable to the member states in the Council. Even then the Commission may struggle for expertise in the fields concerned that matches that of some of the member states.

d) Continue to cooperate in practice but reserve the legal position; secure an express statement on competence

These strategies mirror those available to member states.

e) Seek the adoption of common rules

The adoption of common rules, rather than minimum rules, will generate the ERTA effect of external competence. Coverage of a field to a 'large extent' will suffice.[122]

f) Prefer exclusive negotiations, and sole representation on implementing bodies

We have considered these above. A downside of sole representation, if based on a claim of exclusive competence, is that the EC may only be accorded one vote. This greatly weakens its relative power.

g) Resist declarations of competence

As the representative of the Community, the Commission shares with member states a resistance to declarations of competence. If obliged to make such a declaration it will frame its proposal in the most general terms possible. Sometimes the EC has succumbed to pressure to supply a list of the relevant legislation.[123]

h) Assert external competence based on Articles 100 and 235, even if that competence has not been exercised internally

This scope of this strategy has been greatly limited by the ECJ in

122. See ch. 4 above on *Opinion 2/91* (ILO).
123. See E. Denza, 'Groping Towards Europe's Foreign Policy', in D. Curtin and T. Heukels (eds) *Institutional Dynamics of European Integration: Essays in Honour of H.G. Schermers*, vol. II (1994), p. 586.

its interpretation of the *Opinion 1/76* (Rhine Navigation Case) doctrine in *Opinion 1/94* (WTO), *Opinion 2/92* (OECD National Treatment Instrument), and by the interpretation of Article 235 in *Opinion 2/94* (ECHR).

i) Seek an opinion of the ECJ on Article 228; bring proceedings under Article 173

The Commission has made use of this option on a number of occasions. All but one of the Article 228 opinions delivered as of 1 July 1996 have been sought by the Commission.[124] They are usually requested as a final resort to resolve continuing disputes with member states relating to competence. The results have usually been very favourable to the Commission, though less so recently. The ECJ is institutionally disposed to the same kinds of Community interests as the Commission. The threat to resort to the ECJ is a powerful weapon and can induce political agreement. As Ehlermann has commented: 'Article 228 offers a less conflictual procedure than Article 169 or 170 of the EEC Treaty. But if it is used in order to recognize exclusive Community competence, it is nevertheless considered as an instrument of coercion and a struggle for power.'[125]

Article 173 proceedings are another avenue through which the Commission can assert its institutional powers.

j) Approach to the system of annual approval of bilateral commercial agreements by member states

The Commission stresses that these are under EC control and that Commission approval is required.[126] In its absence there would be no member states competence to maintain these agreements, subject to pre-existing obligations protected by Article 234.[127]

The Parliament

As well as using its increased powers under the TEU, the EP

---

124. See n. 28 above.
125. C.-D. Ehlermann, 'Mixed Agreements: A List of Problems', in O'Keeffe and Schermers, *Mixed Agreements*, p. 7.
126. On national measures of commercial policy see Case 41/76, *Criel, née Donckerwolke et al. v Procureur de la République au Tribunal de Grande Instance, Lille et al.* [1976] ECR 1921; ch. 10, p. 197 below.
127. See ch. 7, pp. 123–4 below.

pushes its competence informally through its Rules of Procedure and Inter-Institutional Agreements.[128] At the IGC it is seeking equal status with the Council in all fields of legislative and budgetary competence.[129] Interestingly, its formal exclusion from involvement from Article 113 agreements[130] puts it in conflict with the Commission which advocates a wide reading of Article 113 because it generates exclusive EC competence. Conversely, a narrower scope for CCP is conversely in the EP's interest in the sense of its own powers. The EP naturally tends to press for whatever interpretation will increase its own powers notwithstanding that national parliaments generally have a limited role in international treaty making.[131] Many of the decisions of the ECJ on legal base have favoured the EP. The EP wants to have the right to request opinions from the ECJ under Article 228(6).[132]

The EP has two committees which principally deal with international relations. These are the Foreign Affairs, Security and Defence Policy Committee and the External Relations Committee (REX).[133] The work of many of the other EP Committees is also of international importance, for example, the Development Cooperation Committee. The EP has also had resort to Article 173 to defend its prerogatives in relations to external relations.[134]

Third states and interest groups[135]

Perceptions of third states are naturally mixed. They do not want the EC to gain advantages *per se* from its unique status though it is worth noting Ehlermann's comment that, 'in reality, the conclusion of mixed agreements is not due to external but to internal reasons'.[136] Fears of 'Fortress Europe' arose particularly but not exclusively in the context of the 1992 Single Market

---

128. See R. Gosalbo Bono, 'The International Powers of the European Parliament, The Democratic Deficit and the Treaty on European Union' (1994) 12 YEL 1992, 85–138; W. Nicholl, 'The European Parliament's Post-Maastricht Rules of Procedure' (1994) 32 JCMS, 403–10; Monar (1994) 31 CMLRev, 693–719.
129. EP Report to the IGC, pr. 22(iii).
130. Article 228(3). In practice it is normally consulted.
131. See its submissions in *Opinion 1/94* (WTO).
132. EP Report to the IGC, pr. 22(v).
133. See Westlake, *A Modern Guide to the European Parliament*.
134. See, e.g., Case C-316/91, n. 111 above (the EDF case).
135. See J. Groux and P. Manin, *The European Communities in the International Order* (Brussels, EC Commission, European Perspective Series, 1985), pp. 67–9.
136. See Ehlermann, op. cit., p. 4.

programme.[137] Lobbying and negotiation solely with the Commission can be helpful in terms of simplicity, clarity to negotiate only with the EC, knowing that its terms will be acceptable to the member states. The complexities of competence can be more difficult and raise doubts as who should be dealing with whom. Competence may be disputed internally. The EC, supported by the ECJ, regard the matter as an internal one of no concern to third states but this is a somewhat arrogant view. The concerns of third states may mean though that they insist on a mixed agreement which EC and member states sign so they are covered wherever competence is found to lie.[138] They may also demand declarations of competence. The UN Convention on the Law of the Sea (1982) is a leading example.[139] Declarations are resisted by EC and member states, or kept general. As the EC a single international entity is an economic superpower, that power alone gives it political power in negotiations. Third states can face being told that if they do not accept the exclusive competence of the EC there will quite simply be no negotiations. Whatever the theoretical difficulties most third states have in practice adapted to the existence of the EC.[140] Some difficult questions of substance are rasied though. A good contemporary example is what it means for a third country to be entitled to most favoured nation treatment or non-discrimination under the General Agreement on Trade in Services, where there is shared competence.[141]

---

137. See P. Eeckhout, *The European Internal Market and International Trade* (Oxford, Clarendon Press, 1994); M. Davenport and S. Page, *Europe: 1992 and the Developing World* (London, Overseas Development Institute, 1991); J. Redmond, *The External Relations of the European Community: the International Response to 1992* (Basingstoke, Macmillan, 1992).
138. Cremona (1982) 2 OJLS, 393–428, p. 412.
139. See Simmonds (1986) 23 CMLRev, 521–44.
140. See Denza op. cit., n. 123; ch. 2 above.
141. The answer may depend upon whether it is the EC or the member state which is regarded as the party for the purposes of the matter at issue.

CHAPTER SEVEN

International agreements and the Community legal order

Introduction

The fundamental issues raised here concern (i) the reception of international agreements into community law, and (ii) whether the provisions of international agreements can be directly effective. If a provision of an international agreement is directly effective it means that it grants rights that must be upheld by the national courts of the member states. It is important to remember that the fact that whether the provisions of an international agreement do not have direct effect does not, of course, affect the Community's obligation to ensure that its provisions are observed in its relations with non-member states.[1] As the number of Treaties to which the EC is a party, or is otherwise bound,[2] these issues have increasingly had to be faced. They raise difficult policy issues for the ECJ over the interface between international law and EC law, and the degree of judicial control over the EC's conduct of external relations.[3]

[1.] Case 266/81, *SIOT v Ministero delle Finanze* [1983] ECR 731, pr. 28 (hereinafter *SIOT*).

[2.] See pp. 118, 121 below (on substitution).

[3.] See J. Bourgeois, 'Effects of International Agreements in European Community Law: Are the Dice Cast?' (1984) 82 MichLRev, 1250–73; I. Cheyne, 'International Agreements and the European Community Legal System' (1994) 18 ELRev, 581–98; L. Hancher, 'Constitutionalism, the Community Court and International Law' (1994) 25 NYIL, 259–98; J. Boulouis, 'Le Droit Des Communautés Européennes Dans Ses Rapports Avec Le Droit International Général' (1992) 235 *Recueil Des Cours* (1992–IV), 9–80, pp. 65–79.

The relationship between international law and community law

In international law theory there are essentially two views on the relationship between international law and national law. In the *monist* view there is a single system of law. This embraces both international and national law. European community law simply enters into that single system of law. The *dualist* view is that there are two separate systems of law, the national system and the international system. Community law must therefore descend from the international system and be incorporated into the national system by some kind of bridge or link. In the UK this is through an Act of Parliament. The monist conception is more in line with the ECJ's conception of the European Community legal system,[4] and it has applied it in its consideration of the relationship between international agreements and community law.

International agreements in the community legal order

The ECJ has applied a very extensive interpretation of Article 177 in the context of international agreements. A Council Decision or Regulation concluding an international agreement (in the sense of internal EC acceptance) is one of the 'acts' of a Community institution for the purposes of Article 177(1)(b).[5] So too are the Decisions of an Association Council since they are 'directly connected' with the agreement to which they give effect and the Association Council is entrusted with responsibility for the

---

4. See K. Meessen, 'The Application of Rules of Public International Law within Community Law' (1976) 13 CMLRev, 485–501, pp. 500–1; J. Groux and P. Manin, *The European Communities in the International Order* (Brussels, EC Commission, European Perspective Series, 1985); Hancher, 'Constitutionalism, the Community Court and International Law', pp. 276–7.

5. Case 181/73, *Haegeman v Belgium* [1974] ECR 449, pr. 4 (hereinafter *Haegeman*); Case 104/81, *Hauptzollamt Mainz v Kupferberg* [1982] ECR 3641 (hereinafter *Kupferberg*). Often a '*sui generis* decision' is used. 'If the agreement contains provisions which are capable of having direct effect, or which, if promulgated as internal legislation within the Community, would take the form of a regulation, the Council act concluding the agreement will often take the form of a regulation. Otherwise, the decision *sui generis* is used', I. Macleod, I. Hendry and S. Hyett, *The External Relations of the European Communities: A Manual of Law and Practice* (Oxford, OUP, 1996), p. 81.

implementation of the agreement.[6] Therefore, the ECJ has jurisdiction to rule on the 'validity' and 'interpretation' of those acts under the preliminary reference procedure.[7] In the *SPI and SAMI Case* the ECJ ruled that that jurisdiction also extended to an agreement, the GATT, to which the EC had succeeded as a matter of law and so there was no Community act all.[8]

In the *International Fruit Co Case* it was submitted that validity extended to 'validity under international law'.[9] The ECJ accepted this. Thus the validity of a measure, 'may be affected by reason of the fact that it is contrary to a rule of international law'.[10] The 'rule of international law' could be derived from an international agreement, customary international law, or be a general principle of international law.[11] However, only rules deriving from international agreements have been argued before the ECJ. Moreover, the ECJ has in fact never held a community measure invalid because it was contrary to international law. As the court of the Community it is institutionally disposed to uphold the validity of community measures against rules in international agreements.[12] However, where an international agreement can be given effect without having to invalidate a community measure, then the ECJ has been more receptive.[13] It is also interesting to note two arguments of the Commission in cases decided in 1982. In *Kupferberg* it submitted that, 'As a subject of international law particularly dependent on the proper functioning of the

---

6. Case C-192/89, *Sevince v Staatssecretaris van Justitie* [1990] ECR I-3461, prs. 9–10 (hereinafter *Sevince*); Case 30/88, *Greece v Commission* [1989] ECR 63, pr. 13; Case 351/95, *Selma Kadiman v Freistaat Bayern* on the interpretation of Article 7 of Decision 1/80 of the EEC/Turkey Association Council.

7. For a claim of alleged illegality of a bilateral fishing agreement concluded between the EC and Canada see Case T-194/95, *Area Cova and Others v Council*. See also n. 108 below.

8. Joined Cases 267 and 269/81, *Amministrazione delle Finanze dello Stato v SPI and SAMI* [1983] ECR 801. The succession by the Community is thus treated as having the same effect as an act of the Community. See AG Reisch in the *SPI and SAMI Case*; T.C. Hartley, 'International Agreements and the Community Legal System: Some Recent Developments', 8 ELRev (1983), 383–92.

9. Joined Cases 21 and 24/72, *International Fruit Company NV v Produktschap voor Groenten en Fruit* [1972] ECR 1219 (hereinafter *IFC Case*).

10. *IFC Case*, pr. 5.

11. See Article 38 of the Statute of the ICJ.

12. This partially explains the ECJ's restrictive interpretation of *locus standi* under Article 173. See T.C. Hartley, *The Foundations of European Community Law*, 3rd edn (Oxford, Clarendon Press, 1994), pp. 361–92.

13. See P. Craig and G. De Burca, *EC Law – Text, Cases and Materials* (Oxford, OUP, 1995), pp. 171–2.

international legal order the Community has no interest in impeding that process by an a priori restrictive attitude to the direct effect of international agreements'.[14] At the same time, however, the Commission argued in the *Polydor* case that, 'the concept of direct effect, as developed in Community law, must not as such be transposed to the field of the Community's international relations'.[15]

In the *International Fruit Co Case* the ECJ stated two conditions that would have to be satisfied before a community measure could be held invalid due to its incompatibility with international law. First, the Community must be bound by the provision of international law concerned. Secondly, the provision of international law must have direct effect in community law. We consider these conditions in turn.

The Community must be bound by the provision of international law concerned: the binding nature of Treaties concluded by the Community

Treaties concluded by the Community and one or more states or international organisations, 'shall be binding on the institutions of the Community and on Member States' (Article 228(7)).[16] As a consequence of this, 'it is incumbent upon the Community institutions, as well as upon the Member States, to ensure compliance with the obligations arising from such agreements'.[17] When the member states ensure respect for such obligations they are fulfilling obligations in relation to the Community as well as to the non-member country concerned.[18] This obligation to the Community explains the ECJ's view that when an international agreement to which the EC is a party comes into force its provisions 'form an integral part of community law',[19] and of the 'community legal system'.[20] So too the Decisions of an Association Council.[21] This integration into community law means that the provisions have, for the purposes of community law, a community nature or character. Given this character, the interpretation and

---

[14] *Kupferberg*, p. 3654.
[15] Case 270/80, *Polydor Ltd. v Harlequin Record Shops Ltd.* [1982] ECR 329, p. 343 (hereinafter *Polydor*).
[16] Formerly Article 228(2).   [17] *Kupferberg*, pr. 11.   [18] Ibid., p. 12.
[19] *Haegeman*, pr. 5. Internal implementation does not appear to be necessary as a matter of principle.
[20] *Kupferberg*, pr. 13.
[21] *Sevince*, pr. 9; *Greece v Commission*, n. 6 above, pr. 13.

effect of such provisions should not vary between member states, for example, by having direct effect in some but not others.[22] Similarly it should not be dependent on whether the application of the provisions is the responsibility of the Community institutions or the member states.[23]

The requirement of consistent and 'uniform application throughout the Community',[24] is ensured by the ECJ, though its jurisdiction to interpret the provisions of such agreements.[25] However, it is important to be clear that the ECJ has no direct jurisdiction under the EC Treaty to interpret an international agreement as between the EC and a non-member state party.[26] It only has jurisdiction to interpret an international agreement, 'where its interpretation is relevant to the question of the validity of an act of a Community Institution or to the question of the interpretation to be given to such an act'.[27] Its interpretation of the provisions concerned is, 'for the purposes of [their] application in the Community'[28] and 'in so far as that agreement is an integral part of the Community legal order'.[29] That interpretation is obviously not binding on the non-member state, though in practice it may be very influential.[30] An international agreement could confer jurisdiction on the ECJ to interpret it for the purposes of its application in non-member countries.[31] The original EEA

---

22. The concept appears elsewhere in EC law, for example, over regulations not being transposed by national laws and thereby losing their community character, Case 39/72, *Commission v Italy* [1973] ECR 101.

23. *Kupferberg*, pr. 14; Case 12/86, *Demirel v Stadt Schwäbisch Gmund* [1987] ECR 3719, pr. 10 (hereinafter *Demirel*).

24. *Kupferberg*, pr. 14.

25. See also *Sevince*, pr. 11. Jurisdiction to interpret an international agreement could arise by way of a preliminary ruling or in a direct action, see *Opinion 1/91* (First EEA Opinion), pr. 38.

26. Cf. Only states can be parties before the ICJ. A third state could refer a dispute over the interpretation of a Community agreement to the ICJ. Presumably a member state could also do in relation to the interpretation of the Agreement itself rather than matters of EC competence. Under Article 219 EC only the ECJ is to have jurisdiction over EC matters, see *Opinion 1/91* (First EEA Opinion), pr. 35, and the discussion in *Opinion 2/94* (ECHR). A dispute over CFSP could go to the ICJ though politically this is unlikely.

27. AG Warner, in *Haegeman*, p. 473.   28. *Kupferberg*, pr. 45.

29. *Opinion 1/91* (First EEA Opinion), pr. 39.

30. In effect the position of the ECJ is the same position as that of a national court interpreting an international agreement.

31. *Opinion 1/91* (First EEA Opinion), pr. 59. Note also the 1971 Protocol to the Brussels Convention on Jurisdiction and the Enforcement of Judgments in Civil and Commercial Matters (1968) which provides for the ECJ to have jurisdiction to interpret the Convention. Only member states are parties. See C-389/92, *Mund and Fester v Hatrex International Transport* [1994] ECR I-467; pp. 30–1 above.

Agreement did this. However, the ECJ has taken the view that such a jurisdiction would only be compatible with the EC Treaty if the ECJ's judgments have binding effect.[32] Alternatively, an international court could be established or given jurisdiction to interpret an international agreement to which the EC is a party. The decisions of such a court would be binding on the community institutions, including the ECJ.[33] Such a system of courts is, in principle, compatible with Community law:

> The Community's competence in the field of international relations and its capacity to conclude international agreements necessarily entails the power to submit to the decisions of a court which is created or designated by such an agreement as regards the interpretation and application of its provisions.[34]

As well as being bound as a party, the ECJ has also accepted that the EC can become bound by an international agreement by a process of substitution or replacement for the member states.[35] This has been the case with the GATT,[36] and two customs conventions.[37] Thus in the *International Fruit Co Case* the ECJ found that the provisions of the GATT agreement were binding on the Community.[38] The ECJ appears to treat such agreements as an integral part of the Community legal order in the same way as agreements expressly adopted by the EC.[39] The ECJ has not

---

32. *Opinion 1/91* (First EEA Opinion), pr. 61. The agreement was changed to make the judgments of the ECJ binding, see *Opinion 1/92* (Second EEA Opinion), [1992] ECR I-2821. See also Case C-188/91, *Deutsche Shell AG v Hauptzollamt Hamburg-Harburg*, [1993] ECR I-363.
33. *Opinion 1/91* (First EEA Opinion), pr. 39.
34. *Opinion 1/91* (First EEA Opinion), pr. 40. See Schermers (1992). This would be of significance in relation to the jurisdiction of the European Court of Human Rights to interpret the ECHR in relation to the EC. See the discussion in *Opinion 2/94* (ECHR).
35. There are a number of possible explanations for this process including an analogy with Article 228 or the transfer of sovereignty from the member state to the EC with the consent of the third parties concerned. See Cheyne, 'International Agreements and the European Community Legal System', p. 587.
36. *IFC Case.* The ECJ has also held that it has exclusive competence to interpret the GATT for the purposes of EC law, *SIOT.*
37. The Convention on the Nomenclature for the Classification of Goods in Customs Tariffs and the Convention Establishing the Customs Cooperation Council. See Case 38/75, *Douaneagent der NV Nederlandse Spoorwegen v Inspecteur der Invoerrechten en Accijzen* [1975] ECR 1439.
38. See also Joined Cases 267 and 269/81, *Amministrazione delle Finanze dello Stato v SPI and SAMI* [1983] ECR 801.
39. See Cheyne, 'International Agreements and the European Community Legal System', p. 587; G. Bebr, 'Agreements Concluded by the Community and their Possible Direct Effect: from International Fruit Company to Kupferberg'

accepted that the EC has succeeded to the European Convention on Human Rights.[40]

In the 1990s the EC has increasingly been faced with questions of state succession to treaties. German reunification, the disintegration of the USSR[41] and of Yugoslavia, the separation of Czechoslovakia and the agreed secession of Eritrea from Ethiopia raised a series of issues for which Community practice had to develop. The results were inevitably variable and pragmatic with the 1978 Vienna Convention on Succession of States in Respect of Treaties providing analogous rules which have served 'as a useful point of reference but no more'.[42] The international law rules of state succession are themselves far from clear.

In *Demirel* the UK and Germany argued that in the case of a mixed agreement the ECJ's jurisdiction only extends to those parts of the agreement which are within EC competence. Arguably, it does not extend to those parts of the agreement which are within member state competence.[43] The ECJ responded that the question did not arise because Article 238 empowered the Community to guarantee commitments towards non-member countries in all fields covered by the Treaty. That obviously included the provisions on the free movement of workers that were in issue in the case. It made no difference to this conclusion that it was for member states to lay down the rules which were necessary for giving effect in their territory to the provisions of an international agreement or the decisions adopted by an Association Council.[44] The ECJ recalled its ruling in *Kupferberg* that the obligation of member states to lay down such rules was a community obligation.[45]

39. *(continued)* (1983) 20 CMLRev, 35–73, p. 43; Case C-69/89, *Nakajima All Precision Co. v Council* [1991] ECR I-2069 concerning the GATT Antidumping Code to which the EC is party. E.L.M. Völker, 'The Direct Effect of International Agreements in the Community's Legal Order', LIEI, 1983/1, 131–45, pp. 142–3, expresses a contrary view.

40. See Cases 50–52/82, *Administrateur des Affaires Maritimes, Bayonne v Dorca Marina* [1982] ECR 3949. *Opinion 2/94* (ECHR) would seem to reinforce that view.

41. On the application of the Community's anti-dumping procedures to a successor state see Case T-164/94, *Ferchimex SA v Council* [1995] ECR, II-2681.

42. See P.J. Kuyper, 'The Community and State Succession in Respect of Treaties', in D. Curtin and T. Heukels (eds), *Institutional Dynamics of European Integration: Essays in Honour of H.G. Schermers* (Dordrecht, Nijhoff, 1994, vol. II), p. 640. See also H.G. Schermers and N.M. Blokker, *International Institutional Law*, 3rd edn (The Hague, Nijhoff, 1995), pp. 986–8.

43. *Demirel*, see p. 3725 (Germany) and p. 3729 (UK).   44. *Demirel*, pr. 10.

45. Ibid., pr. 11. See T.C. Hartley, 'International Agreements and the Community Legal System: Some Recent Developments' (1983) 8 ELRev, 383–92, p. 389.

Pre-existing international commitments and the EC legal order

Article 234 protects third states by providing for the continuing effect of pre-existing international agreements:

> The rights and obligations arising from agreements concluded before the entry into force of this Treaty between one or more Member States on the one hand, and one or more third countries on the other, shall not be affected by the provisions of this Treaty.

Those international agreements with third states do not become part of the EC legal order. Whether the agreement has direct effect will depend on the national law of the member state concerned rather than on EC law.[46] The agreements do not become binding on the EC,[47] subject to the rare possibility of succession.[48] Article 234 continues by providing that if there are incompatibilities between the international agreements and the EC Treaty then the member state concerned 'shall take all appropriate steps to eliminate the incompatibilities concerned'. Member states are to 'assist each other to this end' and, 'where appropriate, to adopt a common attitude'.[49] This obligation should not be interpreted to the point of requiring member states to denounce agreements with third states.[50] The number of cases in which member states seek to rely on Article 234 is increasing steadily.

Article 234 will effectively provide a member state with a defence when they would otherwise be in breach of their obligations under the EC Treaty.[51] For example, in the *Levy*[52] and *Minne*[53] cases the effect of Article 234 was that Article 5 of the Equal Treatment Directive 76/207 could not be relied upon to

---

46. See Case 812/79, *Attorney General v Burgoa* [1980] ECR 2787, pr. 10 (hereinafter *Burgoa*).

47. Ibid., at 2808.   48. See pp. 118, 121 above.

49. A particular problem that can arise is where one member state interprets similar international obligations in a different way to other member states, see J.M. Grimes, 'Conflicts Between EC Law and International Treaty Obligations: A Case Study of the German Telecommunications Dispute' (1994) 35 Harv.ILJ, 535–64, pp. 554–5.

50. See Grimes, 'Conflicts Between EC Law and International Treaty Obligations'. See also *Opinion 1/76* (Rhine Navigation Case), pr. 2, on Article 234 justifying participation in an international agreement.

51. See R. Churchill and N. Foster, 'European Community Law and Prior Treaty Obligations of Member States: The Spanish Fisherman's Cases' (1987) 36 ICLQ, 504–24.

52. Case C-158/91, *Ministère public et direction du travail et l'emploi v Levy* [1993] ECR I-4287.

53. Case C-13/93, *Office Nationale de l'emploi v Minne* [1994] ECR I-371.

prevail over the national provisions adopted to comply with an ILO Convention of 1948. The institutions of the Community are bound not to impede the performance of those obligations by the member state concerned.[54] The third paragraph of Article 234 emphasizes the common advantages to member states of EC membership. This would be consistent with an interpretation of Article 234 which only allows member states to rely on it when it has an obligation to a third state that is relevant. A member state should not be able to rely on Article 234 to gain a benefit or advantage.[55] Article 234 cannot be relied upon in intra-community relations if the rights of non-member states are not involved.[56]

The direct effect of international agreements

The concept of direct effect has been of fundamental importance in the development of the European Community Law system. The EC Treaty does not contain the concept of 'direct effect'. There is an similar sounding concept of 'direct applicability' in Article 189 EC but that only refers to Regulations. The subject matter is similar to, but more extensive than, the international law concept of 'self-executing Treaties'.[57] The ECJ uses the terms 'directly effective' and 'directly applicable' interchangeably.[58] This work uses the term 'directly effective'. If a provision of an international agreement is directly effective, as a matter of EC law, then it grants natural and legal persons rights that must be upheld by the national courts of the member states.[59] One or more provisions of

---

54. *Burgoa*, at 2808.
55. See Case 10/61, *Commission v Italian Republic* [1962] ECR 1, at 10; Case 812/79, *Attorney General v Burgoa* [1980] ECR 2787; Case C-158/91, *Ministère public et direction du travail et l'emploi v Levy* [1993] ECR I-4287.
56. Cases C-241/91P and C-242/91P, *Radio Telefis Eireann (RTE) and Independent Television Publications v Commission* [1995] ECR I-743. On the replacement by Community regulations of social security conventions concluded between member states see Case C-475/93, *Jean-Louis Thevenon and Others v Landesversicherungsanstalt* [1995] ECR I-3813.
57. See J. Jackson, 'Status of Treaties in Domestic Legal Systems: A Policy Analysis' (1992) 86 AJIL, 310–40.
58. In Case C-58/93, *Yousfi v Belgian State* [1994] ECR-I 1353, A-G Tesauro considered the alleged distinction between direct applicability and direct effect and stated that, 'the difference between the expressions used, at least in the case-law, is merely terminological and non substantive', pp. 1357–8. Cf. Cheyne, 'International Agreements and the European Community Legal System'.
59. See Bebr, 'Agreements Concluded by the Community'; Völker, op. cit, n. 39; Bourgeois, 'Effects of International Agreements in European Community Law'.

an international agreement can have direct effect even if other provisions of the same agreement do not have direct effect.[60]

In accordance with *Van Gend En Loos*[61] and subsequent case law, the general test for direct effect of community law measures is threefold:

(1) The provision must be clear and unambiguous.
(2) It must be unconditional.
(3) Its operation must not be dependent on further action being taken [by the community or by national authorities or international bodies such as an Association Council].

These strict criteria were intended to make the doctrine more acceptable to states. In practice, although these tests appeared rigorous when first introduced, over time they have been considerably relaxed in their application. To an extent they are not even applied as successive tests any more. For internal measures direct effect may now be regarded as the norm rather than the exception. The test is essentially a practical one. If a provision lends itself to judicial application it will be held to be directly effective. Only when direct effect would create serious practical problems will the provision be held not to be directly effective. This supports the view that the test has became little more than one of justiciability, 'A rule can have direct effect whenever its characteristics are such that it is capable of judicial application'.[62] It is possible that only part of an EC law can have direct effect.

This jurisprudence on direct effect of EC measures is important because there has been substantial legislative implementation of international agreements within Community law by means of Regulations and Directives. If a provision in such a measure has direct effect there may be no need to consider as a separate issue whether the international agreement concerned can have direct effect in its own right. This issue is particularly important, however, if no internal implementation measures have been taken.

---

60. So *Polydor* and *Kupferberg* concerned the same agreement with Portugal.
61. Case 26/62, [1963] ECR 1.
62. See P. Pescatore, 'The Doctrine of Direct Effect – An Infant Disease of Community Law' (1983) 8 ELRev, 155–77.

Does the general test for direct effect also apply to international agreements?

Formally, the answer appears to be yes.[63] According to the ECJ's well established jurisprudence:

> A provision in an international agreement concluded by the Community with non-member countries must be regarded as being directly applicable when, regard being had to its wording and the purpose and nature of the agreement itself, the provision contains a clear and precise obligation which is not subject, in its implementation or effects, to the adoption of any subsequent measure.[64]

The decisions of an Association Council must satisfy the same conditions as those applicable to the provisions of the agreement itself.[65] However, the result of the practical application of this test has been that direct effect of international agreements has been the exception rather than the norm. This the reverse of the situation with internal EC measures. We need to consider closely the ECJ's approach to the interpretation of international agreements.

How does the ECJ approach the interpretation of international agreements?

The ECJ has rarely referred expressly to the generally accepted rules of interpretation in international law in the Vienna Convention on the Law of Treaties (1969).[66] According to the ECJ, to determine the effect in the community legal system of the

---

63. Ibid., pp. 171–4.

64. *Demirel*, pr. 14; Case C-18/90, *Office National de l'Emploi v Kziber* [1991] ECR I-199, pr. 15. N. Neuwahl suggests that it is 'not clear whether these criteria are sufficient in the case of an international agreement', 'Individuals and the GATT: Direct Effect and Indirect Effects of the General Agreement on Tariffs and Trade in Community Law', in N. Emiliou and D. O'Keeffe (eds), *The European Union and World Trade Law – After the GATT Uruguay Round* (Chichester, Wiley, 1996), p. 319.

65. *Sevince*, prs. 14–15.

66. Examples are *Opinion 1/91* (First EEA Opinion), pr. 14, and C-432/92, *R v Ministry of Agriculture, Fisheries and Food, ex p Anastasiou*, [1994] ECR I-3087, both referring to Article 31 VCLT. The Vienna Convention on the Law of Treaties between States and International Organizations or between International Organizations (1986) contains broadly analogous rules. The EC is not a party. See P. Manin, 'The European Communities and the Vienna Convention on the Law of Treaties between States and International Organizations or between International Organizations' (1987) 24 CMLRev, 457–81.

provisions of an international agreement, its 'international origin' has to be taken into account.[67] Parties to an agreement can '[i]n conformity with principles of public international law', expressly specify the effect of the provisions of an agreement in their respective legal orders.[68] In practice they rarely do this and, in default, the question can come before the ECJ.[69] It is then a question of interpretation of the agreement concerned.

The general approach of the ECJ to the interpretation of an international agreements is to examine its provisions in the light of the general structure of the agreement and any amending or additional Protocols to it.[70] Simultaneously, '[T]he spirit, the general scheme and the general terms of the . . . Agreement must be considered'.[71] In *Haegeman* the ECJ clearly read the international agreement concerned in the light of the EC provisions concerned. There was no reference to GATT or to the international background.

The aims and context of the agreement must also be considered, and its provisions analysed in the light of its object and purpose.[72] The considerations which lead to a certain interpretation in a Community context do not necessarily apply in the context of an international agreement. The ECJ has stressed on many occasions that the EC Treaty creates a new and unique legal order notwithstanding that it was concluded in the form of an international agreement.[73] The Treaty constitutes the constitutional charter of a Community based on the rule of law.[74] Member States have limited their sovereign rights. Community law has primacy over the law of the member state and many of its provisions have direct effect.[75] The Treaty pursues certain aims and objectives, and in particular, 'by establishing a common

---

[67]. *Kupferberg*, pr. 17.

[68]. Ibid. Presumably the parties could all specify that an agreement does or does not have direct effect.

[69]. *Kupferberg*, pr. 17.

[70]. *Haegeman*, pr. 10. AG Warner at 469 stated that the expressions in question must be interpreted in the context of the association agreement read as a whole and against the background of the provisions of the EEC Treaty. This suggests a broader framework than just the EC. In *Opinion 1/91* (First EEA Opinion) the ECJ's interpretation of some of the Protocols to the EEA Agreement were very significant for its opinion.

[71]. *IFC Case*, pr. 20; Case C-280/93, *Germany v Council* [1994] ECR I-4973, pr. 105; Case 87/75, *Conceria Daniele Bresciani v Amministrazione delle Finanze Stato* [1976] ECR 129, pr. 16 (hereinafter *Bresciani*).

[72]. *Kupferberg*, pr. 23.

[73]. *Opinion 1/91* (First EEA Opinion), pr. 21. See ch. 1, pp. 21–5 above on the 'new legal order' of the EC.

[74]. Ibid.   [75]. Ibid.

market and progressively approximating the economic policies of the Member States, seeks to unite national markets into a single market having the characteristics of a domestic market'.[76] The provisions of the Treaty are not an end in themselves. They are only means to attaining the objectives of the EC and, 'making concrete progress towards European unity'.[77] The interpretation and application of the Treaty, even against the same provisions in an international agreement, uses 'different approaches, methods and concepts in order to take account of the nature of each Treaty and its particular objectives'.[78] Stress is also often placed on the institutional structure of the Treaty system and that the Community has at its disposal instruments to achieve the uniform application of EC law and the progressive abolition of legislative disparities.[79]

By contrast, the various classes of international agreements to which the EC is a party[80] pursue different and more limited objectives than the EC.[81] In contrast to the EC Treaty, such an international agreement, 'merely creates rights and obligations as between the Contracting Parties and provides for no transfer of sovereign rights to the inter-governmental institutions which it sets up'.[82] This is the case with free trade and cooperation agreements. Similarly, with association agreements[83] but, to the extent that they seek to prepare the associating state for membership, they are closer on the spectrum to the EC Treaty than mere free trade and cooperation agreements.[84] In *Bresciani* it was important that the international agreement concerned was intended to promote the development of the Associated States.[85] The function of the provisions concerned is important and whether it is the same as that performed by similarly worded provisions of

---

76. *Polydor*, pr. 16.
77. *Opinion 1/91* (First EEA Opinion), pr. 17.
78. *Opinion 1/91* (First EEA Opinion), pr. 51.
79. *Polydor*, pr. 20; *Opinion 1/91* (First EEA Opinion), pr. 21.
80. See ch. 10 below.
81. Reference is often made to the Preamble or the first article of those agreements to determine their objectives and purpose; see, for example, *Polydor*, pr. 10; Case C-280/93, *Germany v Council* [1994] ECR I-4973, pr. 106.
82. *Opinion 1/91* (First EEA Opinion), pr. 20.
83. See *Opinion 1/91* (First EEA Opinion), pr. 15; *Polydor*, pr. 18–20.
84. In *Demirel* the Commission analysed the Association agreement concerned as 'a combination of an association for the purposes of development and an association prior to accession', p. 3730. Also, 'The concept of association has a very wide scope and covers various forms of relationship', p. 3730.
85. *Bresciani*, pr. 22.

the EC Treaty.[86] In any event the result is the same in that the interpretation given to the provisions of the EC Treaty cannot be applied by way of simple analogy to the provisions of other kinds of international agreements even if the wording is similar or even identical.[87] 'Such similarity of terms is not a sufficient reason for transposing to the provisions of the Agreement', the case law of the Community.[88] This is important because many of the EC's international agreements reproduce the language of the EC Treaty. For example, the provisions of the EEA Agreement are textually identical to the corresponding provisions of EC law.[89] Similarly, each of the different classes of EC agreements, for example, free trade, partnership and cooperation, Europe agreements tend to use identical provisions. Thus, the interpretation of any one agreement has significance for others in the same class, and sometimes for agreements in other classes.[90]

In a small number of cases the ECJ held that provisions of association agreements can have direct effect.[91] So too can the Decisions of an Association Council which are directly connected with the agreement to which they give effect. In *Kupferberg* (1982) the same reasoning was extended, in principle, to free trade agreements.[92] The ECJ proceeded from one of the general rules of international law that there must be bona fide performance of every agreement.[93] It observed that in the absence of specific provisions on implementation in the agreement itself, international law did not specify the legal means appropriate for the full execution of a party's commitments under an agreement. It was a

---

86. See Case 17/81, *Pabst & Richarz KZ v Hauptzollamt Oldenburg*, [1982] ECR 1331, pr. 26. For an important decision on the interpretation of 'charges having equivalent effect' in bilateral or multilateral agreements concluded by the Community see Case C-125/94, *Aprile Srl, en liquidation v Amministrazione delle Finanze dello Stato* [1995] ECR I-2919.

87. *Kupferberg*, pr. 30; *Polydor*, pr. 14; *Opinion 1/91* (First EEA Opinion), pr. 22; Case C-312/91, *Metalsa Srl v Italy*, [1993] ECR I-3751.

88. *Polydor*, pr. 15.   89. *Opinion 1/91* (First EEA Opinion), pr. 5.

90. In the *Polydor* case the UK submission noted that the provision in issue appeared in seven free trade agreements with the EFTA countries, all of the Community's agreements with Mediterranean countries, and in the GATT, p. 340. See also Case C-103/94, *Zoulika Krid v Caisse Nationale d'assurances Vieillesse des Travailleurs Salariés* [1995] ECR I-719.

91. For example, *Haegeman, Bresciani.*

92. *Kupferberg*, pr. 22. See Bebr, 'Agreements Concluded by the Community and their Possible Direct Effect'.

93. Ibid., pr. 18. Article 26 of the VCLT provides that 'Every treaty in force is binding upon the parties to it and must be performed by them in good faith'.

matter of discretion for the party concerned.[94] Accordingly, that the legal system of one party accorded direct effect to the provisions of an agreement, while the other party's legal system did not, was simply a reflection of how the parties exercised their discretion as to methods of implementation. Such a situation did not in itself constitute a lack of reciprocity in the implementation of the agreement. In the context of an agreement on development, an imbalance in the obligations of the parties may be inherent in the special nature of the agreement itself.[95] Similarly, that the parties have established a special institutional framework for consultations and negotiations on implementation is not in itself a justification for excluding the possibility of direct effect in principle.[96] Provisions in an international agreement which set out a programme to be achieved would not normally satisfy the standard conditions for direct effect. However, this 'does not prevent the decisions of Council of Association which give effect in specific respects to the programmes envisaged in the Agreement from having direct effect'.[97] The non-publication of a decision of an Association Council will also not serve to deprive a private individual of the rights which that decision confer on him.[98] Finally, the existence of 'safeguard clauses' which enable parties to derogate from certain provisions of the agreement is also not in itself sufficient to exclude the possibility of direct effect in principle.[99] In principle then, neither the nature or structure of a Free Trade Agreement prevented it from having direct effect in the community legal system.[100]

The direct effect of the decisions of an Association Council cannot be affected by the fact that under those decisions the rights concerned are to be established under national rules. Such provisions 'merely clarify the obligation of the Member States to take such administrative measures as may be necessary for the implementation of those provisions, without empowering the Member States to make conditional or restrict the application of

[94]. This is clearly correct. For example, the UK has not incorporated the European Convention on Human Rights.
[95]. *Bresciani*, pr. 23.   [96]. *Kupferberg*, prs. 19–20. Similarly in *Fediol*, pr. 21.
[97]. *Sevince*, pr. 21.
[98]. Ibid., pr. 24. Non-publication would prevent the Decision being applied adversely to a private individual, ibid.
[99]. *Kupferberg*, pr. 21; *Sevince*, pr. 25 in the context of an Association Agreement.
[100]. Interestingly, AG Rozes had taken a different view, stressing the lack of reciprocity, the flexibility of the provisions, the limited objectives of the agreement, and the difference in the wording of the provisions concerned.

the precise and unconditional right which the decisions of the Council of Association grant . . . '[101]

Of major interest has been the question of the possible direct effect of the GATT.[102] The ECJ has consistently taken the view that analysis of the GATT showed that its provisions were not capable of having direct effect.[103] The factors the ECJ regarded as important were the great flexibility of its provisions, in particular those conferring the possibility of derogation, the measures to be taken when confronted with exceptional difficulties, the various possibilities for the settlement of conflicts, and the possibilities to suspend obligations and to withdraw or modify concessions. Whether the provisions of the new 'GATT 1994', or the other agreements that resulted from the Uruguay Round of the GATT, can have direct effect has not yet been tested before the ECJ. These agreements are now under the institutional structure and dispute settlement procedures of the WTO.[104] The EC is an original member of the WTO in its own right and a party to the various agreements. Of particular importance is the 'Understanding on Rules and Procedures Governing the Settlement of Disputes'.[105] This removes the veto power of the contracting parties at various stages in the dispute resolution process,[106] and adds an appellate process. Also under the understanding, the unilateral suspension of concessions is replaced by collectively controlled suspension. In the absence of direct effect this understanding is very important for the EC and for the other WTO members as a much more powerful dispute settlement process.[107] The general strengthening of the GATT structure and system are factors that would weigh with the ECJ when it is considering the direct effect of the 'GATT 1994'

---

101. *Sevince*, pr. 22.
102. See Bebr, 'Agreements Concluded by the Community and their Possible Direct Effect'; M. Hilf, F.G. Jacobs and E.-U. Petersmann (eds), *The European Community and GATT*, 2nd edn (Deventer, Kluwer, 1989); F.C. de la Torre, 'The Status of GATT in EC Law, Revisited' (1995) 29(1) JWTL, 53–68; N. Neuwahl, 'Individuals and the GATT'.
103. See, for example, *IFC Case*; Case C-280/93, *Germany v Council*, [1994] ECR-I 4973; Case C-469/93, *Amministrazione delle finanze dello state v Chiquita Italia*, [1995] ECR nyr.
104. See A. Qureshi, *The World Trade Organization* (Manchester, Manchester University Press, 1996). For the WTO Agreement see [1994] OJ L336/1.
105. Annex 2 of the WTO Agreement. This constitutes an integral part of the WTO Agreement.
106. The EC has blocked the adoption of GATT Panel Reports.
107. For example, in relation to the GATT compatibility of extra-jurisdictional measures by the EC which pursue environment objectives. See Cheyne, 'International Agreements and the European Community Legal System', p. 595.

and the other WTO agreements.[108] As for derogations the ECJ accepted in the *Sevince Case*[109] that the mere existence of powers to derogate will not always prevent direct effect.

In the decision adopting the WTO Agreement there is a statement in the Preamble that the GATT/WTO Agreements are not directly effective.[110] This would not be legally conclusive but it might engender caution on the ECJ's behalf. In the end result, whatever view is taken on the ECJ's jurisprudence on the original GATT Agreement, the specific reasons it has given for denying direct effect would appear to have substantially been met.

As Torre notes:

> Most of the features which the Court considered as weaknesses of the system have been reinforced ... Is this regime substantially different from that of a free trade agreement or an association agreement in respect of which the Court has consistently recognized the possibility to directly apply its provisions?[111]

The direct effect of the GATT 1994 and the other WTO Agreements must be open to serious argument. If the ECJ is to deny direct effect it will have to articulate new policy reasons.[112]

Vertical and horizontal direct effect

Another preliminary question concerns the nature of direct effect in terms of vertical and horizontal direct effect. *Vertical effect* concerns the relationship between an individual or other private legal person and the state.[113] For example, in cases concerning the direct effect of international agreements, the disagreement is often between the state (customs authorities, tax authorities) and an individual or a company. However, the 'state' has a particular community law meaning in this context (*Foster v British Gas*

---

108. See J. Scott, 'The GATT and Community Law: Rethinking the Regulatory Gap', in J. Shaw and G. More (eds), *New Legal Dynamics of European Union* (Oxford, OUP, 1995), pp 147–64. A preliminary ruling on the interpretation of Article 50 of the Agreement on Trade Related Aspects of Intellectual Property Rights has been sought in Case C-53/96, *Hermes International Société en Commandite par Actions v FHT Marketing Choice BV*.

109. See n. 99 above.

110. Council Decision 94/800, [1994] OJ L336/1.

111. Torre, 'The Status of GATT in EC Law, Revisited', pp. 66, 67.

112. For a very good analysis of the ECJ's policy approach to the original GATT see Hartley, op. cit., n. 8.

113. In a general sense, this regulation of the individual-state relationship is one familiar to constitutional lawyers.

plc)[114] and therefore covers 'emanations of the state' which for other purposes would be considered as private bodies.[115] *Horizontal effect* concerns the relationship between one individual or private legal person and another individual or private legal person. Again, given the wide community interpretation of the state, this would be more accurately expressed as one 'non-state emanation' and another 'non-state emanation'. For our purposes, the important question is whether the direct effect of international agreements is limited to vertical direct effect. Provisions of the Community Treaties can have both horizontal and vertical effect.[116] Many provisions of the EC Treaties have been held to be directly effective both vertically and horizontally. The fact of their being addressed to states has been no bar to their horizontal effects. The same argument can be applied to international agreements. In all of the cases considered by the ECJ to date the argument has been one of the vertical direct effect of an international agreement, for example, against a customs authority. However, the *Polydor Case* (1982) represented an example of an attempt to rely on the direct effect of a Treaty against a private party.

Finally, Regulations and Directives are often used to implement international agreements it is important to note the possibility of them having direct effect. Regulations can have both vertical and horizontal direct effect. Directives, however, can have vertical direct effect, but not horizontal direct effect.[117] Secondary legislation implementing an international agreement must, as far as possible, be interpreted in a manner that is consistent with it.[117A]

Policy considerations

Although the ECJ has stated that the meaning of a Treaty provision may not necessarily be transposed by a similar or identical provision of a Community Treaty or legislation, this often appears strange to outside observers. In some of the early cases the Court was concerned with institutional structures and dispute settlement procedures (*International Fruit Co*) but

---

114. Case C-188/89, *Foster v British Gas* [1990] ECR I-3133. It does not matter in which capacity the state is acting.
115. For example, in the context of international personality or state immunity.
116. Case 43/75, *Defrenne v SABENA* [1976] ECR 455.
117. Case 152/84. *Marshall v Southampton & SWHAHA (Teaching)* [1986] ECR 723; Case C-91/92, *Paola Faccini Dori v Recreb Sri* [1994] ECR I-3325.
117A See Case C-64/94, *Commission v FRG* [1996] ECR nyr.

subsequent cases have been less concerned with this (*Pabst*). Similarly, with respect to whether there existed a judicial mechanism for ensuring a uniform interpretation. In *Polydor* the Court seems to have deplored the lack of any such provision in the agreement with Portugal. But in *Kupferberg* concerning the same free trade agreement, the Court no longer mentioned this. The factual background of the two cases was, of course, different. *Polydor* dealt with an exercise of a copyright as a possible measure having the equivalent effect of a quantitative restriction. In *Kupferberg* the Court declared the provision prohibiting fiscal discrimination of imported products to be directly effective. Another problem has concerned, in terms of direct effect, the unconditional nature of an obligation which is one of its essential requirements. Under the various community agreements with third states there are safety clauses permitting a derogation from the obligations presumed. Is this compatible with the unconditional nature of an obligation, and if so under what conditions and to what extent? In *Kupferberg* the Court considered that such clauses may not preclude direct effect. The Court referred in that case to the specific conditions on derogation and the joint examination by the contracting parties within the joint committee. This kind of approach parallels broad approach to whether obligations in internal measures are conditional. The importance of reciprocity has also varied in the ECJ's jurisprudence and may be less important in some kinds of agreements than others.

The complexity and variety of the ECJ's jurisprudence can be best explained by policy considerations.[118] Its jurisprudence on the direct effect of the ECJ Treaty and secondary legislation was controversial and had faced some national resistance. Extending direct effect to international agreements raised even more difficult questions of consistency and effectiveness. Differential interpretation of the same wording appears curious whatever the legal reasoning and policy considerations behind it. That other EC remedies are more restricted[119] means that allowing international agreements to have direct effect would establish an easy means of enforcement and bypass the member states. There have been an

---

118. T.C. Hartley, *The Foundations of European Community Law*, 2nd edn (Oxford, Clarendon Press, 1988), pp. 250–4; H.G. Schermers, 'The Direct Application of Treaties with Third States: Note Concerning the Polydor and Pabst Cases' (1982) 19 CMLRev, 563–9; Boulouis, 'Le Droit Des Communautés Européennes Dans Ses Rapports Avec Le Droit International Général', pp. 74–9.

119. Especially Article 173.

increasing number of challenges to EC rules as incompatible with the GATT. Denying direct effect to the GATT means that the ECJ avoids ruling on such alleged conflicts. The ECJ faces similar policy considerations to states. It is bound by the GATT/ WTO rules and has a long-term, systemic interest in agreed multilateral rules being followed. Its natural instinct is to make the EC legal order effective and consistent with international standards. However, as an EC institution, it also has to take account of the EC's own interests. Longer term policy considerations are tempered by the realities and limitations of conducting an international trade policy on a uniform basis and the EC's political policy of establishing a range of preferential agreements.[120] EC interests thus have to be pursued within WTO framework (formerly GATT). This enhances the role of the policy making institutions of the EC, the Council, the Commission and, to some extent, the EP. It can thus create a rare alliance of these institutions both seeking to deny the direct effect of international agreements.[121] At the same time, by refusing to apply its normal methods of interpretation to such agreements, it has ensured that non-Community countries will not be given too great an advantage.[122]

Reliance on international agreements in the absence of direct effect

In the *Fediol* case an agricultural federation (Fediol) brought an action under Article 173(2) seeking the annulment of a Commission decision.[123] The Commission decision rejected Fediol's complaint which had requested the Commission to initiate the procedure under Regulation 2641/84 to examine certain commercial practices of Argentina. Fediol argued that various commercial practices were contrary to Articles of the GATT. Interestingly, a GATT panel had ruled that the import regime violated GATT rules.[124] The ECJ recalled its jurisprudence that provisions of the GATT did not have direct effect. However, it

---

[120.] See the *SPI and SAMI Case*, [1983] ECR 801. On the range of agreements see ch. 10 below.

[121.] See Torre, 'The Status of GATT in EC Law, Revisited', pp. 64–7.

[122.] Hartley, *The Foundations of European Community Law*, p. 230. See also p. 228, n. 37.

[123.] Case 70/87, *Fediol v Commission* [1989] ECR 1781 (herinafter *Fediol*).

[124.] The Report had not been adopted by the contracting parties. As noted above, the dispute settlement rules under the WTO are stronger.

ruled that as –

> Regulation 2641/84 entitles the economic agents concerned to rely
> on the GATT provisions in the complaint in which they lodge with
> the Commission in order to establish the illicit nature of those
> commercial practices which they consider to have harmed them,
> those same economic agents are entitled to request the Court to
> exercise its power of review over the legality of the Commission's
> decision applying those provisions.[125]

In such a case reliance on an international agreement is obviously
dependent on the terms of the internal EC measure concerned.[126]
In *Germany v Council*[127] Germany sought to challenge the
lawfulness of a Community Regulation as contrary to the GATT,
regardless of any question of direct effect.[128] The ECJ held that –

> 109. Those features of the GATT, from which the Court concluded
> that an individual within the Community cannot invoke it in a court
> to challenge the lawfulness of a Community act, also preclude the
> Court from taking provisions of GATT into consideration to assess
> the lawfulness of a regulation in an action brought by a Member
> State under the first paragraph of Article 173 of the Treaty.
> 110. The special features noted above show that the GATT rules
> are not unconditional and that an obligation to recognize them as
> rules of international law which are directly applicable in the
> domestic legal systems of the contracting parties cannot be based on
> the spirit, general scheme or terms of GATT.
> 111. In the absence of such an obligation following from the GATT
> itself, it is only if the Community intended to implement a particular
> obligation entered into within the framework of GATT, or if the
> Community expressly refers to specific provisions of GATT, that the
> Court can review the lawfulness of the Community act in question
> from the point of the GATT rules . . .[129]

---

125. *Fediol*, pr. 21. The ECJ found that the practices concerned did not fall within
the scope of the GATT Articles concerned and that the other GATT articles
invoked did not provide for a general prohibition or for any specific
substantive rule.
126. See Cheyne, 'International Agreements and the European Community Legal
System', pp. 592–3.
127. Case C-280/93, [1994] ECR-I 4973.
128. Ibid., pr. 103.
129. Citing the *Fediol* and *Nakajima* cases. See also Cases T-163/94 and 165/94,
NTN Corporation and Others v Council, [1995] ECR II-1381: the provisions of
the basic regulation on anti-dumping must be interpreted in the light of the GATT
and its 1979 Anti-Dumping Code. The EC is a party to the 1979 code. See Case
T-162/94, *NMB France SARL and Others v Commission* [1996] ECR nyr.

On the merits of the case the German challenge failed but this jurisprudence clearly opens up another approach to using the GATT.[130] It is increasingly important because internal EC measures increasingly refer to their being consistent with the GATT rules. Moreover, in principle, it also opens up the possibility of using other international obligations in the same way. Obvious difficulties may arise is assessing whether, in the absence of an express reference in the EC measure, the EC 'intended to implement a particular obligation'.[131] Finally, there is a principle of interpreting EC law to conform with international law where possible.[132] The basis for this interpretative principle would lie in Article 5 of the Treaty.[133]

[130.] See Neuwahl, 'Individuals and the GATT', pp. 325–8.
[131.] Torre, 'The Status of GATT in EC Law, Revisited', pp. 59–62.
[132.] See *NTN Case* in n. 127 above; *Commission v FRG*, n. 117A above.
[133.] See J. Temple Lang, 'Community Constitutional Law: Article 5 EEC Treaty' (1990) 27 CMLRev, 645–81.

CHAPTER EIGHT

From European political cooperation to a common foreign and security policy

Introduction

European political cooperation (EPC)

This developed on a relatively informal basis after 1970.[1] It was formalized to a greater extent in the Single European Act of 1986, Article 30.[2] The Foreign Ministers of the member states and a representative from the Commission met at least four times a year with the 'framework of EPC'. They also discussed foreign policy within the 'framework of EPC' when the Council met. The general aim was to determine *common policies* to be asserted by the Community in its dealings with the rest of the world so that positions and responses are co-ordinated and made consistent. Although the pace of progress varied in response to political circumstances, practice developed across a very wide range of issues and the boundaries of EPC were gradually extended. The TEU furthered this process by providing for the development of a common foreign and security policy (CFSP).[3] An interesting

---

[1.] See D. Allen, R. Rummel and W. Wessels (eds), *European Political Cooperation* (London, Butterworths, 1982); M. Holland (ed.), *The Future of European Political Cooperation* (London, Macmillan, 1991); S. Nuttall, *European Political Cooperation* (Oxford, Clarendon Press, 1992).

[2.] [1987] OJ L169/1.

[3.] See F. Fink-Hooijer, 'The CFSP of the EU' (1994) 5 EJIL, 173–98; M. Cremona, 'The Common Foreign and Security Policy of the European Union and the External Relations Power of the European Community', in D. O'Keeffe and P. Twomey (eds), *Legal Issues of the Maastricht Treaty* (Chichester, Wiley Chancery, 1994), pp. 247–58; M.R. Eaton, 'Common Foreign and Security Policy', in O'Keeffe and Twomey (eds), *Legal Issues of the Maastricht Treaty*, pp. 215–25; N. Neuwahl, 'Foreign and Security Policy and the Implementation of the Requirement of "Consistency" under the Treaty on European Union', in O'Keeffe and Twomey (eds), *Legal Issues of the Maastricht Treaty*, pp. 227–46; I. Macleod, I. Hendry and S. Hyett, *The External Relations of the European Communities: A Manual of Law and Practice* (Oxford, OUP, 1996),

question to bear in mind in this chapter is how much could have been achieved under the continuing evolution of EPC in any event?

Common foreign and security policy

One of the objectives of the Union is to, 'assert its identity on the international scene, in particular through the implementation of a common foreign and security policy including the eventual framing of a common defence policy, which might in time lead to a common defence'.[4] Prior to the TEU the assertion of an international identity by the EC was made through a combination of the EC's external relations policy and through EPC.[5] The challenge of responding to the revolutionary changes in Central and Eastern Europe after 1989, and the experience of the European response to the Iraqi invasion of Kuwait in 1990–91, convinced the member states that the process of EPC needed to be moved on a stage further although they differed on how far it was necessary to go, and the means.[6] Ultimately, EPC was replaced by CFSP.[7] Title V of the TEU makes provision for CFSP. Title V contains an Article J, which is divided into Articles J and J.1–J.11. A number of Declarations to the TEU are also of importance.[8]

In as much as the TEU represented a major structural evolution into a three-pillared EU,[9] then the interests of the member states and of the institutions in the development of CFSP may differ. For those who saw the structural changes as a weakening of the concept of a European Community, then the intergovernmental

---

3. (continued) pp. 409–24; P. de Schoutheete, 'The Creation of the CFSP in the Maastricht Treaty', in E. Regelsberger et al. (eds), Foreign Policy of the European Union: From EPC to CFSP and Beyond (Boulder, Lynne Reinner, forthcoming 1997). See also the annual review of EPC, and now CFSP, in YEL and in JCMS.

4. Article B of the TEU.

5. See G. Edwards, 'Interaction Between European Political Cooperation and the European Community' (1988) 7 YEL 1987, 211–49.

6. See G. Edwards and S. Nuttall, 'Common Foreign and Security Policy', in A. Duff, J. Pinder and R. Pryce (eds), Maastricht and Beyond: Building the European Union (London, Routledge, 1994), pp. 84–103; P. Tsakaloyannis, 'Risks and Opportunities in the East and South', in A. Pijpers, The European Community At The Crossroads (Dordrecht, Nijhoff, 1992); Pijpers, The European Community At The Crossroads.

7. Article P(2) of TEU.

8. The legal interpretation and evaluation of the Declarations on CFSP are not within the competence of the ECJ, see Article L of the TEU.

9. See ch. 1, p. 14 above.

pillars are inherently flawed and cannot be successful. For those who welcomed the structural changes (especially, but not only, the UK) then it is important that practical progress is made so that the charge of deliberately retarding the development of the concept of a European Union can be met.

The member states share the view that they can often achieve their own interests by acting together and cooperating. For example, during the debate in the UK on the TEU the Foreign Secretary gave three examples of where the combined influence of EC cooperation had added to the effectiveness of British foreign policy without reducing the protection of British interests. In addition to the sending of a team of EC observers to South Africa alongside those from the Commonwealth and the UN, and the role of the EC in the multilateral talks on the Arab-Israeli peace process, he stated that:

> The concept of safe havens for the Kurds was originally a British proposal, but it gave immediate and decisive impetus once it was adopted by the European Council at the urging of ... the Prime Minister. It was a clear example of how a decisive move at the European level achieves worldwide acceptance ... [10]

The more challenging question is the degree to which CFSP seeks to achieve 'European interests' rather than simply further separate national interests of the member states or the aggregate of those interests. Moreover, the development of a public consciousness and acceptance of 'European interests' may be related to the evolution of the concept of European citizenship.[11] Thus, there may be different measurements of the effectiveness of CFSP depending on which interest assessment is being made.

The scope of CFSP

CFSP is built on the EPC's *acquis*,[12] its intergovernmental structure, and indeed, is 'largely a codification of existing practice'.[13] CFSP is thus evolutionary rather than revolutionary. None the less, CFSP is a move forward in terms of scope. Article

---

[10]. D. Hurd, Secretary of State for Foreign and Commonwealth Affairs, *Hansard*, HC Debs., 30 March 1993, col. 170. See ibid., cols. 160–245 for an interesting debate.

[11]. See ch. 9 below.

[12]. See Article C of the TEU. EPC could in a sense have been described as a second pillar even before the TEU.

[13]. M.R. Eaton, 'Common Foreign and Security Policy', in O'Keeffe and Twomey (eds), *Legal Issues of the Maastricht Treaty*, p. 215.

J.1 of Title V provides that, 'The Union and its members *shall* define and implement a common foreign and security policy, governed by the provisions of this Title and covering *all areas* of foreign and security policy'.[14] The formulation 'The Union and its member states', was used at the insistence of the UK to stress the intergovernmental character of CFSP.[15] The scope of CFSP seems to be unlimited, viz, 'all areas'. New and evolving perceptions of interests can bring matters within the perceived scope of foreign and security policy.

The foreign and security policy is to be a 'common' one but it is not necessarily common in the same sense as the 'common policies' of the EC. A common policy is not necessarily a single policy. Some of the differences between the member states in their approach can be explained by whether CFSP is seen as a substantive objective in itself, a policy in itself, or as merely as creating 'a procedural framework within which specific substantive issues can be treated'.[16]

Neither 'foreign policy' nor 'security policy' are defined or explained in the TEU.[17] The concept of a 'European foreign policy' is not necessarily the same as national foreign policy, or as an aggregation of national foreign policies.[18] In any event, the practice under EPC thus remains relevant for determining the scope of foreign policy.[19] EPC had developed to cover the economic and political aspects of security, but not its military aspect.[20] The clear incorporation in CFSP of the military aspects of security is an

14. Article J 1(1) (emphasis added)
15. In EPC the expression used was 'the Community and its Member States'. Edwards and Nuttall comment that intergovernmental procedures 'are better suited to the continued coordination of national policies than the stated purpose of a common policy' ('Common Foreign and Security Policy', in Duff, Pinder and Pryce (eds), *Maastricht and Beyond*, p. 85).
16. Eaton, 'Common Foreign and Security Policy', in O'Keeffe and Twomey (eds), *Legal Issues of the Maastricht Treaty*, p. 225.
17. See Neuwahl, 'Foreign and Security Policy and the Implementation of the Requirement of "Consistency" ', in O'Keeffe and Twomey (eds), *Legal Issues of the Maastricht Treaty*, pp. 229–33; P. de Schoutheete, *La Coopération Politique Européenne*, 2nd edn (Brussels, Editions Labor, 1986), p. 269.
18. See W. Carlsnaes and S. Smith, *European Foreign Policy – The EC and Changing Perspectives in Europe* (London, Sage, 1994).
19. See European Political Cooperation Documentation Bulletin, 8 vols published to date (European Commission/Bonn). The German Foreign Ministry has also published EPC/CFSP Documents on a regular basis.
20. See 'Report on European Political Co-operation', adopted by the Foreign Ministers of the Ten Member States of the European Community on 13 October 1981. 'Solemn Declaration on European Union', Stuttgart, 19 June 1983, Bull-EC, 6-1983, 24–29. Nuttall, *European Political Cooperation*, pp. 175–91.

important expansion of substantive scope, and in part is a reflection of the weaknesses revealed in the European response to the Gulf crisis in 1990–91.[21] Possible evolution to cover defence matters is also signalled. CFSP includes, 'all questions related to the security of the Union, including the eventual framing of a common defence policy, which might in time lead to a common defence'. Thus CFSP can, with the agreement of all the member states, develop to cover a 'common defence policy' and a 'common defence'. Although the language is tentative and the 'words were much fought over',[22] this represents an important expansion beyond EPC.[23] CFSP also extends to the powers member states retain in relation to international economic matters.

The objectives of CFSP

Some indication of the scope of CFSP can be deduced from its objectives established for it by the TEU and by the European Council and the Council. The TEU provides that the objectives of CFSP are:

(1) to safeguard the common values, fundamental interests and independence of the Union;[24]
(2) to strengthen the security of the Union and its members in all ways;
(3) to preserve peace and strengthen international security, in accordance with the principles of the United Nations Charter as well as the principles of the Helsinki Final Act[25] and the objectives of the Charter of Paris;[26]
(4) to develop and consolidate democracy and the rule of law and respect for human rights and fundamental freedoms.[27]

21. See Articles J.1(1) and 4(1); G. Edwards and S. Nuttall, 'Common Foreign and Security Policy', in A. Duff, J. Pinder and R. Pryce (eds) *Maastricht and Beyond – Building the European Union* (London: Routledge, 1994), pp. 84–103 p. 89.
22. Eaton, 'Common Foreign and Security Policy' in O'Keeffe and Twomey (eds), *Legal Issues of the Maastricht Treaty*, p. 218.
23. See Article J.4(1).
24. It may be wondered what is meant by safeguarding the independence of the Union? From whom?
25. On the development of the OSCE from the HFA through to the Charter of Paris and beyond see D. McGoldrick, 'The Development of the Conference on Security and Cooperation in Europe – from Process to Institution', in B.S. Jackson and D. McGoldrick, *Legal Visions of the New Europe* (London, Graham and Trotman/Nijhoff, 1993), pp. 135–82.
26. On the Charter of Paris see McGoldrick, ibid.   27. Article J.1(2).

These are wide-ranging and worthy objectives for CFSP, but they cannot be judicially enforced at the ECJ.[28] It clearly places the EU in a broader framework of externalising its values and interests, including its economic and social order, democracy and human rights.[29]

The level of obligations under CFSP

The language of CFSP is pitched at a higher level of obligation than EPC. Member states *shall* inform and consult one another and, whenever it deems it necessary, the Council *shall* define a common position (Article J.2). Member states *shall* ensure that their national positions conform to the common positions (Article J.2), rather than their merely constituting a 'point of reference' as under EPC.[30] The member states *shall* support CFSP and shall refrain from action impairing its effectiveness (Article J.1(4)), rather than 'endeavour to avoid impairing ... '[31] Moreover, a *common* policy is also qualitatively different from a policy to *cooperate*.

The roles of the institutions and decision making

In theory, integration into a 'single institutional structure' should systemically result in more coherent and consistent policy formulation and implementation.[32] However, as we shall see, although the structure is singular, the powers of the institutions under CFSP differ markedly from under the EC pillar.[33] The 'Community method' is not followed. CFSP is essentially intergovernmental.[34]

The European Council

In political and policy terms the role of the European Council is crucial.[35] 'The European Council shall provide the Union with the

---

28. See Article L. See the consideration below.   29. See also chs. 10–11 below.
30. Article 30(2)(c) SEA.   31. Article 30(2)(d) SEA.
32. See Articles A and C of the TEU.   33. See Article E of the TEU.
34. See the critique by Cremona, 'The Common Foreign and Security Policy of the European Union', in O'Keeffe and Twomey (eds), *Legal Issues of the Maastricht Treaty*, pp. 247–58.
35. See B.C. Ryba, 'La Politique Etrangère Et De Sécurité Commune (PESC) – Mode D'Emploi Et Bilan D'Une Année D'Application (Fin 1993/94)', 384 Revue Du Marche Commun Et De L'Union Européenne, 1995, 14–35.

necessary impetus for its development and shall define the general political guidelines thereof'.[36] Specifically in relation to CFSP, the European Council, 'shall define the principles of and general guidelines for the common foreign and security policy'.[37] This includes general guidelines on joint action.[38] This role in providing general guidelines is much the same as under EPC. We note the steps it has taken below.

The Council

The involvement of the Council as the main executive body is the most important institutional change brought about by CFSP.[39] The Council would normally be composed of the Foreign Ministers or their Deputies. If CFSP evolves a 'common defence policy' and possibly towards a 'common defence', the involvement of defence ministers either separately or jointly may well occur.[40]

The Council has a variety of functions under CFSP. It takes the decisions necessary for defining and implementing CFSP on the basis of the 'general guidelines' provided by the European Council.[41] It shall ensure the, 'unity, consistency and effectiveness of action by the Union'.[42] It shall ensure that the principles in Article J.1(4) of support and solidarity by the member states for the Union's external and security policy are complied with.[43] It is within the Council that member states shall inform and consult one another on any matter of CFSP of general interest.[44] Whenever it deems it necessary, the Council shall define a common position.[45] On the basis of general guidelines from the European Council, the Council decides whether a matter shall be the subject of joint action.[46]

The member states are to support the Union's external and security policy actively and unreservedly in a spirit of loyalty and mutuality.[47] In addition, they are to refrain from an action which is contrary to the interests of the Union or likely to impair its

---

36. Article D of the TEU.   37. Article J.8.   38. Article J.1(3).
39. See Eaton, 'Common Foreign and Security Policy', in O'Keeffe and Twomey (eds), *Legal Issues of the Maastricht Treaty*, pp. 220–1.
40. This could then create tensions within the Ministries of the member states.
41. Article J.8(2).
42. Ibid. See Neuwahl, 'Foreign and Security Policy and the Implementation of the Requirement of "Consistency"', in O'Keeffe and Twomey (eds), *Legal Issues of the Maastricht Treaty*, pp. 227–46.
43. Article J.1(4).   44. Article J.2(1).   45. Article J.2(2).
46. See pp. 153–7 below for more detail.
47. Article J.1(4).

effectiveness as a cohesive force in international relations.[48] The Council is to ensure that these principles are complied with. These solidarity provisions are analogous with Article 5 EC which has been built on as a constitutional foundation by the ECJ.[49] The important point here is that CFSP decisions are to be taken unanimously, subject to the proviso that the Council can define by unanimity those matters on which decisions are to be taken by qualified majority.[50] In Declaration No. 27 to the TEU the member states agreed that they, 'will, to the extent possible, avoid preventing a unanimous decision where a qualified majority exists in favour of that decision'.[51] Again, this reflected the existing practice of seeking consensus. This is not a legally binding obligation. It is an admonition to the member states to seek to agree decisions where the majority are in favour. It effectively makes the decision making process one of consensus in the sense of agreeing not to oppose. No vote is actually taken. However, if the decisions or action have been agreed unanimously or by consensus, then the solidarity provisions essentially demand the member states must support those policies and not undermine them. A move away from unanimity or consensus would risk undermining the solidarity of the member states in following CFSP decisions.[52]

The Presidency

The TEU strengthened the role of the Presidency which represents the Union in all matters of CFSP.[53] The Presidency is responsible for the implementation of common measures.[54] In that capacity the Presidency shall, in principle, express the position of the Union in international organizations or conferences.[55] In representation and implementation the Presidency is assisted by the operation of the troika, i.e., the previous and next member states to hold the

---

48. Ibid.   49. See ch. 1, pp. 19–20 above.
50. Articles J.8(2) and J.3(2). The QMV requirement is 62 votes cast by at least ten member states. The QMV requirement also applies for procedural questions.
51. See Commission report on this.
52. See Edwards and Nuttall, 'Common Foreign and Security Policy', in Duff, Pinder and Pryce (eds), *Maastricht and Beyond*, p. 99.
53. Article J.5. This imposes an extremely heavy burden on the smaller member state. The Commission had hoped to be given a wider role.
54. On the role of the Presidency under EPC see P. de Schoutheete, 'The Presidency and the Management of Political Cooperation', in A. Pijpers, E. Regelsberger and W. Wessels (eds), *European Political Cooperation in the 1980s* (Dordrecht, Nijhoff, 1988), pp. 71–83.
55. See Article J.5(2).

Presidency. The Commission is 'fully associated' with these tasks.[56] In practice this means that the Commission always accompanies the troika. This 'four-person troika' is used for external representation at all levels whether Council, Political Committee, Heads of Mission, or Working Group.[57]

COREPER; Political Committee; Council Secretariat; Working Groups

On CFSP the Council is principally served by the Political Committee. It provides input, monitors implementation and contributes to the definition of policies by delivering opinions to the Council at its request or on its own initiative.[58] COREPER remains as the normal channel for the preparation of Council business and this extends to checking points of CFSP, and adding comments on the work done by the Political Directors.[59] This assists consistency. When an issue raises an aspect of the Community system the role of COREPER may be crucial. This was the case, for example, in the issue of financing of CFSP.[60]

The central role of the Council under CFSP necessarily carries with it an expanded role for the Council Secretariat. As foreseen in Declaration No. 28 to the TEU, the EPC Secretariat was subsumed into the General (Council) Secretariat as a special autonomous division under the Secretary-General. It has been expanded in size as is now composed of twelve seconded diplomats and twelve Council officials. The CFSP Unit reports directly to the Presidency.[61] The transfer of EPC Working Groups into the Council Secretariat also caused bureaucratic problems, particularly where there were existing EC Working Groups.[62]

As CFSP continues to develop, questions of international law increasingly arise. Sources of legal advice on international law include the Legal Service of the Council, the Legal Service of the Commission, the national legal advisers of the member state holding the Presidency, and the national legal advisers of the other

---

[56.] Article J.5(3).
[57.] Fink-Hooijer, n. 3 above , p. 186.
[58.] Article J.8(5).
[59.] See G. Edwards, 'Common Foreign and Security Policy' (1994) 13 YEL 1993, 497–509, p. 499; G. Edwards, 'Common Foreign and Security Policy' (1995) 14 YEL 1994, 541–56, pp. 542–3.
[60.] See Declaration No. 28 to the TEU; J. Monar, n. 68 below.
[61.] See CFSP Forum 3 (1994), p. 2.
[62.] See Edwards, 'Common Foreign and Security Policy' (1994), p. 499.

member states. In addition there is the ad hoc Working Group on International Law, but this meets infrequently.

The Commission

The formal right of initiative for the Commission enhances its relative institutional position[63] although, again, in practice, the Commission had made proposals under EPC.[64] Although initially very cautious it is beginning to make more active use of its right.[65] The Commission is 'fully associated with the work carried out' in the CFSP field.[66] This association extends to implementation. This is obviously important in terms of ensuring consistency with action in the EC pillar where the role of the Commission is more central. The Commission shares with the Council responsibility for ensuring the consistency of the Union's external relations, security, economic and development policies.[67] It does not have any role under CFSP which is comparable to that which it has under Article 155 EC as guardian of the EC Treaty. The Commission is increasingly caught between the Council and the Commission, for example, in relation to the procedures on CFSP financing.[68]

In 1993 the Commission established a new directorate-general for external political affairs (DG1A) to reflect the wider dynamics of CFSP.[69] There is also an interesting division of work between the Commissioners. President Santer shares responsibility for CFSP with Mr van den Broek. After some political infighting, Mr van den Broek's responsibilities include external relations with Central and Eastern Europe and the former Soviet Union. This responsibility was clearly perceived within the Commission as more important than external relations for the developed world which went to Sir Leon Brittan.[70] Manuel Marin has responsibility

---

63. See Article J.8.(3).
64. See S. Nuttall, 'The Commission and Foreign Policy Making', in G. Edwards and D. Spence (eds), *The European Commission* (London, Longman, 1994), pp. 287–302.
65. See Article J.8(3). A rather Machiavellian idea is that it was in the Commission's interest for CFSP to fail under the current structure. It now realizes that it is probably here to stay so it needs to play its role to the full.
66. Article J.9. This is the same as under EPC, see Article 30(3) (b) SEA.
67. Article C of the TEU.
68. See J. Monar, 'The Financial Dimension of the Common Foreign and Security Policy', in M. Holland (ed.), *Common Foreign and Security Policy: The Record and the Reforms* (London, Pinter, forthcoming 1997).
69. See S. Nuttall, 'The European Commission's Internal Arrangements for Foreign Affairs and External Relations' (1995) CFSP Forum 2.
70. See Bull-EU, 1/2-1995, pp. 8–30. Sir Leon Brittan considered resigning when he did not get the external political relations portfolio.

for external relations with the developing world. Others members of the Commission have responsibilities which can impact on external relations and CFSP.

European Parliament

The EP's role in CFSP is limited and was clearly intended to be so. The Presidency is to consult the EP on the 'main aspects and the basic choices' of CFSP and is to ensure that the views of the EP are duly taken into consideration.[71] The Presidency and the Commission are to keep the EP 'regularly informed' of the development of CFSP.[72] The EP has been pressing for a wide interpretation of these provisions so that consultation takes place at a time when its views can have an impact rather than afterwards. It has used its role in the financing of CFSP under the EC budget to press its claims.[73] It should not be allowed to use its budgetary powers to effectively subvert the clear decision of the member states on the intergovernmental nature of CFSP. A problem the EP is facing in the IGC[74] in seeking wider powers over CFSP is that the argument that it cannot have wider powers than national parliaments have. That raises the policy question of whether national parliaments should have wider powers.[75]

The European Court of Justice

The TEU does not accord the ECJ jurisdiction over CFSP. The same was true in respect of EPC.[76] However, the ECJ does have jurisdiction over the 'Final Provisions' of the TEU in Articles L–S. Of particular importance is Article M, which provides that, other than the amendments expressly provided for by the TEU, nothing in the TEU shall affect the Treaties amending the European Communities. Thus CFSP cannot be used to modify or amend the

---

71. Article J.7.   72. Ibid.
73. See Edwards, 'Common Foreign and Security Policy' (1995), p. 344; Monar, 'The Financial Dimension', in Holland (ed.), *Joint Actions*.
74. The EP has a very limited role in the IGC negotiations.
75. See E. Denza, 'Groping Towards Europe's Foreign Policy', in D. Curtin and T. Heukels (eds), *Institutional Dynamics of European Integration: Essays in Honour of H.G. Schermers* (Dordrecht, Nijhoff, 1994), vol. II, 575–93, p. 592. On democratic control of foreign policy see R. Bieber, 'Democratic Control of European Foreign Policy' (1990) 1/2 EJIL, 148–73, who comments that 'At present, the activities of CFSP enjoy neither popular understanding nor popular support', p. 103.
76. See Article 31 SEA. See D. Freestone and S. Davidson, 'Community Competence and Part III of the Single European Act' (1986) 23 CMLRev, 793–801.

Community Treaties. 'The effect is that the Court can and must police the borderline between the Community pillar and the CFSP'.[77] The Commission or a member state could bring an action before the ECJ for failure to implement EC sanctions even if they were adopted under Article 228a following a decision under CFSP. That is because the obligation to implement the sanctions would be a Community law obligation. However, no member state or institution can bring an action before the ECJ concerning compliance with obligations arising under CFSP, or the validity of a CFSP instrument. Rather, it is the Council's responsibility at a political level to ensure that the obligations of support and solidarity under CFSP are complied with.[78]

As with any other international law obligations, it is possible that a member state could invoke the jurisdiction of the International Court of Justice.[79] This would require the consent of the state concerned and in some cases it might be brought under the Optional Jurisdiction provision in Article 36(2) of the statute of the ICJ. Although politically such a course of action may seem unlikely, the possibility of high level disputes between member states on implementation means it remains an option for consideration.

The instruments of CFSP

The concept of legally binding 'joint action' opened new possibilities for practical developments. The joint actions taken are considered below. Even before the TEU entered into force, European Councils had begun to express the will to engage in proactive rather than reactive foreign policy.

The instruments of CFSP are neither Community law measures not international conventions.[80] Rather, the Union has two general

---

77. See Eaton, 'Common Foreign and Security Policy', in O'Keeffe and Twomey (eds), *Legal Issues of the Maastricht Treaty*, p. 221.
78. Article J.1(4).
79. See Article 36 of the Statute of the ICJ. The bringing of such a case would not contravene Article 219 EC because it would not concern the interpretation or application of the EC Treaty but rather the TEU.
80. See Neuwahl, 'Foreign and Security Policy and the Implementation of the Requirement of "Consistency"', in O'Keeffe and Twomey (eds), *Legal Issues of the Maastricht Treaty*. Conventions would appear to be excluded if the lack of international personality of the Union is maintained, see ch. 2 above. In its proposals to the 1990–91 IGC on Political Union the Commission proposed that the Council should be able to conclude international agreements in the field of CFSP, see Bull-EC, Supp 2/91 at 94, Article 25Y.

techniques for pursuing its objectives in relation to CFSP. First, by establishing systematic cooperation between member states in the conduct of policy. At the formal level these can be expressed as 'common positions'. These can find expression in 'Political Declarations', or in a Council Decision sui generis. Secondly, by gradually implementing 'joint action' in the areas in which member states have important interests in common. These also take the legal form of a Council Decision sui generis.[81] The distinction between these two concepts is a new development.[82] In practice there has been some inconsistency and confusion about the different roles of the two instruments.[83] What became known as 'theological disputes' arose reflecting concerns by the Commission and member states that the EC and CFSP pillars would contaminate each other's procedures. For example, could common positions in CFSP on a strategy towards a particular country also refer to EC matters.[84] It would obviously have been nonsensical for all EC matters to be excluded. Indeed, they are often a central part of the EU's CFSP and this is reflected in both CFSP common positions and joint actions. However, although a CFSP instrument can cover matters within the EC's competence, the implementation of such matters must be done through the EC structure and in accordance with the EC's institutional requirements and voting rules.

Although the European Union may at present lack international legal personality,[85] it was decided at the General Affairs Council of 8 and 9 November 1993 that all political declarations under CFSP will be made on behalf of the European Union.[86] The use of

---

81. The Sui Generis Decisions on CFSP are published in the OJ.
82. Eaton, 'Common Foreign and Security Policy', in O'Keeffe and Twomey (eds), *Legal Issues of the Maastricht Treaty*, p. 217. Under EPC joint action was merely an aspect of cooperation, see Articles 3(c) and 30(2)(c) SEA.
83. See Edwards, 'Common Foreign and Security Policy' (1995). In June 1996 the Foreign Affairs Council adopted 'Guidelines on Working Methods of the Council' which were intended in part to achieve consistency in the use of the different instruments. Nonetheless, at the IGC 'there is a fairly general desire to clarify the scope of CFSP instruments, particularly joint actions and common positions', Progress Report on IGC, p. 42.
84. See M.R. Eaton, 'Common Foreign and Security Policy (non-security aspects)', in *The Treaty on European Union: Suggestions for Revision* (The Hague), TMC Asser Instituut Conference on European Law (Sept 1995), pp. 293–4; A. Dashwood, *Reviewing Maastricht: Issues for the 1996 IGC* (London, Sweet and Maxwell/Law Books in Europe, 1996), pp. 222–3.
85. See pp. 36–9 above.
86. The statements and Declarations are usually published in the capital of the Presidency and in Brussels.

statements and Declarations,[87] well established under EPC and an important part of any foreign policy, has continued at a high level.[88]

Systematic cooperation between member states in the conduct of policy

This is governed by Article J.2. It builds heavily on, and largely corresponds to, the practice of EPC. Member states are to, 'inform and consult one another within the Council on any matter of foreign and security policy of general interest in order to ensure that their combined influence is exerted as effectively as possible by means of concerted and convergent action'. Although the scope is again wide, viz, 'any matter', it is limited to matters of 'general interest'. Difficulties may arise if a member state argues that the matter is only of specific concern to it, or to a limited number of members.[89] Given the unanimity requirement,[90] their view would prevail in such a situation and, with no common position, there would be no solidarity obligation. In terms of information sharing and cooperation, there is a 'massive flow of diplomatic business already through this channel of European cooperation'.[91] There are approximately 300 telexes per day passing through the Foreign Offices of the member states. Daily contact between the respective personnel of the member states administrations is now the norm.

Whenever it deems it necessary the Council shall define a 'common position'.[92] This will set out the EU's view on the matter concerned. It is the responsibility of the Presidency to elaborate a position paper which meets the common will of the member states. The normal practice is for text to be prepared and agreed upon by way of coded telexes through the COREU network.[93] As compared to the substantial number of EU statements and declarations only

---

87. These are used in particularly important cases. All Declarations are communicated to the Secretary-General of the UN. Cf. UN practice of using Declarations to designate GA resolutions of particular significance.
88. Over 100 per year.
89. See Neuwahl, 'Foreign and Security Policy and the Implementation of the Requirement of "Consistency" ', in O'Keeffe and Twomey (eds), *Legal Issues of the Maastricht Treaty*, p. 230.
90. Article J.8(2).
91. D. Hurd, Secretary of State for Foreign and Commonwealth Affairs, *Hansard*, HC Debs., 30 March 1993, col. 170.
92. Article J.2(2).
93. See above on this. See the Declaration 29 to the TEU on the use of languages in the field of CFSP.

a small number of formal common positions have been adopted. These take the form of a sui generis decision. Member states are obliged to make sure that their national policies conform to the common positions.[94] This is part of the solidarity obligation in respect of positions arrived at unanimously.[95] European cooperation has been a particularly important phenomena in international organizations and conferences.[96] Such coordination of action is to continue under CFSP.[97] If not all members participate, then those members that do shall uphold the common positions.[98] There is an important but carefully worded provision relating to the UN Security Council in Article J.5(4):

> Member States which are also members of the United Nations Security Council will concert and keep other Member States fully informed. Member States which are permanent members of the Security Council will, in the execution of their functions, ensure the defence of the positions and the interests of the Union, without prejudice to their responsibilities under the provisions of the United Nations Charter.

It has occasionally been suggested that, if there were Charter reform, the permanent seats held by the UK and France could be replaced by a single seat in the name of the EU. Such a development appears extremely unlikely.[99]

The common positions adopted

The number of formal common positions adopted under Article J.2 has risen steadily. They have dealt with a range of matters, sometimes in great detail. These have concerned the reduction of economic relations with Libya;[100] an embargo on arms, munitions and military equipment to Sudan;[101] the reduction of economic relations with Haiti and their subsequent termination;[102] various aspects of sanctions against the former Yugoslavia;[103] arms exports

---

94. See Articles J.1(3) and J.2(1).   95. See above.
96. See ch. 2 above and ch. 11 below.   97. Article J.2(3).   98. Ibid.
99. See M. Wood, 'Security Council Working Methods and Procedure: Recent Developments', 45 ICLQ (1996), 150–61.
100. Council Decision 93/614/CFSP, [1993] OJ L295/7.
101. Council Decision 94/165/CFSP, [1994] OJ L75/1.
102. Council Decisions 94/315/CFSP, [1994] OJ L139/10, and 94/681/CFSP, [1994] OJ L271/3.
103. Council Decisions 94/336/CFSP, [1993] OJ L165/1; 94/672 CFSP, [1994] OJ L266/10; 94/673/CFSP, [1994] OJ L266/11; 95/11/CFSP, [1995] OJ L20/1; 95/150/CFSP, [1995] OJ L99/2; 95/213/CFSP, [1995] OJ L138/2; 95/254/CFSP, [1995] OJ L160/2; 95/378/CFSP, [1995] OJ L227/2; 95/511/CFSP, [1995] OJ L297/4.

to the former Yugoslavia;[104] the objectives and priorities of the EU towards Rwanda[105] and Ukraine;[106] the situations in Angola,[107] Burundi,[108] East Timor,[109] and Nigeria;[110] blinding lasers;[111] and the Fourth Review Conference of the Convention on the Prohibition of the development, production and stockpiling of bacteriological (biological) and toxin weapons and on their destruction.[112] There has also been a decision of the representatives of the governments of the member states, meeting within the Council of 25 June 1996 on the establishment of an emergency travel document.[113]

Joint action[114]

Member states have acted jointly before, for example, over the recognition of new states,[115] but 'joint action' is new in the sense that it is now a formal instrument. It is governed by Article J.3.[116] What exactly a 'joint action' is, is not defined. Fink-Hooijer comments that, 'It can be understood as a joint policy or as a specific action, restricted to solving, for example, a given conflict'.[117] Joint action can be taken in any matter of CFSP but it is restricted to areas in which members states have 'important interests in common'.[118] Again this will need to have unanimous support.[119] Joint actions commit the member states in the positions they adopt and in the conduct of their activity.[120]

104. Council Decision 96/184/CFSP, [1996] OJ L58/1.
105. Council Decision 94/697/CFSP, [1994] OJ L283/1.
106. Council Decision 94/779/CFSP, [1994] OJ L313/1.
107. Council Decision 94/413/CFSP, [1995] OJ L245/1.
108. Council Decisions 95/91/CFSP, [1995] OJ L72/1; 95/206/CFSP, [1995] OJ L130/2.
109. Council Decision 96/407/CFSP, [1996] OJ L168/2.
110. Council Decisions 95/515/CFSP, [1995] OJ L298/1; 95/544/CFSP, [1995] OJ L309/1; 96/361/CFSP, [1996] OJ L143/1; 96/677/CFSP, [1996] OJ L315/3. On Burma see 96/635/CFSP, [1996] OJ L287/1.
111. Council Decision 95/379/CFSP, [1995] OJ L227/3.
112. Council Decision 96/408/CFSP, [1996] OJ L168/3.
113. Council Decision 96/409/CFSP, [1996] OJ L168/4.
114. See Holland (ed.), *CFSP: The Record and the Reforms.*
115. See C. Warbrick, 'Recognition of States' (1992) 41 ICLQ, 473–82. Though recognition itself is an act of the member state.
116. The idea of joint action can be found in Article 30 SEA but it was never developed operationally.
117. See Fink-Hooijer, 'The CFSP of the EU', 5 EJIL, 173–98, pp. 180–1; Dashwood, *Reviewing Maastricht*, p. 217.
118. Article J.1(3).   119. Article J.8(2).
120. Article J.(3)4. There are further safeguard provisions on adopting national positions or taking national action pursuant to a joint action, cases of imperative need and major difficulties in implementing a joint action, see

The European Council in Lisbon 1992 set out the factors to be used to determine important common interests, and which are to be taken into account when defining issues and areas for joint action. These are:

- the geographical proximity of a given region or country;[121]
- the existence of important political interests in the political and economic stability of a region or country;
- the existence of threats to the security interests of the Union.[122]

The idea of 'gradual implementation' suggests that the development of joint action should be a cautious and evolutionary process. Joint actions are not available for issues having defence implications, as opposed to purely security implications.[123]

General guidelines for joint action have to be laid down by the European Council. It quickly set about this task. In Lisbon in 1992 it approved a report establishing the first set of general guidelines for joint action.[124] The report reaffirmed the conditions relating to subsidiarity, acquis communautaire, consistency, and the objectives expressly stated in the TEU.[125] It then set out further specific objectives to be taken into account when adopting joint action. These were:

---

120. (*continued*) Articles J.(3)5–7. See also Declaration 25 to the TEU on the representation of the interests of overseas countries and territories. See Eaton, 'Common Foreign and Security Policy', in O'Keeffe and Twomey (eds), *Legal Issues of the Maastricht Treaty*.
121. This criterion would thus be affected by future enlargement.
122. For an academic assessment of the EU's future security threats and challenges see M. Clarke, 'Future Security Threats and Challenges', in S.A. Pappas and S. Vanhoonacker (eds), *The European Union's Common Foreign and Security Policy: The Challenges of the Future* (Maastricht, EIPA, 1996).
123. Article J.4(3). Eaton gives the example of Disarmament Conference, Eaton, 'Common Foreign and Security Policy', in O'Keeffe and Twomey (eds), *Legal Issues of the Maastricht Treaty*, p. 218. He also notes that CFSP must be compatible with the NATO Treaty and that bilateral cooperation is not excluded.
124. Lisbon Report, 'Report to the European Council on the likely development of CFSP', 27 June 1992.
125. See Fink-Hooijer, 'The CFSP of the EU', pp. 178–9. Edwards and Nuttall suggest that CFSP is a prime candidate for the application of the principle of subsidiarity, 'which would result in most foreign policy decisions being taken at the level of the Union'. This view seems to lose sight of the series of questions that need to be asked in application of the subsidiarity principle ('Common Foreign and Security Policy', in Duff, Pinder and Pryce (eds), *Maastricht and Beyond*, p. 101).

- strengthening democratic principles and institutions, and respect for human and minority rights;
- promoting regional political stability and contributing to the creation of political and/or economic frameworks that encourage regional cooperation or moves towards regional or sub-regional integration;
- contributing to the prevention and settlement of conflicts;
- contributing to more effective international coordination in dealing with emergency situations;
- strengthening existing cooperation in issues of international interest such as the fight against arms proliferation, terrorism and traffic in illicit drugs;
- promoting and supporting good government.

The Lisbon Council also identified a number of areas where joint action in relation to individual countries or groups of countries appeared to be particularly beneficial, in a first phase, for the attainment of the objectives of the EU. These were Central and Eastern Europe, especially the ex-USSR and former Yugoslavia, the Mahgreb and the Middle East.

Looking to the future the Council identified areas of common interest which would require joint action. These were all aspects of North-South relations, the continuation of relations with the USA, Japan and Canada, and the coordination of action in international organizations and conferences. At the Edinburgh Council in 1992 a further report was adopted which set out a non-exhaustive list of potential areas or issues in the security field suitable for early joint action by the EU. The Extraordinary European Council in 1993 requested the Council to engage in preparatory work for the implementation of joint action on the promotion of stability and peace in Europe – the Balladur Pact on Stability[126] – on the Middle East, on South Africa, on former Yugoslavia, and on election observation in Russia.

The European Council has given specific attention to the field of security, the clear addition of which was an advance on EPC. In Maastricht (1991) in a 'Declaration on Areas which could be the subject of Joint Action' it identified four areas in the security field in which the member states have important interests in common and which could, therefore, lend themselves to the implementation of joint actions. These were the OSCE process, the policy of

126. See Bull-EU, 3-1995, point 2.2.1.

disarmament and arms control in Europe, nuclear non-proliferation issues and the economic aspects of security. Further detail was provided on each of these in a Report on Joint Action and the development of the CFSP in the field of security adopted by the Edinburgh Council in 1992.

In 1993 the European Council in Brussels defined the general objectives of European security as the territorial integrity and political independence of the EU, its democratic character, its economic stability and the stability of neighbouring regions.

If it decides on the principle of joint action, the Council shall also, 'lay down the specific scope, the Union's general and specific objectives in carrying out such action, if necessary its duration, and the means, procedures and conditions for its implementation'.[127] The Council can define those matters concerning a joint action on which decisions can be taken by qualified majority.[128]

The joint actions adopted

The number of joint actions adopted has also risen steadily. They have covered an interesting range of matters and in some cases complement or develop common positions. In some cases their content has been very detailed. The joint actions adopted have concerned the convoying of humanitarian aid to Bosnia-Herzegovina,[129] continued support for the EU administration of the city of Mostar,[130] implementation of the peace plan for Bosnia-Herzegovina,[131] support for the electoral process in Bosnia-Herzegovina,[132] the dispatch of a team of observers to Russian Parliamentary elections,[133] support for transition towards a democratic and multiracial South Africa,[134] the Conference and implementation of the Stability Pact on Europe, limits on the

---

127. Article J.3(1).   128. Article J.3(2).
129. See Council Decisions 93/603/CFSP, [1993] OJ L286/1; 93/729/CFSP, [1993] OJ L339/3; 94/158/CFSP, [1994] OJ L70/1; 94/308/CFSP, [1994] OJ L134/1; 94/501/CFSP, [1994] OJ L205/3; 95/516/CFSP, [1995] OJ L298/3.
130. See Council Decisions 94/790/CFSP, [1994] OJ L326/2; 95/23/CFSP, [1995] OJ L33/1; 95/517/CFSP, [1995] OJ L298/4; 95/552/CFSP, [1995] OJ L313/1; 96/442/CFSP, [1996] OJ L185/2; 96/476/CFSP, [1996] OJ L195/1; 96/508/CFSP, [1996] OJ L212/1.
131. Council Decision 95/545/CFSP, [1995] OJ L309/2.
132. Council Decision 96/406/CFSP, [1996] OJ L168/1.
133. See Council Decision 91/604/CFSP, [1994] OJ L286/3.
134. See Council Decision 93/678/CFSP, [1993] OJ L316/45. See M. Holland, 'Bridging the Credibility-Expectations Gap: A Case Study of the CFSP Joint Action on South Africa' (1995) 33 JCMS, 555–72, for an assessment.

production and distribution of anti-personnel mines,[135] support for the Middle East peace process,[136] preparation for the 1995 Conference on the Non-Proliferation Treaty,[137] control on the export of dual-use goods,[138] participation of the EU in the Korean Peninsula Energy Development Organization,[139] and the nomination of a Special Envoy for the African Great Lakes Region.[140]

Financing[141]

There has been a rapid growth in the CFSP budget,[142] and financing has developed into a major issue.[143] Adequate and timely financing, and the existence of available reserves, are essential pre-conditions to the effectiveness of CFSP. Article J.(11)2 provides that (i) 'administrative expenditure' which the CFSP provisions entail shall be charged to the EC budget. 'Operational expenditure to which the implementation' of CFSP provisions gives rise can, if there is unanimity, come from either the EC budget, or it can from national financial contributions. If recourse is made to the EC budget then the EC budgetary procedure is applicable.[144] This obviously gives the EP an enhanced role in CFSP. No clear practice has developed on the distinction between 'administrative expenditure' and 'operational expenditure'. Not surprisingly, the Council has sought to apply an extensive interpretation of the former. Another factor favouring this is that under a 'Gentleman's Agreement' the EP refrains from intervening in the administrative expenditure of the Council and the Council,

---

135. Council Decisions 95/170/CFSP, [1995] OJ L115/1; 96/251/CFSP, [1996] OJ L87/3.
136. See Council Decisions 94/276/CFSP, [1993] OJ L119/1; 95/205/CFSP, [1995] OJ L130/1; 95/403/CFSP, [1995] OJ L238/4; 96/676/CFSP, [1996] OJ L315/1.
137. See Council Decision 94/509/CFSP, [1994] OJ L205/1.
138. Council Decisions 94/942/CFSP, [1994] OJ L367/8, as corrected by [1996] OJ L52/18 and as amended by Council Decision 96/423/CFSP, [1996] OJ L176/1; 95/127/CFSP, [1995] OJ L90/2, as corrected by [1996] OJ L52/24; 95/128/CFSP, [1995] OJ L90/3; 96/173/CFSP, [1996] OJ L52/1.
139. Council Decision 96/195/CFSP, [1996] OJ L63/1.
140. Council Decisions 96/250/CFSP, [1996] OJ L87/1; 96/441/CFSP, [1996] OJ L185/1.
141. See Monar, 'The Financial Dimension of the Common Foreign and Security Policy', in Holland (ed.), *Joint Actions* (1996) for an excellent analysis of the problems and practice.
142. ECU 110m budgeted for 1995. For the 1996 budget see [1996] OJ L22/1, pp. 1617–27.
143. Ibid.; T. Hagleitner, 'Financing the Common Foreign Security Policy – A Step Towards Communitarisation or Institutional Deadlock' (1995) CFSP Forum 2, 6.
144. The legal basis is Article 199. For expenditure charged to the member state a scale of charges has to be decided.

rather than the Commission, is responsible for administering it. Difficulties soon arose between the Council and the EP in relation to the adoption of the EC budget in the years after 1993. The Commission found itself pressured by the Council and then criticized by the EP.[145] However, event within the EP there were differences between its 'Committees on the Budget' and its 'Committee on Foreign Affairs and Security'.[146] As for operational expenditure member states proved reluctant to contribute from their national budgets. When there was agreement to contribute there were serious delays in the actual contributions, for example, relating to the provision of humanitarian aid.[147] The result was that EC financing as the norm seemed increasingly inevitable. A likely model is the Joint Action on Anti-Personnel mines, Decision 95/170/CFSP.[148] In this it was agreed that, without prejudice to possible contributions from the member states, that the Union would contribute ECU 160,000 for the organization of the UN conference on mine clearing and a contribution of up to ECU 7 million to the UN Voluntary Fund for Assistance in Mine Clearing. Both of these sums were charged to the EC budget.[149]

The effect is an indirect communitarization of CFSP because the Commission presents the budget and the EP can decide in relation to non-obligatory expenditure. The EP has gone along with this so far, but it has sought to use the resort to the EC budget as a means of extending its rights over CFSP by pressing for stronger pre-consultation rather than information and post-consultation. The difficulty is to devise a system using the EC budget which allows the EP oversight but not control.[150]

CFSP and Community instruments: sanctions[151]

Practice had developed which effectively required the achievement of consensus rather than the QMV which action under Article 113

145. See [1994] OJ C305, p. 29.
146. See Monar, 'The Financial Dimension of the Common Foreign and Security Policy', in Holland (ed.), *Joint Actions* (1996).
147. This meant that the time period for Joint Actions had to be extended.
148. [1995] OJ L115/1.
149. [1995] OJ L112/2. CFSP actions are attributed to the Commission section of the budget. By contrast under JHA all of the financing has come from national financing, see D. O'Keeffe, 'Recasting the Third Pillar' (1995) 32 CMLRev, 893–920.
150. See Progress Report on IGC, Presidency Conclusions, European Council in Florence, 21–22 June 1996, Doc. SN 300/96, Annexes. p. 22.
151. See Macleod, Hendry and Hyett, *The External Relations of the European Communities*, pp. 352–66; P.J. Kuijper, 'Trade Sanctions, Security and Human Rights and Commercial Policy', in M. Maresceau (ed.) *The European*

would require.[152] Article 228a provides for action in the EC pillar to be predicated on a common position or on a joint action taken in CFSP. This was used for the first time for sanctions against Libya.[153] Article 228a now provides the appropriate legal base. This does not undermine general community competence to take sanctions in relation to its commercial policy.[154] Hitherto the Community had only ever imposed sanctions on the basis of a Commission proposal under Article 113 when UN sanctions had been imposed and the relevant agreement had been reached in EPC.[155] There had always been doubts about the adequacy of Article 113 as a legal basis. It was used for the first time only in 1982, sanctions prior to that being implemented at member states level after consultation under Article 224.[156] CFSP therefore creates more room for economic counter-measures, particularly given the wider objectives of the EU[157] and the specific objectives of CFSP.[158] For example, sanctions against Haiti in 1993 and 1994 were imposed as part of an international response to an assumption of power by the military and human rights abuses.[159] The EU response to the US Helms-Burton Act on Cuba consisted of an EC regulation, a common position and a joint action.

A common defence policy and a common defence

This is one of the most sensitive and controversial issues for the development of CFSP.[160] The TEU clearly looks to the future

---

151. (continued) Community's Commercial Policy after 1992 – The Legal Dimension (Dordrecht: Nijhoff, 1993), pp. 387–422.
152. That practice had been based on the Regulation on chemical precursors, Reg 428/89, [1989] OJ L50/1.
153. See Regulation 3274/93, [1993] OJ L295/1, and Regulation 3275/93, [1993] OJ L295/4.
154. See S. Bohr, 'Sanctions by the United Nations Security Council and the European Community' (1993) 4 EJIL, 256–68.
155. See P.J. Kuijper, 'Community Sanctions Against Argentina: Lawfulness under Community and International Law', in D. O'Keeffe and H.G. Schermers (eds), Essays in European Law and Integration (Deventer: Kluwer, 1982), pp. 141–66; Bohr, 'Sanctions by the United Nations Security Council and the European Community'.
156. See Denza, 'Groping Towards Europe's Foreign Policy', in Curtin and Heukels (eds) Institutional Dynamics of European Integration.
157. See Article B of the TEU. See Case C-84/95, Bosphorus Hava Yollari Turizm ve Ticaret AS v Minister for Transport, Energy and Communications and Others [1996] ECR nyr, on sanctions against Yugoslavia (Serbia and Montenegro).
158. See Article J.1(2).
159. See Regulation 1608/93, [1993] OJ L155/2; Regulation 1263/94, [1994] OJ L139/1; Regulation 1296/94, [1994] OJ L139/4; Regulation 2543/94, [1994] OJ L271/1.
160. See L. Martin and J. Roper (eds), Towards a Common Defence Policy (Paris,

evolution of defence matters. Article J.4.2 provides that the 'Union requests the Western European Union (WEU), which is *an integral part of the development of the Union*, to elaborate and implement decisions and actions of the Union which have defence implications'.[161] The Council and the institutions of the WEU are to agree the necessary arrangements.[162] The importance of not undermining the NATO system is stressed. The Union's policy under Article J.4, 'shall not prejudice the specific character of the security and defence policy of certain Member States and shall respect the obligations of certain Member States under the North Atlantic Treaty and be compatible with the common security and defence policy established within that framework'. One of the declarations to the TEU is an elaborate 'Declaration on WEU' by the members of the WEU who are also members of the EU.[163] This very much points to a 'gradual process involving successive stages' in which 'the objective is to build up WEU in stages as the defence component of the European Union'. Under Article J.(4)5 further bilateral cooperation in the framework of the WEU and NATO is foreseen, provided it does not run counter to cooperation under CFSP. Defence is one of the matters for which the possibility of revision at the 1996 IGC is specifically provided for.[164]

Reform of CFSP

The TEU provided that CFSP was to be reviewed in 1996 at the IGC.[165] Indeed, it has been one of the principal concerns of the IGC because there is general recognition by member states, the institutions and academics that it needs some reform.[166] The very

---

160. (*continued*) WEU/Institute for Strategic Studies, 1994). Defence was one of the major issues in the Danish referendum in 1992 on the TEU. Denmark secured a Decision of the Heads of State or Government meeting within the European Council concerning its problems. Section C of that Decision dealt with Defence Policy. See Bull-EU, 12/1992, pp. 25–9.

161. Emphasis added.

162. See O. Waever, 'European Security Identities' (1996) 34(2) JCMS, 103–32. The WEU moved its location from London to Brussels in 1993.

163. Declaration No. 30.   164. Article J.(4)6.

165. Articles J.(4)6, J.(4)10. The review is based on the report from the European Council, see Council: Report of the Council of Ministers on the Functioning of the TEU (Luxembourg/Brussels, 10 April 1995) Doc. 5082/95; Dashwood, *Reviewing Maastricht*, pp. 211–75.

166. See P. Ludlow and N. Ersboell, *Towards 1996: The Agenda of the Intergovernmental Conference* (Brussels, Centre for European Policy Studies, 1994); Justus Lipsius, 'The 1996 Intergovernmental Conference' (1995) 20

concept of a 'foreign and common security policy' was an ambitious one[167] and raised both internal and external expectations. The reality has been more pragmatic and conservative.[168] The approach of member states ranges across the familiar integrationist to intergovernmentalist spectrum.[169] As with EPC, different member states have different interests in CFSP.[170] Political culture and diplomatic experience, engagement and resources varies widely across the EU. Some of the member states which are most reluctant in respect of CFSP or particular aspects of it such as security or defence, are those which are more strongly integrationist and communitarian in respect of EC matters, such as Ireland and Greece. Germany is pushing CFSP strongly. The UK is much more cautious.[171] France has always been more ambivalent but there is a consistent theme of intergovernmentalism running

166. (continued) ELRev, 235–67; P. Sutherland, 'The European Union – A Stage of Transition' (1995) EIPASCOPE, 1995/2, 2–9; W.F. Van Eekelen, 'The Common Foreign and Security Policy', in *The Treaty on European Union: Suggestions for Revision* (The Hague, TMC Asser Instituut Conference on European Law (Sept 1995); Eaton, 'Common Foreign and Security Policy (non-security aspects)', in *The Treaty on European Union: Suggestions for Revision* (The Hague), TMC Asser Instituut Conference on European Law (Sept 1995); *The Treaty on European Union: Suggestions for Revision*, TMC Asser Instituut Conference on European Law (The Hague, 1996); Pappas and Vanhoonacker (eds), *The European Union's Common Foreign and Security Policy*; Council Report to the IGC Doc. 5082/95; Commission Report to the IGC (Report on the Operation of the Treaty on European Union, Brussels, 10 May 1995, SEC (95) 731 final), pp. 56–66; EP Report to the IGC (Report of the European Parliament on the Functioning of the Treaty on European Union, 19 May 1995, EP Doc. A4-0102/95), pp. 6–7; Progress Report on IGC, pp. 40–55; UK Government White Paper, *A Partnership of Nations* (CM 3181, London, HMSO, 1996); E. Regelsberger and W. Wessels, 'The CFSP Institutions and Procedures: A Third Way for the Second Pillar' (1996) I EFARev, 29–54.
167. The member states could not agree to use the words 'common foreign and security policy' in the SEA 1986.
168. See Edwards, 'Common Foreign and Security Policy' (1994), (1995).
169. See EIPA, 'The European Union's Common Foreign and Security Policy: the Positions of the Main Actors, (Conference, Maastricht, 19–20 October 1995); Reflection Group Progress Report (Brussels, September 1995) Doc. SN509/1/95, Rev 1 (Reflex 10); Reflection Group Final Report (Brussels, December 1995) (sometimes referred to as the Westendorp Report) Doc. SN520/95.
170. See W. Wallace and W. Paterson (eds), *Foreign Policy Making in Western Europe* (Farnborough, Saxon House, 1978); C. Hill, 'The Capability- Expectations Gap, or Conceptualising Europe's International Role' (1983) 31 JCMS, 305–28; F. Pfetsch, 'Tensions in Sovereignty – Foreign Policies of EC Members Compared', in Carlnaes and Smith, *European Foreign Policy*, pp. 120–37.
171. See D. Hurd, 'Developing the CFSP' (1994) Int. Affairs, 421–8; M. Rifkind, 'Principles and Practice of British Foreign Policy', Speech Delivered at the Royal Institute of International Affairs, Chatham House, London, 21 September 1995; UK Government White Paper, *A Partnership of Nations*.

through its initiatives and this appears to continue to be French policy. The enlargement from twelve to fifteen member states has also had an effect on attitudes. Member states that may have generally favoured a CFSP in a small grouping of like-minded states are coming to realize that new member states bring with them a different set of interests and objectives.[172] This will be further accentuated by further enlargement. This may partly explain current French policy on CFSP particularly in the light of the critical reaction of many of the member states of the Union to the resumption of French nuclear tests in the South Pacific in 1995.[173]

The Reflection Group's Progress Report (RGP) referred to the 'major changes taking place outside the Union as the end of the century approaches: major political instability in the European region following the end of the cold war, major migrations of populations which are particularly acute in Europe, risks of ecological imbalances which the Union cannot afford to ignore, etc., coupled with an increasing globalization of the economy which highlights Europe's loss of some comparative historical advantages gained through its social and technological innovations, and which can only be met by adopting an equally global approach'.[174] The Union's responses had to put it in a position to continue acting as the principal factor of peace and prosperity on the European continent.[175] It had to achieve the highest possible levels of external stability and security:

> The key task, here, therefore, is to take all the steps necessary to provide the Union with a genuine external identity that will enable it to become a world force in international relations, so that it can promote its values, defend its interests and help shape a new world order. This will clearly only be possible if the foreign policy really functions, with full consistency being ensured between the political and economic aspects of the Union's external action.[176]

It was also stressed that the forthcoming enlargement, which has

172. See J. Sedivy, 'Common Foreign and Security Policy – A Central European View', in S.A. Pappas and S. Vanhoonacker (eds) op. cit., n. 122.

173. Some member states were vehement in their opposition. Some applications were also brought to the ECJ. See, for example, Case T-219/95, *Danielsson and Others v Commission* [1995] ECR II-3051. The UK and Germany were the least critical. Interestingly the French position on CFSP now appears to be very close to that of the UK.

174. Reflection Group's Progress Report, pp. 1–2. See also Reflection Group's Final Report, pp. I–II, 2–3.

175. Reflection Group's Progress Report, p. 2; Reflection Group's Final Report, pp. II–III, 4–5.

176. Reflection Group's Progress Report, p. 3; Reflection Group's Final Report, pp. 5–6.

been accepted in principle, required reform of the functioning of the Union, so that enlargement did not weaken or break up the Union. Objectives need to be clarified and the Union's instruments for external action strengthened.

The discussions in the Reflection Group and at the IGC (General Outline for a draft revision of the Treaties, CONF 2500/96, 5 December 1996) suggest that the main issues and themes for CFSP reform are fairly well set.[177] We consider these in turn, along with the positions of the Institutions on them. Attention is focused on CFSP but it must not be forgotten that many of the IGC issues interrelate and progress in one area can impact on others.

Analysis and planning

There is a concensus that an 'analysis, forecasting, planning and proposal unit or body' should be set up for CFSP.[178] The more difficult question is as to the status of such a unit within the Institutions of the Union and its possible effects on the institutional balance. The RG considered that reform should respect the institutional balance as a whole.[179] A majority of the RG thought that the Commission should be involved with planning and analysis work in the interests of the necessary consistency in all aspect's of the Unions external action. Similarly a majority was opposed to the creation of a new institution to handle the CFSP.

One possibility is a further increase in the staffing, facilities and resources of the CFSP Department in the General Secretariat of the Council.[180] The UK has argued for a distinction between analysis and planning. While is can see an analysis role for such a unit, it argues that planning is best done by the working groups and COREPER. The RG referred to the 'difficulty of separating analysis, planning and proposals'.[181] These rightly seen as a continuum. The unit's mandate should embrace all of them and include a right of initiative. It is submitted that the most important

---

177. A Special European Council was held in Dublin in October 1996 to move the IGC process forward.

178. Reflection Group's Progress Report, p. 27; Reflection Group's Final Report, pp. 41–2; Progress Report on IGC, p. 40. See also the Group of Experts on CFSP of the High Level Working Group (HLWG) to Mr Van Den Broek entitled, 'European Security Policy Towards 2000: ways and means to establish genuine credibility' (19 December 1994). See 'General Outline', p. 71.

179. Reflection Group's Progress Report, p. 7; Reflection Group's Final Report, pr. 79.

180. This has already grown since the TEU.

181. Reflection Group's Progress Report, p. 28; Reflection Group's Final Report, pr. 152.

thing is that it should be placed clearly and directly under the control of the Council. This would ensure that the units work remained concentrated on central issues and concerns identified by the Council. Speculative planning would be avoided and the Council could ensure that existing planning reports are completed before new ones are undertaken.

Much concern in the last decade has been centred on the concept of 'crisis management' as distinct from crisis avoidance.[182] The EU must use the eyes and ears of its member states and the Commissions' Representatives. CFSP and COREU are potentially very good at this. The planning and analysis unit would need access to the best available information throughout the Union. However, on past experience, some member states can be reluctant to share information with their partners under EPC. Global communications makes information harder to keep anyway except for very short periods.

Whether a planning and analysis unit can be set up without Treaty amendment depends on the model chosen. It may be preferable for the IGC to clearly set out its role, function and place in the institutional balance.

A High Representative for CFSP – A Mr or Ms CFSP?

A related but distinct proposal concerns a proposal, made by France, for the establishment of single figurehead for CFSP – a Mr or Ms CFSP.[183] One possibility is for the Secretary-General of the General Secretariat to be raised in rank to ministerial level and thus be this figure-head. The more ambitious possibility is to establish a separate figure, a 'High Representative for CFSP', appointed by the European Council.[184] The designations 'Foreign Minister for Europe' or 'Secretary-General for Europe' are studiously avoided but they capture the essential ideas.[185] Mr/Ms

182. See, for example, the UN Secretary-General's *Agenda for Peace* (New York, UN, 1992); D. McGoldrick, 'The Development of the Conference on Security and Cooperation in Europe – from Process to Institution', in B.S. Jackson and D. McGoldrick, *Legal Visions of the New Europe* (London, Graham and Trotman/Nijhoff, 1993) on OSCE developments.
183. M. or Mme PESC in French; Herr or Frau GASP in German. This idea was strongly supported by the HLWG. See 'General Outline', p. 70.
184. Reflection Group's Progress Report, p. 27; Reflection Group's Final Report, prs. 157–62; Progress Report on IGC, p. 41. The person could possibly also be approved by the European Parliament but that might raise questions as to who the person is serving.
185. It would also give the telephone number required by Henry Kissinger's famous question as to whom he should ring when he wanted to speak to Europe.

CFSP, ranking at least on a par with a minister, would conduct the Union's external political affairs and represent it. Mr/Ms CFSP would be responsible to, and would represent, the Council. They would chair the Political Committee and head the proposed planning and analysis unit. The unit would be a tripartite body composed of member states, the Council and the Commission. Consistency with Community external policy would have to be ensured. In practical terms this would mean that Mr/Ms CFSP would always be accompanied by a representative of the Commission. Together they would represent the total sum of the Union's external relations. This would appear much clearer to non-EU States who presently face a bewildering and changing array of EU representatives.

The relationship with the operation of the Presidency would also have to be closely examined, but the central point would be that Mr/Ms CFSP would serve the Presidency and not be its equal or seek to represent some separate interest. The establishment of such a figure would take a lot of the representational function of the Presidency away from it. This is an increasingly demanding and onerous function both for large and small member states, particularly when allied to the operation of the troika system and the association of the Commission. The Presidency would be left to provide internal dynamism, drive, initiative, impulses and implementation, but not be burdened by the public relations and ceremonial demands. For particular situations or crises the Council could also establish 'personal representatives' on the model of the EU representatives to the former Yugoslavia or the EU Administrator for Mostar.[186] This solution would appear to preserve the best features of the rotating Presidency but make it more manageable for the member states. Member states outside the Presidency could contribute the most appropriate personnel if that was appropriate.

Legal personality

In the RG and at the IGC several member states considered that the EU should be given international legal personality.[187] We have

---

[186.] 'experience (with Mostar in particular) has shown that there should be some procedure whereby the Council can, under certain conditions, assign the Presidency, the Troika, the CFSP High Representative or the Commission special responsibility in implementing joint action', Progress Report on IGC, p. 42.
[187.] See Progress Report on IGC, pp. 36–7.

considered the general matter above.[188] The UK in particular is opposed. Practical solutions have had to be found to the argument that the EU does not have treaty making capacity.[189] For the administration of the Yugoslav city of Mostar a memorandum of understanding was used which was signed by the Presidency of the EU on behalf of the member states of the EU acting within the framework of the CFSP and in full association with the Commission.[190]

The Presidency

Possibilities being considered are the ideas of Presidencies for an extended term, for example, one year or eighteen months, or 'Team Presidencies' though the detail of how these would work is not yet clear.[191] The aim would be greater consistency and less frequent changes of personnel. In any event they would not be inconsistent with the above idea of a Mr/Ms CFSP. Yet another possibility would be the establishment of a permanent Political Subcommittee which would be staffed by the political counsellors in the Permanent Representations of the member states and the respective experts in the Commission.[192] This could relieve the Political Committee of more routine and lower-level matters.

Planning is easier once objectives have been established and these now exist to some extent.[193] Similarly, once common positions have been established and joint actions agreed, challenges or threats to them are more readily identifiable. The development of other common positions and joint actions for analogous problems or situations can be foreseen and considered. However, there will necessarily be a limit to the efficacy of planning and policy preparation in the field of CFSP. This is essentially because foreign and security policy is inherently unpredictable. The variables involved are to a greater or lesser degree outside the control of Europe. If the national policies of the

188. See ch. 2 above.
189. See the 'Guidelines for Concluding Third Party Agreements', agreed by COREPER on 5 April 1995, subject to a Danish reserve; Dashwood, *Reviewing Maastrict*, p. 252.
190. The other signatories were the Presidency of the WEU and various Bosnian authorities.
191. See Justus Lipsius, 'The 1996 Intergovernmental Conference'. See 'General Outline', p. 69.
192. See E. Regelsberger, 'Reforming the CFSP – An Alibi Debate or More', in S.A. Pappas and S. Vanhoonacker (eds), op. cit. n. 122.
193. See pp. 142–3, 153–6 above.

member states had been reactive, it is unrealistic to expect that the EU policy would suddenly become active. This unpredictability must not be overstated. Indeed, much of the EU's external relations and the CFSP is premised on the values of the EU and that the EU can have and influence upon third states and external situations, for example, in Central and Eastern Europe, and in the Middle East.

The Institutional structure in CFSP

As for progress on adopting common positions and joint actions, numerically the record is clearly limited. However, the EU can claim that some of them have had a considerable political impact.[194] The Stability Pact in Europe was a high profile diplomatic endeavour and could lead on to a number of bilateral Treaties.[195] The EU has also claimed some credit for setting the agenda for the successful conclusion of the Non-Proliferation Review. The administration of Mostar is perhaps an idiosyncratic joint action but must be recognized as having been a creditable achievement.[196] Humanitarian aid in Bosnia-Herzegovina has relieved massive suffering despite being open to criticism in terms of its planning and speed of implementation.[197] Useful support has been provided to the Middle East peace process, the democratic process in South Africa, election monitoring in Russia. However, it must be noted that there has also been major foreign policy activity pursued on a national basis, outside the EU framework. This was the case with the Contact Group on Yugoslavia, on Namibia, South Africa,

In the RG the member states differed on the causes of the inadequacies of CFSP and its lack of consistency.[198] While some of the member states argued that new systems will always have early

194. See Holland, 'Bridging the Credibility–Expectations Gap'; M. Holland (ed.), *Joint Actions*.

195. One of the major treaties to emerge so far is the Hungary-Slovakia Treaty. There are continuing problems of interpretation and dispute.

196. See M. Levy, *L'Administration De La Ville De Mostar Par l'Union Européenne* (Bruges, 1995).

197. ' . . . the humanitarian aid operation for Bosnia-Herzegovina last winter is particularly dismaying. Approved within weeks, without any proper study of the conditions in the field, bogged down in the minutiae of budgetary wrangles about which the public, fortunately, remained in ignorance, it was not implemented until the winter was over – too late', High Level Working Group, op. cit, n. 178, p. 3.

198. Reflection Group's Progress Report, p. 26; Reflection Group's Final Report, prs. 146–51.

problems, and that there have been a number of internal CFSP procedural developments to improve these,[199] others pointed to the lack of political will and fixed attitudes. The strongest critics argued that the system was structurally flawed in separating the Union's political dimension from its economic dimension. The Commission also argues that the pillar system is an obstacle to the development of common European interests.[200] Either the pillar system needed to be wholly or partially collapsed[201] or, at the very least, there had to be a greater injection of the 'community method' into CFSP. Common action, a more integrated approach, a reflex of consulting the EU first, needed to become the norm. Action at the European level had to be seen as the best way to achieve national interests. National foreign policies were not excluded but they had to be complementary to a European foreign policy. The Commission should have an enhanced role. It could exert a greater dynamism to CFSP and best formulate the European interest and the concept of a 'European foreign policy'. It could be given an exclusive right of initiative but it would not seem to be credible or even intellectually defensible to exclude initiatives from the member states.[202] Moreover, on the evidence, the Commission made no use of its right of initiative for the first twelve to eighteen months of CFSP. In any event, the analogy with the EC pillar is misleading because both the Council and the EP can invite proposals from the Commission and the latter has always acceded.[203]

The majority of the RG accepted that the EP could not play the same role in the field of CFSP as in EC matters.[204] Several of them referred to the very limited powers that national parliaments have over the conduct of foreign policy and were strongly of the view

199. See Eaton 'Common Foreign and Security Policy (non-security aspects)', in *The Treaty on European Union: Suggestions for Revision* (The Hague), TMC Asser Instituut Conference on European Law (Sept 1995), p. 292.
200. See H. van den Broek, 'The Common Foreign and Security Policy: The Challenges of the Future', in Pappas and Vanhoonacker (eds), *The European Union's Common Foreign and Security Policy*.
201. Note that the Commission did not expressly argue for an end to the pillar structure in its Report to the IGC. See also the discussion in Dashwood, *Reviewing Maastricht*, pp. 247–50, on the idea of communitizing 'foreign policy' but keeping security and defence policy separate.
202. An alternative argument is that a Commission proposal could be adopted by something less than unanimity. This is obviously linked to more general changes in decision making which are considered below.
203. See Articles 138b and 152 respectively.
204. Reflection Group's Progress Report, p. 29; Reflection Group's Final Report, pr. 164; Progress Report on IGC, p. 44.

that the EP could not have greater powers.[205] The most that seems likely is more regular and substantial information and consultation requirements.[206] The EP may achieve these by inter-institutional agreement, by using financial power over the EC budget being used for CFSP or by limited Treaty amendment.

A change in the pillared structure for CFSP appears very unlikely.[207]

Decision making procedures

The most controversial question on CFSP under consideration at the IGC is perhaps that of the decision making procedures.[208] Some member states, and the Commission, see this as an essential cause of the effectiveness of CFSP. It leads to paralysis and inaction. National interests prevail over the common European interest. Unanimity requirements should therefore be replaced by QMV. Other member states, including the UK, remain of the view that foreign policy cannot be assimilated to matters within the EC pillar. The common policies of the EC may be credible even if decided by majority vote, but a foreign policy decided by majority would not be.

The RG explored, and the IGC continues to examine, a number of arrangements including 'consensus bar one',[209] a 'super-qualified majority', or 'positive abstention'.[210] Commissioner van den Broek has recognized that the role of the larger member states must be recognized but that a directorate by these must be avoided.[211]

Decision making other than by unanimity (consensus in practice) might appear to be more acceptable if it was confined to

---

205. In Denmark the Parliament has increasingly sought to exercise a greater role of foreign policy leading to confrontations with the Danish government (EIPA, 'The European Union's Common Foreign and Security Policy: the Positions of the Main Actors (Conference, Maastricht, 19–20 October 1995).

206. The scope of this, for example, whether it covers specific actions, is being discussed at the IGC.

207. See Eaton, 'Common Foreign and Security Policy (non-security aspects)' in *The Treaty on European Union: Suggestions for Revision* (The Hague), TMC Asser Instituut Conference on European Law (Sept 1995).

208. See Progress Report on IGC, pp. 42–3; 'General Outline', pp. 73–6, 127–31.

209. This is the formula used in the OSCE in certain cases, see McGoldrick 'The Development of the Conference on Security and Cooperation in Europe', in Jackson and McGoldrick, *Legal Visions of the New Europe*.

210. Progress Report on IGC, p. 43.

211. See van den Broek, 'The Common Foreign and Security Policy: The Challenges of the Future', in Pappas and Vanhoonacker (eds), *The European Union's Common Foreign and Security Policy*.

common positions and did not extend to joint actions. However, this still requires a member state to accept that a policy which they were positively opposed to would become the Union's foreign policy. The RG considered that the solidarity principle in general, and financial solidarity in particular, would apply. This does not seem to be very realistic in terms of a government of a member state having to explain its position to its domestic population and its national Parliament. If some form of majority voting is adopted, it might be more sensible to exempt a member state from the general solidarity principle except in the sense that it should not undermine the EU policy. However, it will be very difficult for a member state to say nothing in relation to a problem when it is positively opposed to the EU policy. Similarly, it would seem more credible to exempt the dissenting member state from having to provide financial support. However, even this might be very difficult if the finance is provided from the EC budget.[212]

A more limited possibility is to move the text of Declaration No. 27 to the body of the TEU.[213] This would only be of psychological importance, given that it is only an admonition to the member state and would not be enforceable before the ECJ either as a matter of substance, and because of the bar on the ECJ in Article L of the TEU.

Security and defence

This will be one of the most complex areas for possible revision. Any progress is likely to be incremental and pragmatic.[214] Many of those complexities stem for the variations in membership of the EU, NATO and the WEU. The WEU has ten full members who are also members of the EU and NATO. The other five members of the EU are observers at the WEU (Ireland, Finland, Austria, Sweden and Denmark).[215] Of these five only Denmark is a member of NATO. Thus, eleven members of the EU are members of NATO.[216]

It is only possible here to outline some of the major problems

212. Cf. under Article 2 of the Protocol on Social Policy the UK only pays its share of the 'administrative costs' of the institutions.
213. As suggested by Regelsberger, op. cit., n. 192.
214. See J.M. Gabriel, 'The Integration of European Security: A Functionalist Analysis' (1995) 50 Aussen-Wirtschaft, 135–59; 'General Outline', ch. 12.
215. There are also three associate members and nine associate partners.
216. However, France and Spain continue to operate partly outside NATO in respect of particular matters. In June 1996 France agreed to reintegrate into NATO.

and issues that will have to be considered.[217] The options for the relationship between the EU and the WEU range from rapid merger, the WEU being politically or legally subordinate to the EU, or the WEU continuing its separate existence.[218] Will neutrality be a continuing option for the member states of the EU?[219] As the RG put it, 'Where must flexibility stop if it is to be compatible with collective security and the consistency of the European design?'.[220] The operational, institutional and administrative capability of the WEU needs to be significantly expanded in line with the new aspects of defence set out in the St Petersberg Declaration of the WEU in 1992.[221] Much of the attention will be focused on the development of the WEU's operational capability in the fields of crisis management, crisis prevention and peace-keeping.[222] The WEU/NATO relationship will have to be developed and strengthened in all its aspects including sharing data, intelligence and communications.[223] The concept of Combined Joint Task Forces (CJTFs) is likely to be further developed. The rationale of a European defence may require some elucidation in terms of the threats and security challenges to the interests of Europe, particularly in the context of enlargement,[224] and its relationship to the world's major geo-political actors, the US, Russia, Japan and China.

[217] See Progress Report on IGC, pp. 45–7.
[218] See Reflection Group's Progress Report, pp. 31–3; Reflection Group's Final Report, prs. 166–77; J. Cutiliero, 'CFSP and the Role of the Western European Union (WEU)', in Pappas and Vanhoonacker (eds), *The European Union's Foreign and Security Policy.*
[219] See T.C. Salmon, 'Ireland: A Neutral in the Community?' (1982), 3 JCMS, 205–27; D. Spring, '1996 Intergovernmental Conference: an Irish View', in *'The European Union's CFSP: The Challenges of the Future* (Maastricht: EIPA, 1995), Document Collection; S.P. Subedi, 'The Common Foreign and Security Policy of the European Union and Neutrality', XLII (1996) NILR, 399–412; 'Norway and defence', *The Times*, 4 October 1995, p. 12.
[220] Reflection Group's Progress Report, p. 33; Reflection Group's Final Report, prs. 168, 172–3; Progress Report on IGC, pp. 45–7.
[221] St. Petersberg Declaration, 19 June 1992 (Paris: WEU). This sought to clarify the WEU's role as the defence component of the WEU. See S. Duke, 'The Second Death (or the Second Coming?) of the WEU' (1996) 34(2) JCMS, 167–90.
[222] The OSCE has also been developing a role in these fields and cooperation and consistency with its work will also be required. See McGoldrick, 'The Development of the Conference on Security and Cooperation in Europe', in Jackson and McGoldrick, *Legal Visions of the New Europe.*
[223] See H. van Forrest, 'NATO and the New European Security Landscape', in Pappas and Vanhoonacker (eds), *The European Union's Common Foreign and Security Policy* (1996). For example, Europe urgently needs to develop a satellite intelligence capability.
[224] See Clarke, 'Future Security Threats and Challenges', in Pappas and

Objectives and interests

Some members of the RG sought a more specific statement of the Union's fundamental interests beyond those in Article J.1(2). One proposal is that these be defined by geographical area. The difficulty with such a proposal is that it can change over time and very rapidly. Moreover, in as much as it seeks to establish itself as a world power in international relations then the EU's interests may extend to all geographical regions of the world. The present system under which the Council can and has established areas of fundamental interests seems to be more sensible and flexible. Other members argued that the objectives should cover solidarity between member states and the upholding of and defence of human rights and democracy. This does seem to add much to the existing Article J.1. At the IGC there has been a suggestion of adding to the CFSP objectives a reference to maintaining the integrity of member states' territory and of common external frontiers.[225] Another suggestion has been the insertion of a provision stating that membership of the Union creates between member states a security relationship entailing close, practical solidarity, without constituting a commitment to an alliance.[226]

The EU's projection of its international interests is also linked to its own perception of itself. Thus, further developments on internal questions of the EU's identity, values, character, and self-confidence will, in turn, have an international impact.[227] What does being European mean at the dawn of the twenty-first century?[228]

Financing

As noted above this is a major issue. There was consensus in the RG on the need to establish specific procedures ensuring availability of the necessary funds for rapid action when required. A 'broad majority' were in favour of CFSP being financed out of the EC budget.[229] At the IGC there is agreement that operational expenditure should in principle be charged to the Community budget, provided that: (i) financing by member states remains a

---

224. *(continued)* Vanhoonacker (eds), *The European Union's Foreign and Security Policy*; J. Sedivy, ibid. (1996); A.J. Figueiredo Lopes, ibid. (1996).
225. Progress Report on IGC, p. 46.   226. Ibid. See 'General Outline', ch. 10.
227. See G. De Burca, 'The Quest for Legitimacy' (1996) 59 MLR, 349–76.
228. See Reflection Group's Final Report, pp. I–X.
229. Reflection Group's Progress Report, p. 29; Reflection Group's Final Report, pr. 63.

possibility in exceptional circumstances; (ii) the Council has the final say in budgetary decisions; and (iii) financing out of the EC budget is subject to compliance with the financial perspective.[230]

230. Progress Report on IGC, pp. 43–4. See 'General Outline', p. 117.

CHAPTER NINE

Justice and home affairs; international human rights; citizenship

Introduction

This chapter briefly considers the third pillar of the TEU, which covers cooperation on justice and home affairs. For convenience it also makes reference to international human rights and the international aspect of EU citizenship.

Justice and home affairs

One of the objectives of the Union, set out in Article B of the TEU, is –

> to develop close cooperation on justice and home affairs.

Cooperation on matters of justice and home affairs had taken place under the broad aegis of EPC and under separate frameworks.[1] Title VI of the TEU now makes express provision for 'Cooperation in the Fields of Justice and Home Affairs'.[2] Title VI contains an Article K, which is divided into Article K and K.1–K.9. Two of the Declarations to the TEU relate to JHA. These are Declaration No. 31 on asylum and Declaration No. 32 on police cooperation. As with CFSP, the third pillar is essentially intergovernmental and based on unanimous voting,[3] and disputes over competence were perhaps inevitable.[4]

---

1. See S. Nuttall, *European Political Cooperation* (Oxford: Clarendon Press, 1992), pp. 294–308.
2. See I. Hendry, 'The Third Pillar of Maastricht: Cooperation in the Fields of Justice and Home Affairs' (1993) 36 GYIL 1993, 295–327; R. Bieber and J. Monar, *Justice and Home Affairs in the European Union: The Development of the Third Pillar* (Brussels, European Inter-University Press, 1994).
3. Article K.4. See P.-C. Muller-Graff, 'The Legal Basis of the Third Pillar and its Position in the Framework of the Union Treaty' (1995) 31 CMLRev, 493–510.
4. See S. Peers, 'The Visa Regulation: Free Movement Blocked Indefinitely' (1996) 21 ELRev, 150–5.

The scope of justice and home affairs

Article K.1 specifies a series of matters which are considered to be of 'common interest'. Many of these will clearly have implications for the international relations of the EU. In outline these matters are asylum policy; rules governing the crossing by persons of the external borders of the member states and the exercise of controls thereon; immigrations policy and policy regarding nationals of third countries;[5] combatting drug addiction; combatting fraud on an international scale; judicial cooperation in civil and criminal matters; customs cooperation; police cooperation for the purposes of preventing and combatting terrorism, unlawful drug trafficking and other serious forms of international crime, including if necessary certain aspects of customs cooperation, in connection with a Union-wide system for exchanging information with a European Police Office (Europol).[6] According to Article K.2 these matters 'shall be dealt with in compliance with' the European Convention on Human Rights (1951) and the Convention Relating to the Status of Refugees (1951).

The instruments of JHA

Article K.3 makes provision information, consultation and collaboration between member states, and for the adoption by the Council of 'joint positions' (usually referred to as 'common positions') and 'joint actions'. These parallel the instruments available for CFSP in Title V.[7] In addition under Article K.3(2)(c) the Council may –

> without prejudice to Article 220 of the Treaty establishing the European Community,[8] draw up conventions which it shall recommend to the Member States for adoption in accordance with their respective constitutional requirements.

[5.] See Article K.1(3) (a) – (c) for more detail on the scope of this matter.

[6.] See Bruggemann, 'Europol: Wanted or Tolerated?', in *The Treaty on European Union: Suggestions for Revision* (The Hague, TMC Asser Instituut Conference on European Law, Sept 1995).

[7.] See ch. 8 above. 'The legal instruments provided for in Title VI have been modelled on those of Title V (CFSP). They are not well suited to the essentially legislative nature of JHA action. The idea of creating a new legal instrument (which might be called a "common measure") has been generally welcomed', Progress Report on IGC, Presidency Conclusions, European Council: Florence, 21–22 June 1996, Doc. SN 300/96, Annexes, p. 18 at 3(a).

[8.] Article 220 provides for member states to enter into negotiations in certain areas to secure benefits to their nations in certain areas. See ch. 2, pp. 31–2 above.

Unless the conventions adopted provide otherwise, measures implementing them shall be adopted within the Council by a majority of two-thirds of the High Contracting Parties.[9] This option has not been used. The conventions adopted may stipulate that the ECJ shall have jurisdiction to interpret their provisions and to rule on any disputes concerning their application.[10] A whole series of proposed conventions have been held up because of the lack of unanimity on this matter.[11] Article K.5 provides that, 'Within international organisations and at international conferences in which they take part, Member States shall defend the common positions adopted' under Article K.3.[12] Under Article K.9 the Council may unanimously decide to apply Article 100c to action in certain of the matters listed in Article K.1.1.[13]

Legally, the financing of JHA raises similar legal problems as with the CFSP though the sums involved are much smaller. To date all financing has been charged to the member states.[14] Subject to the exception noted above, the jurisdiction of the ECJ does not extend to Title VI,[15] though again it may have to make decisions on the borderline between matters of EC competence and Title VI.[16] The roles of the Commission and the EP under JHA are very limited. There are also practical problems relating to the interface between the EC pillar and the JHA pillar.

Practice under JHA[17]

There has been limited progress under JHA and this has generated very strong criticism of, and calls for reform of, the third pillar.[18] A

9. Article K.3(2)(c), para 2.   10. Article K.3(2)(c), para 3.
11. In particular, the UK would not accept the compulsory jurisdiction of the ECJ.
12. See the Justice and Home Affairs Council's 'Conclusions on the implementation of Article K.5 of the TEU: expression of common approaches in international organizations and conferences', and its 'Conclusions on relations with third countries in the JHA field', 30 November – 1 December 1994, Press Release 11321/94 (Presse 252-G).
13. More precisely those in Article K.1(1)–(6). Article K.9 is known as the 'passerelle' provision.
14. See O'Keeffe, 'Recasting the Third Pillar' (1995) 32 CMLRev, 893–920.
15. Article L of the TEU.   16. Article M of the TEU.
17. See 'Overview of work in progress, work accomplished and obstacles that remain in areas falling within the Third Pillar of the Maastricht Treaty', *Agence Europe*, No. 6638, 5 January 1996.
18. See European Parliament, Report on the Functioning of the Treaty on European Union, 19 May 1995, EP Doc. A4–0102/95, p. 7, para. B; Commission, Report on the Operation of the Treaty on European Union, Brussels, 10 May 1995, SEC (95) 731 final, prs. 117–27; Reflection Group's Final Report, Doc. SN520/95, Brussels, 5 December 1995, prs. 45–60; Progress Report on IGC, Presidency Conclusions, European Council: Florence, 21–22 June 1996, Doc. SN300/96, Annexes, 17–19; O'Keeffe, 'Recasting the Third Pillar'; 'General Outline', chs 2–3.

substantial number of recommendations, resolutions, statements, conclusions and reports have been adopted.[19] Although these range across many important matters affecting international relations, they are not legally binding. In any event, these instruments existed and were used before the TEU.

No formal common position was adopted until 1996. Those now adopted concern (i) the harmonized application of the definition of the term refugee in Article 1 of the Geneva Convention of 28 July 1951 relating to the status of refugees;[20] an alert and emergency procedure for burden-sharing with regard to the admission and residence of displaced persons on a temporary basis;[21] a framework for the exchange of liaison magistrates to improve judicial cooperation between the member states of the EU.[22]

A small number of joint actions have been adopted.[23] These have included (i) travel facilities for school pupils from non-member countries resident in a member state;[24] (ii) extending the field of action of the EUROPOL drugs unit;[25] (iii) measures implementing Article K.1 of the TEU;[26] airport transit arrangements;[27] action to combat racism and xenophobia, Council Decision 96/443/JHA, [1996] OJ L185/5. In terms of international conventions progress has been slow. Those adopted have concerned (i) simplified extradition subject to the consent of the person concerned;[28] (ii) the establishment of EUROPOL but in a form which provides that states have to opt in to the jurisdiction of the ECJ;[29] (iii) asylum;[30] the Uses of Technology for Customs Purposes;[31] the Protection of the Community's Financial Interests;[32] (iv) extradition.[33] There are also draft conventions on

---

[19.] See Commission, Report on the Operation of the Treaty on European Union, Annex 15; M. Den Boer, 'Justice and Home Affairs Cooperation in the European Union: Current Issues' (1996) 1996/1 EIPASCOPE, 12–16.

[20.] Council Decision 96/196/JHA, [1996] OJ L63/2.

[21.] Council Decision 96/198/JHA, [1996] OJ L63/10.

[22.] Council Decision 96/227/JHA, [1996] OJ L105/1.   [23.] Notably less than in CFSP.

[24.] Council Decision 94/795/JHA, adopted on 30 November 1994, [1994] OJ L327. There were arguments over competence on this matter.

[25.] Council Decision 94/73/JHA, adopted on 10 March 1995, [1995] OJ L62/1.

[26.] Council Decision 95/401/JHA, [1995] OJ L238/1. There has also been a Council Decision concerning the implementation of this Joint Action, Council Decision 95/403/JHA, [1995] OJ L238/2.

[27.] Council Decision 96/197/JHA, [1996] OJ L63/8.

[28.] Adopted 10 March 1995, [1995] OJ C78.

[29.] Article K.3(2)(c), para 3. See Progress Report on IGC.

[30.] Known as the Dublin Convention.   [31.] Signed in July 1995.

[32.] Signed in July 1995. A Protocol was also signed in October 1996.

[33.] Agreed in July 1996. No competence was given to the ECJ but this will be reviewed after one year.

the Crossing of External Frontiers, and the fight against corruption of European and national officials and members of Community institutions. None of the signed conventions has yet been ratified by all of the member states.

International human rights and the EC/EU

Under Article F of the TEU, the Union –

> shall respect fundamental rights, as guaranteed by the European Convention for the Protection of Human Rights and Fundamental Freedoms signed in Rome on 4 November 1950 and as they result from the constitutional traditions common to the Member States, as general principles of community law.

Article F gave expression to the jurisprudence of the ECJ on community law.[34] EC accession to the ECHR has long been under consideration and the EC's competence to accede was considered and rejected by the ECJ in an Article 228 Opinion.[35] In its international agreements with non-member states the EU has increasingly inserted provisions on human rights. Development policy has also evolved and now clearly covers human rights issues, without making it a distinct objective, as well as economic matters.[36] International agreements have been suspended as reaction to human rights abuses in Serbia and Montenegro, Nigeria.

One of the objectives of CFSP is 'to develop and consolidate democracy and the rule of law, and respect for human rights and fundamental freedoms'.[37] The Commission has submitted a Communication to the Council and the EP on the EU and the external dimension of human rights policy.[38]

EU citizenship: international aspects

Another of the Union's objectives is –

---

34. A recent Article 177 reference raises the question of the Community character of the ECHR provisions and the effects of a finding by the European Court of Human Rights of an infringement of the Convention, Case C-299/95, *F. Krezmow v Austria*.
35. *Opinion 2/94* (ECHR), 28 March 1996. See F. Jacobs, *Human Rights in the European Union* (Durham, Durham Law Institute, 1994).
36. See Case C-268/94: *Portugal v Council* (3 December 1996) ch. 10 below.
37. Article J.1(2).
38. 'The European Union and the external dimension of human rights policy: from Rome to Maastricht and beyond', COM(95)567.

to strengthen the protection of the rights and interests of the nationals of its Member States through the introduction of a citizenship of the Union; (Article B)

The TEU introduced the concept of citizenship of the Union, though interestingly it is in part of the EC Treaty, namely Article 8. Under Article 8, 'Every person holding the nationality of a Member State shall be a citizen of the Union'. Thus EU citizenship is predicated on member state nationality. The granting of nationality remains a prerogative of member states (Declaration No. 2 to the TEU on the nationality of a member state).[39]

EU citizenship is in fact a rather limited concept.[40] It gives some additional rights and protection but does not in anyway take the place of national citizenship.[41] It has also attracted criticism for being divisive.[42] Its potential for growth is also rather restricted.[43] However, our concern here is with its international aspect. Article 8c provides:

Every citizen of the Union shall, in the territory of a third country in which the Member State of which he is a national is not represented, be entitled to protection by the diplomatic and consular authorities of any Member State, on the same conditions as the nationals of that State. Before 31 December 1993, Member States shall establish the necessary rules among themselves and start the international negotiations required to secure this protection.

This idea of third party diplomatic protection is a novel legal idea but, as so often, it reflects to some degree what was happening in

39. See S. O'Leary, 'Nationality Law and Community Citizenship: A Tale of Two Uneasy Bedfellows' (1994) 12 YEL 1992, 353–84; Decision of the Heads of State or Government, meeting within the European Council, concerning certain problems raised by Denmark on the TEU, Section A on Citizenship, 'The question whether an individual possesses the nationality of a Member State will be settled solely by reference to the national law of the Member State concerned', Bull-EC, 12/1992, 25–6.
40. See E.A. Marais (ed.), *European Citizenship* (Maastricht, EIPA, 1994); *R v Home Secretary, ex parte Vitale and Do Amaral*, [1995] All ER (EC) 946, QBD.
41. Ibid. See also the Unilateral Declaration by Denmark associated with its act of ratification and of which the other 11 member states took cognizance, Bull-EC, 12/1992, 26–7.
42. 'In the very concept of Union citizenship a distinction is created that negates the common humanity of two comparable groups, namely those legally established and residing in a host member state', D. Curtin and M. Guerts, 'Race Discrimination and the European Union Anno 1996: From Rhetoric to Legal Remedy?' (1996) 14/2 Netherlands Quarterly of Human Rights, 147–71, p. 165.
43. No change to that procedure is envisaged, see Progress Report on IGC, pp. 6–7.

practice. It is clearly a sensible development in practical and resource terms. There are a great many countries in the world where not all EU members are represented.[44] Article 8c envisages agreements with the third states concerned. This would appear to be necessary. A member state has no international legal right to exercise any level of diplomatic protection on behalf of a national of another member state.[45] It may be doubtful whether legally third states are under any obligation to recognize the concept of EU citizenship at all. It must at least be logically curious for third states to be presented with an assertion of a form of international citizenship of an entity which does not itself have international legal personality! In practice the political and economic power of the EU may mean that third states will recognize EU citizenship. In November 1995 a decision of the representatives of the governments of the member states, meeting within the Council was agreed, regarding protection for citizens of the EU by diplomatic and consular representatives.[46] As of 1 July 1996, no agreements had been reached with third states on diplomatic and consular protection.

44. So, in practice, it is the member states with the worldwide diplomatic representation, particularly the UK and France, which would be protecting EU citizens.
45. See the *Nottebohm Case (Lichtenstein v Guatemala)*, ICJ Reports, 1955, p. 4; *Flegenheimer Claim* (1958) 25 ILR, p. 91. The intended level of diplomatic protection is not made clear in Article 8c, see I. Macleod, I. Hendry and S. Hyett, *The External Relations of the European Communities: A Manual of Law and Practice* (Oxford, OUP, 1996) p. 219. In 1993 'Guidelines for the protection of unrepresented EC nationals by missions in third countries' were agreed within EPC and have been applied since then. See now the decision in n. 46 below.
46. Council Decision 95/553/EC, [1995] OJ L314; Bull-EU, 11–1995, point 1.1.1.

CHAPTER TEN

The EU as an international actor

Introduction

This chapter outlines the variety of international roles played by the EU, and how the EU conducts and organizes its communication with the world. Section 1 considers the economic and political relations that the EU has established and operated with non-EC states. It examines the different forms of international agreements involved and the bases of political dialogue. These constitute the legal and political instruments which form the sub-structure of the EU's international activities. It also considers the EU's role in promoting international human rights and democracy, and its contribution to humanitarian and development assistance. Section 2 briefly considers the EU's participation in some major international institutions and organizations.[1]

It is difficult to convey the extraordinary range of activities, bilateral and multilateral meetings, conferences, and dialogues, both formal and informal, conducted on a daily basis by the EU.[2] In addition to its extensive participation in international organizations[3] and international treaties,[4] the adoption of formal common positions and joint actions,[5] there are over 100 EU statements or Declarations per year. The EU has clearly sought to play an increased role on the international stage.[6] This can be

1. We have already considered the question of membership, see ch. 2 above.
2. Good sources of current information are *Agence Europe*, *European Briefing* (European Information Service, Brussels), and the monthly Bulletin of the EU (Brussels).
3. See ch. 2 above and pp. 194–7, 202–5 below.   4. See chs. 3–5 above.
5. See chs. 8–9 above.
6. See P. Taylor, 'The European Communities as an Actor in International Society' (1982) 6(1) Journal of European Integration; G. Edwards and E. Regelsberger (eds), *Europe's Global Links* (London, St Martins, 1990); W. Wessels,

observed through the development of an extensive range of international agreements with third states and groupings of states, in the evolution of EPC, and through to CFSP. The political commitment of the member states to the EU playing a role seems consistent. Yet there are clear differences between member states in terms of how far they are willing to let the EU displace them as international actors.[7] However, the member states do have a strong interest in the harmonization of world trade rules on the basis of EU rules and legislation, a kind of EU single market writ large.

1. The EU's relationships with the rest of the world[8]

The EU has economic relationships with almost the whole of the world community and structured political dialogue with around thirty states or groups of states. It is helpful to outline the range and bases of these relationships by arranging them into various categories. However, it must be borne in mind that there is not necessarily a clear division between them and the name used for some agreements is more explained by political factors than by their substance. We then proceed to outline the EUs relations with major states or groupings of states. Fundamental issues underlying the different levels of relationship are (i) the prospect of membership of the EU; (ii) the level of association with the EU; (iii) access to the EU market and the degree of reciprocity involved and (iv) political and security considerations. Each of these can constitute an incentive which the EU can offer to secure international agreements and political and economic conduct that conform with its interests.[9]

---

6. (continued) 'EC-Europe: An Actor Sui Generis in the Internation System', in B. Nelson, D. Roberts and W. Veit, The EC in the 1990s (New York, Berg, 1990); R. Rummel (ed.), The Evolution of an International Actor: Western Europe's New Assertiveness (Boulder, Col., Westview, 1990); B. Soetendorp, 'The Evolution of the EC/EU as a Single Foreign Policy Actor', in W. Carlsnaes and S. Smith, European Foreign Policy – The EC and Changing Perspectives in Europe (London, Sage, 1994).

7. See Taylor (1982) 6(1) Journal of European Integration; C. Hill (ed.), National Foreign Policies and European Political Cooperation (London, Allen and Unwin, 1983).

8. See G.A. Bermann, R.J. Goebel, W.J. Davey and E.M. Fox, Cases and Materials on European Community Law (St. Paul, Minn: West, 1993), pp. 928–64.

9. On the EU's interests see ch. 8, pp. 142–3, 153–7 above.

It is important to keep the broader EU framework in mind. CFSP is increasingly becoming the driving force behind the various levels of international agreements entered into by the EU. What emerges is a distinct hierarchy of relationships. The degree of preference accorded by the EU can depend on a combination of historical, economic and geo-political factors. Any change in relationship by the EU amounts to a relative weakening or strengthening vis-à-vis another state or group of states. The EU is continually seeking to balance the interests of its various partners including the developing states, the states of Central and Eastern Europe, the US, the Mediterranean states, the Asian states. This fact alone evidences the global nature of the EU's interests.

a) Association agreements in general

Article 238 provides that –

> The Community may conclude with one or more States or international organisations agreements establishing an association involving reciprocal rights and obligations, common action and special procedure.

There is a wide variety of what have become known generically as 'association agreements'.[10] Examples are the EEA Agreement, Europe Agreements and Lome Agreements.[11] Their scope and substance can vary enormously. At their heart will usually be issues of access to the EU market and the degree of reciprocity involved.[12] However, their scope has increasingly been broadened to cover political dialogue and human rights.[13] An association agreement may or may not envisage future membership of the EU.

The level of association can be crucial in both economic and political terms. It can be of major importance for a state to gain a higher level of association with the EU. This was the case with Turkey in 1995. Turkey has had an association agreement with the

---

10. See J. Macleod, I. Hendry and S. Hyett, *The External Relations of the European Communities: A Manual of Law and Practice* (Oxford, OUP, 1996), pp. 367–85; 'The Legal Regime of Association Agreements', LLM Thesis, L.S.E., University of London, (1995).
11. Partnership and cooperation agreements are not association agreements but rather are based on Articles 113 and 235.
12. See below on the EC-ACP relationship.
13. See M. Cremona, 'Human Rights and Democracy Clauses in the EC's Trade Agreements', in N. Emiliou and D. O'Keeffe (eds), *The European Union and World Trade Law – After the GATT Uruguay Round* (Chichester, Wiley, 1996).

EC since 1963.[14] One of the objectives of that agreement was the establishment of a customs union and establishing very close ties with the EC. The terms of this were agreed in 1995[15] and its successful conclusion was of major political importance for Turkey.[16]

Association agreements normally establish an Association Council or a Joint Committee. These are composed of representatives of the EC and the non-member states. They can have important functions relating to the implementation of the agreement. The agreement, or the Council Decision concluding it, may specify the arrangement for EU coordination and who will express the position of the Community.[17] It is also worth recalling that the provisions of international agreements entered into by the EC form part of its legal order and may have direct effect.[18] This extends to decisions taken by an Association Council if they are legally binding under the terms of the association agreement.[19]

The conclusion of association agreements

The procedure for the conclusion of association agreements is in Article 228. The Commission negotiates on the basis of a mandate unanimously agreed in the Council (Article 228(1)). The Council must also be unanimous for the conclusion of the agreement and the assent of the EP must have been obtained. These strict requirements indicate the level of importance of such agreements. Given the increasing range and importance of association agreements this puts the EP in an important position, for example, over the customs union with Turkey in 1995.[20] Whether the EC is solely a party to the agreement or whether member states are also parties, i.e. it is a mixed agreement, will be determined by the material scope of the agreement. The early association agreements with Turkey (1963), Cyprus and Malta, which focused on trade aspects, were not mixed. More recently the increasing scope of

14. [1963] JO 217/3687.
15. It was agreed by means of Decision 1/95 of the Turkey-EU Association Council. The legal basis was Article 238, so the assent of the EP was needed.
16. See *The Times*, 23 November 1995, pp. 14, 21. The EP voted strongly in favour of the agreement on 13 December 1995.
17. See, for example, Article 2 of the Decision concluding the Europe Agreement with Hungary, Decision 93/742/Euratom/ESCS/EC.
18. See ch. 7 above.
19. Ibid., pp. 129–31, see n. 15 above.
20. See n. 14 above.

Association Agreements has naturally led to mixed agreements being common. For example, all of the 'Europe Agreements' are mixed.

The legal basis of international agreements

The issue The question of legal basis has become increasingly important within the EU constitutional system. It has important ramifications for the powers of the institutions, the procedures to be adopted and the nature of the Community powers.[21] This is thus one of those areas where simplification and rationalization of the EC's legislative procedures would reduce some of the need for disputes on legal basis. Similarly, if Treaty provisions were agreed on the implementation of mixed agreements. This would facilitate the duty of cooperation between the EC and the member states.[22]

The determination of legal base In principle, the legal basis of an international agreement will depend on its aim, objective and material scope.[23] The ECJ has insisted that the choice of legal basis is not a subjective matter for the institutions. It must be based on objective criteria which can be judicially controlled.[24] It must be ascertainable from the Preamble or from the terms of the measure. Article 113 on the CCP will be used to cover the commercial aspects such as tariff provisions and the elimination of quantitative restrictions, and what are referred to as 'flanking measures' such as safeguard clauses and anti-dumping rules. Article 235 has been commonly used. For example, it was the legal basis for the Agreement on the European Bank for Reconstruction and Development.[25] The extensions of EC competence brought about by the SEA and the TEU have reduced the possibility of using Article 235. The first use of Article 130y on development cooperation as a legal basis, alongside Article 113, was for an agreement with India in 1993.[26] Trade and development have

---

21. See chs. 4–5 above.
22. See ch. 5 above.
23. See Macleod, Hendry and Hyett, *The External Relations of the European Communities*, pp. 81–4; D. Chalmers, 'Legal Basis and External Relations of the European Community', in Emiliou and O'Keeffe, *The European Union and World Trade Law*.
24. See Case 45/86, *Commission v Council* [1987] ECR 1493; Case C-187/93, *Parliamant v Council* [1994] ECR I-2857.
25. See Council Decision 90/674, [1990] OJ L372/1.
26. See Council Decision 94/578, [1994] OJ L223/23. The legal basis was unsuccessfully challenged, see Case C-268/94, *Portugal v Council* (3 December 1996).

become inextricably linked and the distinction between common commercial policy and development cooperation is not an easy one to draw.[27] The aim and objective may not necessarily correspond with the substantive content. A trade instrument can be used to further development aims.[28] By contrast, the Council took the view that content of the Regulation establishing the special system for the traditional suppliers of bananas was of a development policy nature and so used Article 130w rather than Article 113 as the legal basis.[29] To identify the appropriate legal basis the agreement concerned must be assessed having regard to its essential objectives rather than in terms of individual clauses of an altogether secondary nature. Case C-268/94, *Portugal v Council* is an excellent illustration of the ECJ's identification of objectives in an agreement.

If an agreement is very wide ranging in its content and objectives it will have to be based on a number of articles of the EC Treaty.[30] For example, *Opinion 1/94* has clarified the scope of a number of articles of the Treaty. It resulted in the inclusion of a number of additional articles as part of the legal basis for international agreements then being proposed, including the agreements at issue in *Opinion 1/94*.[31] The practice in relation to association agreements is not to cite article 113 or any other provision but only to cite Article 238. For the implementation of association agreements the practice is to use the specific legal basis for the matter in question, for example, Article 113 for the trade aspects. This avoids the need to go through the Article 228 procedure again.

We now consider a range of EU relationships and international agreements. Although the focus is on the central agreements, it is important to bear in mind that these are often supplemented by Protocols and other forms of international agreements.[32]

EU–EFTA relationship: the EEA Agreement[33]

There have long been close economic ties with the EFTA states

[27.] See Case 45/86, *Commission v Council* [1987] ECR 1493.

[28.] See *Opinion 1/78* (Natural Rubber) [1979] ECR 2871; Case 45/86, *Commission v Council* [1987] ECR 1493 (GSP Case). Both instruments fell within Article 113.

[29.] Council Regulation 2868/94, [1994] OJ L286/1.

[30.] See the agreements with India [1994] OJ L223/23 and with Sri Lanka [1995] OJ L85/32, both of which cite Article 113 as well as Article 130w.

[31.] The legal bases for the Uruguay Round Agreements were Articles 43, 54, 57, 66, 75, 84(2), 99, 100, 100a, 113 and 235 in conjunction with the second subparagraph of Article 228(3), see [1994] OJ L336/1.

[32.] For example, an exchange of letters.

[33.] See F. Weiss, 'The Oporto Agreement on the EEA – A Legal Still Life' (1994)

based on free trade agreements.[34] While originally perceived as an alternative, even a competitor, to the EC, the EFTA has increasingly become a precursor to membership. What appeared at the time to be a major development in relations was the Agreement on the European Economic Area.[35] The most astonishing aspect of the agreement is the extent to which the EC is the dominant legal partner.[36] There is provision for the extensive incorporation, both initially and on a continuing basis, of EC law relating to the internal market in the EFTA states.[37] Similarly, provision is made for the extension of various EC policies and measures. Although there is consultation with the EFTA members on EC legislation, there is no actual participation by them. There are sophisticated arrangements for implementation which include an EFTA Court,[38] an EEA Joint Committee and an EEA Council. The EEA Council adopted a Joint Declaration on Political Dialogue in May 1995.[39]

The EEA Agreement appears less important than it did in 1992. Austria, Finland and Sweden have since become EU members. Switzerland rejected the agreement in a referendum and this effectively deferred Lichtenstein's participation for some time. So at present there are only three EFTA states to whom the agreement applies, namely Iceland, Lichtenstein and Norway. However, it may still be an option as a precursor to EU membership.[40]

33. (continued) 12 YEL 1992, 385–431; S. Norberg, 'The Agreement on a European Economic Area' (1992) 29 CMLRev, 1171–98; A. Toledano-Laredo, 'The EEA Agreement: An Overall View' (1992) 29 CMLRev. 1199–1213; Case T-185/94, Geotronics v Commission [1995] ECR II-2795.

34. See F. Laursen (ed.), Europe 1992: World Partner? The Internal Market and the World Political Economy (Maastricht, European Institute of Public Administration, 1991), pp. 67–122; R. Schwok, 'The European Free Trade Association: Revival or Collapse?', in J. Redmond, The External Relations of the European Community: The International Response to 1992 (Basingstoke, Macmillan, 1992).

35. This was a mixed agreement. It had to be modified after an adverse opinion from the ECJ under Article 228(6). See Opinion 1/91 (First EEA Opinion) [1991] ECR 6079; Opinion 1/92 (Second EEA Opinion) [1992] ECR I-2821. See also Case C-188/91, Deutche Shell AG v Hauptzollamt Hamburg-Harburg [1993] ECR I-363.

36. See the two opinions of the ECJ, in n. 35 above.

37. See M. Cremona, 'The "Dynamic and Homogenous" EEA: Byzantine Structures and Variable Geometry' (1994) 19 ELRev, 508–26.

38. See V. Kronenberger, 'Does the EFTA Court Interpret the EEA Agreement as if it were the EC Treaty? Some questions raised by the Restamark Judgment' (1996) 45 ICLQ, 198–212.

39. See Bull-EU, 5-1995, point 1.4.61.

40. See S. Peers, 'The Visa Regulation: Free Movement Blocked Indefinitely' (1995) 21 ELRev 150–5.

Europe Agreements

This form of agreement represented part of the EC's strategic response to the revolutionary developments in Central and Eastern Europe after 1989.[41] The use of the name 'Europe Agreements' is of symbolic rather than legal significance. They are a form of association agreement, but they do create a very close relationship with the EU. The Europe Agreements are mixed agreements.[42] Although originally envisaged for a small, select grouping, there are now ten of them. The ten are with Poland, Hungary, the Czech Republic, Slovakia, Bulgaria, Romania, Latvia, Lithuania, Estonia, and Slovenia.[43] These countries are categorized for EU purposes as the 'Associated Countries'.

Each of the agreements recognized that EU membership was an objective of the associated state, there was no EU commitment and no time period was specified. Although this has not been amended, it has effectively been reinterpreted by the European Council since Copenhagen (1993). The future accession of the associated states is now a common strategy. The Europe Agreements and the pre-accession strategy agreed in 1993 now effectively constitute a programme of preparation for membership.[44]

In relation to the substantive terms of the agreement they specify a transitional period of ten years. Provision is made for the gradual implementation of a free trade area on an asymmetrical basis but there is protection for certain sensitive areas. There are limited provisions relating to workers, establishment, services, payments and capital. Again the EC is the dominant legal partner. The Associated Countries are rapidly adapting their legislation and policies to make them consistent with EC law. Textually the

---

41. See the Conclusions of the European Councils in Copenhagen (1993), Essen (1994), Cannes (1995) and Madrid, Annex 6 (1995). See generally D. Kennedy and D. Webb, 'The Limits of Integration: Eastern Europe and the European Communities' (1993) 30 CMLRev, 1095–117; J. Scott and W. Mansell, 'Trading Partners: The European Community Trade Agreements with Poland, Hungary and Czech and Slovak Republics' (1993) 64 BYIL, 391–408; J. Pinder, *The European Community and Eastern Europe* (London: Pinter, 1991); M. Maresceau and E. Montaguti, 'The Relations Between the European Union and Central and Eastern Europe: A Legal Appraisal' (1995) 32 CMLRev, 1327–67.
42. Their ratification by the member states took a number of years, so interim agreements on the trade parts were used.
43. There has been delay due to a bilateral dispute between Italy and Slovenia concerning their respective minority populations. The agreement contains a title on economic cooperation between Italy and Slovenia.
44. See the Commission's White Paper on the Preparation of the Association Countries for Integration, COM(95)163.

Europe Agreements are virtually identical. One notable feature of the second series of them is the addition of specific references to minority rights. The Essen European Council effectively added a further accession condition of good neighbourly relations.[45]

All of the agreements make provision for regular political dialogue aimed at achieving a convergence of positions on international questions. Each of the Europe Agreements makes provision for an Association Council. An innovation in EU practice is that they also provide for the possibility for resort to international arbitration if the Association Council cannot resolve a dispute.[46] Under a 'Structured Dialogue' Joint Ministerial meetings are also held with the Associated Countries.[47] Under Protocols to the Europe Agreements the Associated Countries have access to various community programmes.[48]

b) African, Caribbean and Pacific States: the Yaounde and Lome Conventions

There have been a series of international agreements regulating relationships between the EU and the grouping of African, Caribbean and Pacific States which now numbers 70 states.[49] They have created what has been described as a 'unique relationship' between them.[50] The fourth Lome Convention of 1990 was revised after a mid-term review.[51] The series of Lome conventions have been predicated on the concept of fostering development. They have thus been based on granting EU market access to the ACP states, rather than on reciprocity. However, these general principles are tempered by specific provisions on rules of origin, fishery and temperate agricultural products, a number of special protocols governing trade in certain products notably bananas,[52]

---

45. Bull-EU, 12-1994, I.1-I.55.
46. The first invocation of this concerned a Polish ban on leather exports to the EU.
47. See, e.g., Bull-EU, 6-1995, p. 19.
48. See Bull-EU, 3-1995, point 1.4.68; G. Edwards, 'Common Foreign and Security Policy' (1995) 14 YEL 1994, 541–56, p. 550.
49. See M. Addo, 'A Critical Analysis of the Perennial International Economic Law Problems of the EEC-ACP Relationship' (1990) 33 GYIL 1990, 37–60.
50. C. Cosgrove and P.H. Laurent, 'The Unique Relationship: The European Community and the ACP', in Redmond, *The External Relations of the European Community*.
51. The revised Convention was signed in Mauritius in November 1995. See Bull-EU, 11-1995, point 1.4.102.
52. The banana protocol has been the subject of increasing political and legal dispute, particularly from Germany. See Case C-280/93, *Germany v Council*, [1994] ECR I-4973. See also *Opinion 3/94*, [1995] ECR I-4577.

trade in services. There is also substantial financial assistance including project aid, the STABEX[53] and SYSMIN[54] systems, support for structural adjustment, enterprise development and trade development. Lome IV provides for an annual ACP-EC Council meeting and an ACP-EC Joint Assembly twice per year.[55]

c) Euro-Mediterranean association agreements

These have been signed initialled with Tunisia, Israel and Morocco.[56] These are wide ranging agreements covering, *inter alia*, human rights and democracy, political dialogue, a free trade area to be established within twelve years,[57] services, capital movements, competition rules, intellectual property rights, approximation of laws,[58] and a dialogue on social and cultural cooperation.[59] An Association Council and Association Committee have implementation[60] and dispute settlement functions.[61]

d) Partnership and cooperation agreements

These represent a lower level of relationship than an Association Agreement. Membership of the EU is not foreseen and has usually been ruled out for the foreseeable future.[62] The PCAs do not establish a free trade zone but some of them contain an undertaking to examine the possibility in the future. In policy terms this is obviously important. Examples of recent PCAs are those with Russia, Ukraine, Belarus, Moldova, Kazakhstan; Kyrgyzstan and Uzbekistan.[63] Further PCAs are foreseen with

53. Stabilization of export earnings scheme.   54. Support system for minerals.
55. See K.R. Simmonds, 'The Fourth Lome Convention' (1991) 28 CMLRev, 521–47.
56. In April, September and November 1995, respectively. Agreements with Egypt, Jordan and Lebanon are planned.
57. Rules of origin for goods are thus crucial.
58. As usual it is approximation to EC laws that is envisaged, though Article 55 of the Israel agreement is an oddity, 'The Parties shall use their best endeavours to approximate their respective legislations in order to facilitate the implementation of this Agreement'. I am grateful to Marise Cremona for noting this. See M. Hirsh, 'The 1995 Trade Agreement between the European Communites and Israel: Three Unresolved Issues', 1 EFARev (1996) 87–123.
59. The breadth of these agreements may be a reflection of the wider competence of the EU after the TEU.
60. This is important bearing in mind that decisions of an Association Council can have direct effect, see ch. 7 above.
61. Reference to arbitration is ultimately possible.
62. See the Commission's Communication of 31 May 1995.
63. See S. Peers, 'Towards Equality: Actual and Potential Rights of Third-Country Nationals in the European Union' (1995) 33 CMLRev, 7–50.

Georgia, Armenia and Azerbaijan. Until these are agreed, their relations with the EU remain governed by the 1989 Agreement with the then USSR.[64]

Due to their wide range, these PCAs have been concluded as mixed agreements based on Article 113 and a number of other articles.[65] Commercial and economic cooperation agreements have been concluded with a wide range of states, often on the basis of Articles 113 and 235. For the future resort is increasingly likely to be had to Article 130y on development cooperation rather than Article 235.[66]

e) Free trade agreements/customs union agreements[67]

Alongside these various forms and levels of association agreements are free trade agreements which may be described in different ways, for example, Economic Agreements, association agreements, Europe Agreements. If they are kept within the broad scope of the CCP then they can be based solely on Article 113. The next level above this is a customs union agreement.[68] The establishment of this may be foreseen in a free trade agreement or an Association Agreement. This was the case with Turkey, Malta and Cyprus. The agreement on an EU-Turkey customs union, foreseen in an association agreement of 1972, was only completed in December 1995.

f) Human rights and democracy provisions in the EC's international agreements

International human rights and freedoms are now reflected in a number of provisions in the TEU and the EC Treaty.[69] In November 1991 an important resolution of the Council and of the member states meeting in the Council was adopted on 'Human Rights, Democracy and Development'.[70] This was part of the impetus in the trend towards the insertion of human rights and democracy clauses into the Preamble and later into the articles of

---

64. [199] OJ L68/1.
65. See Macleod, Hendry and Hyett, *The External Relations of the European Communities*, pp. 286–8.
66. See the Agreement with India, [1994] OJ L223/23.
67. There has been an explosion in international free trade agreements in the 1990s.
68. See the Agreement with Andorra on a customs union, [1990] OJ L374/6.
69. See Articles F, J, K.2 of the TEU; Articles 3q, 130u(2) EC Treaty; N. Neuwahl and A. Rosas (eds), *The European Union and Human Rights* (Hague, Nijhoff, 1995).
70. Bull-EC, 11-1991, p. 122.

the EC's international agreements.[71] Although practice is not yet entirely consistent, the rule of law, human rights and democracy are increasingly set out as the 'basis of', or 'essential to', those agreements.[72] Legally, this is important when the EU has to consider the legal justification for the suspension of an agreement (see Case C-268/94, *Portugal v Council*, pr. 19). Express suspension clauses are found in some agreements, e.g., the first set of agreements with the Baltic states in 1992.[73] In May 1995 the Council approved a suspension mechanism to be included in Community agreements with non-member countries to enable the Community to react immediately in the event of violation of essential aspects of those agreements, particularly human rights.[74] The Commission has urged the EU to support the inclusion of social clauses in multilateral trade agreements.[75] The issue is high on the EU's international agenda.[76]

The EP regularly passes resolutions on the human rights situation in states and regions of the world[77] and an annual resolution on 'Human Rights in the World'.[78] The Council regularly makes statements or declarations on human rights through the Presidency. The 'Conclusions of the Presidency', issued after meetings of the European Councils, the European Council often refers to human rights. Financial assistance is given to states and to non-governmental organizations under a number

71. See P.J. Kuijper, 'Trade Sanctions, Security and Human Rights and Commercial Policy', in M. Maresceau (ed.), *The European Community's Commercial Policy after 1992: The Legal Dimension* (Dordrecht, Nijhoff, 1993); D. Napoli, 'The European Union's Foreign Policy and Human Rights', in Neuwahl and Rosas, *The European Union and Human Rights*; Commission Communication agreed on 22 November 1995 on refining the EU's human rights strategy, COM(95)567; IP/95/1265. The Bulletin of the EU contains a separate section on human rights.

72. See, e.g., the Europe Agreement with Hungary. See Cremona, in Emiliou and O'Keeffe, *The European Union and World Trade Law*.

73. Interestingly, they were not included in later agreements because resort to the European Convention on Human Rights is now possible in the Baltic States, see Cremona, n. 72 above, p. 70. See p. 202 below on Australia's objection to the inclusion of a reference to human rights.

74. Bull-EU, 5-1995, point 1.2.2–1.2.3. See COM(95) 216.

75. See Commission Communication COM(94)669 on the World Summit for Social Development (1995). Note also the references to social and environmental standards in the Regulations on the Generalized System of Preferences, see Regulations 3281/94, [1994] OJ L348/1 and Regulation 3282/94, [1994] OJ L348/57.

76. See C. Barnard, 'The External Dimension of Community Social Policy: The Ugly Duckling of External Relations', in Emiliou and O'Keeffe, *The European Union and World Trade Law*.

77. Reproduced in the Bulletin of the EU and in the Official Journal, C Series.

78. For the resolution for 1993–94 see OJ C126 (22 May 1995).

of programmes in support of international human rights, democracy and development.

We have considered the increasing use of sanctions by the EC on the basis of decisions taken within EPC, and now CFSP.[79] Various kinds of sanctions, trade related, suspension of development cooperation, have been taken in support of international human rights in a number of cases, for example, South Africa, Yugoslavia (Serbia and Montenegro), Haiti, Nigeria.

g) Development cooperation and humanitarian assistance

The EC has an extensive range of development activities. The TEU made provision for a policy in the sphere of development cooperation.[80] Article 130y provides that 'within their respective spheres of competence' the EC and its member states shall co-operate with third states and international organizations. The arrangements for EC development cooperation may be the subject of international agreements negotiated and concluded in accordance with Article 228 (see Case C-268-94 *Portugal v Council*). Competence is clearly shared between the EC and the member states.[81]

The EU is also the world's largest provider of humanitarian aid. In 1991 it established a European Community Humanitarian Office.[82] The ECHO is active in 63 countries and in 1994 had a budget for ECU 760 million. Over 40 per cent of its budget goes to the ACP countries. Substantial financing for development also comes for the EDF which operates outside the EC budget, and from other sources.[83] Important internal measures are the PHARE and TACIS programmes. In the five years to 1994 PHARE was the largest programme of international assistance to the eleven partner countries in Central and Eastern Europe.[84] Other important

79. See ch. 7 above; Macleod, Hendry and Hyett, *The External Relations of The European Communities*, pp. 352–66.
80. See Articles 3, 130u-y; Macleod, Hendry and Hyett, *The External Relations of the European Communities*, pp. 338–51.
81. On complementarity between the development policies and actions of the Union and of the member states, see Commission Communication COM(95)160 and the Council's Resolution, Bull-EU, 6-1995, point 1.4.41.
82. See the 1994 Report of the ECHO (22 February 1995).
83. See Case C-316/91, *Parliament v Council*, [1994] ECR I-625 (the EDF Case); Joined Cases C-181 and C-248/91, *Parliament v Council and Commission*, [1993] ECR I-3885 (the Bangladesh Case).
84. See the Fifth Annual Report on PHARE, COM(95)366. A new Regulation for the TACIS programme was adopted in June 1996 for the period 1996–99 with a reference sum of ECU 2.224 billion. See Case T-185/94, *Geotronics v Commission* [1995] ECR II-2795.

internal measures of international significance deal with common rules for imports from certain countries,[85] a generalized system of tariff preferences (GSP) for developing countries,[86] and research and technological development in third countries and international organizations.[87]

h) Multilateral international economic agreements

The EC is party to an extensive number of multilateral economic agreements. It was never a GATT contracting party but, according to the ECJ, it was bound by the GATT by a process of substitution for the member states.[88] Although the member states remained parties, the EC assumed the dominant legal and practical role in the functioning of the GATT.[89] The EC is an original member of the WTO.[90] *Opinion 1/94* (WTO) of the ECJ substantially clarified the respective competencies of the EC and the member states in relation to the range of agreements that fall within the WTO framework.[91] Whether the EC's preferential arrangements with third countries satisfies the terms of Article XXIV of GATT is increasingly questioned.[92] The essential problem has been the exclusion of agricultural products and, after 'GATT 1994', there will also be the absence of substantial sectoral coverage of services. The EC also faces criticism because of the very limited extent to which the GATT is acknowledged in the EC legal order.[93]

The EC has an extensive range of bilateral agreements within the context of the Multi-Fibre Agreement. The MFA is being integrated within the GATT/WTO system. Along with member

---

85. See Council Regulation 519/94, OJ 1994 L67/89. See also Council Decision 95/131/EC on textile products from third countries, OJ 1994 L94/1.
86. See the scheme for 1995–98 in Council Regulation 3281/94, OJ 1994 L348/1. Sensitive areas in the EU are protected.
87. See Council Decision 94/807/EC, [1994] OJ L334/109, based on Article 130.
88. See ch. 4 above.
89. See M. Hilf, F.G. Jacobs and E.-U. Petersmann (eds), *The European Community and the GATT*, 2nd edn (Deventer, Kluwer, 1989).
90. See A. Qureshi, *The World Trade Organization* (Manchester, MUP, 1996), pp. 164–91.
91. See J. Bourgeois, 'The EC in the WTO and Advisory Opinion 1/94: An Echternach Procession' (1995) 32 CMLRev, 763–87; M. Hilf, 'The ECJ's Opinion on the WTO – No Surprise, but Wise?' (1995) 6 EJIL, 245–59.
92. See E.-U. Petersmann, 'The EEC as a GATT Member: Legal Conflicts between GATT Law and European Community Law', in M. Hilf *et al.* (eds), *The European Community and GATT*, 2nd edn (Deventer, Kluwer, 1989).
93. See ch. 7 above. It is becoming more frequent for Commission and Council Decisions to make reference to ensuring compliance with the GATT obligations.

states, the EC is party to a series of international commodity agreements,[94] and international customs conventions.[95]

i) International fisheries agreements

The EC has competence over fisheries on the basis of the treaty provisions relating to the common agricultural policy, internal Regulations, and Article 102 of the 1972 Act of Accession.[96] The *Kramer case* established that the EC has exclusive competence in relation to fisheries conservation.[97] Whether the competence is exclusive in relation to fisheries conservation in waters which do not border on EU waters is more arguable.[98]

The EC has signed or is a party to a number of international agreements on fisheries. The legal base used is Article 43.[99] Some of these have established international organizations to oversee them and the EC is a member of those organizations.[100] The EC's exclusive competence has meant that it alone may be a member of a fisheries organization. An example is the North Atlantic Fisheries Organisation. If voting does take place on an issue the EU can thus be outvoted as was the case with the EU-Canada dispute in 1995.[101] The EC and the member states have signed but not ratified the extremely important UN Law of the Sea Convention (1982).[102] After an agreement which effectively amends Part IX of the LOSC on the Deep Sea Bed, the likelihood of member states and EC ratification is much greater. The most recent multilateral fisheries agreement negotiated by the EU is the UN Straddling

---

94. See *Opinion 1/78* (Natural Rubber) [1979] ECR 2871; G. Coreu, *Taming Commodity Markets* (Manchester, MUP, 1992).
95. See Macleod, Hendry and Hyett, *The External Relations of the European Communities*, pp. 291–2.
96. See the *Kramer Case*, discussed in ch. 3 above.
97. See also Case C-804/79, *Commission v UK*, [1981] ECR 1045. On the limitations imposed by community law on the discretion of member states concerning the nationality of fishing boats see Case C-221/89, *R v Secretary of State for Trade and Industry, ex p Factortame Ltd* [1990] ECR I-2433.
98. See *Opinion 1/94*, pr. 85.
99. See, e.g., the recent agreement with Canada, Council Regulation 3675/93, OJ 1995 L340/1, and the agreement to promote compliance with international conservation and management by fishing vessels on the high seas, Council Decision 96/428, [1996] OJ L177/24, and the agreement itself at [1996] OJ L177/26.
100. See Macleod, Hendry and Hyett, *The External Relations of the European Communities*, pp. 241–52.
101. See P. Davies, 'The EC/Canadian Fisheries Dispute in the Northwest Atlantic' (1995) 44 ICLQ, 927–39.
102. See K.R. Simmonds, 'The Communities Declaration Upon Signature of the U.N. Convention on the Law of the Sea' (1986) 23 CMLRev, 521–44.

Stocks Convention 1995.[103] This was the first UN multilateral fisheries agreement negotiated by the EC.

j) International environmental agreements

There was no explicit environmental base in the EC Treaty until 1986. After amendments by the SEA and the TEU there are more detailed provisions on the environment. The EC has rapidly developed an extensive internal and international environmental practice.[104] Article 130r(4) provides:

> Within their respective spheres of competence, the Community and the Member States shall cooperate with third countries and with the competent international organisations. The arrangements for community cooperation may be the subject of agreements between the Community and the third parties concerned, which shall be negotiated and concluded in accordance with Article 228.
>
> The previous subparagraph shall be without prejudice to Member States' competence to negotiate in international bodies and to conclude international agreements.

This provision gives express authority for the EC to enter into international agreements on the environment but its competence to do so is clearly shared with the member states.[105] It remains possible for exclusive competence to arise on the basis of the ERTA principle,[106] but the express possibility under Article 130t for member states to maintain or introduce more stringent protective measures will be of importance. In practice international environmental agreements have normally only been entered into by the EC when internal rules already exist.

The EC is a signatory or a party to some of the leading international conventions on the environment.[107] All of those agreements are mixed agreements and declarations of competence

---

103. See D. Anderson, 'The Straddling Stocks Agreement of 1995 – An Initial Assessment' (1996) 45 ICLQ, 463–75.
104. See L. Kramer, *EC Treaty and Environmental Law*, 2nd edn (London, Sweet and Maxwell, 1994); P. Sands, *Principles of International Environmental Law* (Manchester, MUP, 1995), pp. 539–75; P. Sands and R.G. Tarasofsky, *Documents in European Community Environmental Law* (Manchester, MUP, 1995); P. Sands, R.G. Tarasofsky and W. Weiss, *Documents in International Environmental Law* (Manchester, MUP, 1995).
105. See Article 130r; Macleod, Hendry and Hyett, *The External Relations of the European Communities*, pp. 326–7.
106. See Declaration no. 10 to the TEU.
107. See Macleod, Hendry and Hyett, op. cit., pp. 323–37.

are usually required from the EC, and sometimes from the member states. The declaration is to be made initially and a continuing basis if there is significant change or modification.[108] The EC also plays an increasingly active role in their drafting and implementation, for example, at the UN Conference on Environment and Development 1992.[109] In addition, the various kinds of international agreements between the EC and third states that we have considered above (section 1) frequently have provisions on the environment.[110] EC standards and principles are often used as models in those agreements and even in non-EC international agreements such as that on the European Bank for Reconstruction and Development.[111]

k) Use of commercial defence instruments by the EU

Although the details are beyond the scope of this work, a controversial aspect of EC international relations practice has been its resort to commercial defence instruments. These include safeguard measures such as surveillance measures, such as anti-dumping, anti-subsidy measures, the commercial policy instrument, as part of the CCP.[112] The Commission prepares an annual report on these activities. In 1993 the countries which formed the subject of the most measures were, in order, China, Japan, Turkey, and the Republic of Korea.[113] Japan was the most affected country with 50 per cent of the total. The use of commercial defence instruments is controversial and is regularly challenged before the ECJ.[114]

---

[108]. See, e.g., Article 22(3) of the UN Framework Convention on Climate Change 1992.

[109]. See N. Haigh, 'The EC and International Environmental Policy', in A. Hurrell and B. Kingsbury, *The International Politics of the Environment* (Oxford, OUP, 1992); L.J. Brinkhorst, 'The European Community at UNCED: Lessons to be Drawn for the Future', in D. Curtin and T. Heukels (eds), *Institutional Dynamics of European Integration: Essays in Honour of H.G. Schermens*, vol. II (Dordrecht, Nijhoff, 1994).

[110]. See P. Demaret, 'Environmental Policy and Commercial Policy: The Emergence of Trade-Related Environmental Measures', in M. Maresceau (ed.), *The European Community's Commercial Policy after 1992: The Legal Dimension* (Dordrecht, Nijhoff, 1993).

[111]. See D. McGoldrick, 'A New International Economic Order for Europe?' (1994) 12 YEL 1992, 434–64, pp. 448–56.

[112]. See Macleod, Hendry and Hyett, op. cit., pp. 278–83.

[113]. The use of such instruments against the former state trading countries is now significantly reduced.

[114]. See F. Jacobs, 'Judicial Review of Commercial Policy Measures After the Uruguay Round', in Emiliou and O'Keeffe, *The European Union and World Trade Law*; and the regular surveys in the EJIL.

2. Structured dialogue with states

The EU has a structured political dialogue commitment with around thirty states or groups of states.[115] It is worth listing them: Albania, Australia, ASEAN, the Baltic states, the countries of Central and Eastern Europe, Central America, China, Cyprus, the Gulf Cooperation Council, India, Japan, Malta, New Zealand, the non-aligned countries, Pakistan, the Rio Group, Russia, South Korea, Sri Lanka, Turkey, Ukraine, and last but not least, the US. The basis of these varies enormously and can change over time, for example, by being up-graded to an international agreement. The political dialogue can be conducted on the basis of any of the forms of Association Agreement, a decision of an Association Council, a joint seclaration, joint decisions of the EC and the group of states concerned, decisions of the European Council and or of the Council, a declaration on the relations concerned, an exchange of letters, or a decision of the Political Committee.

a) The EU and the major powers[116] and some of the major regions[117]

(i) The United States

Relations between the EC/EU and the US have had a complex and troubled history.[118] The US has been somewhat ambivalent about its attitude to the development of a powerful Union of European States. The basis for political dialogue is the EU/US Declaration of November 1990.[119] This provides for a biannual summit.[120] At the

---

115. See E. Regelsberger, 'Reforming the CFSP – An Alibi Debate or More', in S.A. Pappas and S. Vanhoonacker (eds), *The European Union's Common Foreign and Security Policy: The Challenges of the Future* (Maastricht, EIPA, 1996).

116. Kissinger suggests that the international system of the twenty-first century will contain at least six major powers – the US, Europe, China, Japan, Russia and probably India; H. Kissinger, *Diplomacy* (New York, Simon and Schuster, 1994), p. 23.

117. The regions indicated are illustrative rather than exhaustive. A more strategic approach is clearly evident.

118. See J. Schwarze, *The External Relations of the European Community, in particular EC–US Relations* (Baden-Baden, Nomos, 1989); M. Smith, 'The United States and 1992: Responses to a Changing European Community', in Redmond, *The External Relations of the European Community*; R. Rummel (ed.), *The Evolution of an International Actor*, pp. 199–295; G.C. Hufbauer (ed.), *Europe 1992: An American Perspective* (Washington, D.C., Brookings Institute, 1990).

119. See Bull-EC, 11–90, 1.5.3.

120. There is also a biannual summit with Canada.

EU-US summit on 3 December 1995 an extensive document entitled 'The New Transatlantic Agenda' was signed.[121] A joint action plan was attached. A recurrent suggestion is that of a US-EU Free Trade Agreement.[122]

(ii) ASEAN[123]

There has been political dialogue between the EC and ASEAN since the 1970s. A cooperation agreement was signed in 1980.[124] This provides for a regular EC-ASEAN ministerial meeting. However, in relative terms relations are very much under-developed.[125] The Prime Minister of Singapore has described Europe's links with Asia as a 'missing link'.[126] Given that it is now economic orthodoxy that the ASEAN region will continue to be the worlds fastest economic growth area, this is a matter of the utmost importance for the EU.[127] An EU-Asia summit in March 1996 set out a broad agenda for relations.[128] Framework agreements are foreseen with Bangladesh, Pakistan, Laos and Cambodia.[129]

(iii) Japan

Relations with Japan have generally been dominated by economic issues.[130] There are regular disputes concerning market access, local content rules and the application of voluntary export

---

121. See PRES/95/356 (8 December 1995). See also the Commission's Communication, 'Europe and the US: the Way Forward', COM(95)411; and the Conclusions of the Madrid European Council, Annex 10 (1995). H.G. Krenzler and A. Schomaker, 'A New Transatlantic Agenda' (1996) 1 EFARev, 9–28.

122. There are some eleven EC–US bilateral agreements including the agreement on competition.

123. Brunei, Indonesia, Malaysia, the Philippines, Singapore and Thailand.

124. [1980] OJ L144/1.

125. See J. Redmond, 'The European Community and ASEAN' in Redmond, *The External Relations of the European Community.*

126. Cited in P. Sutherland, 'The European Union – A Stage of Transition' (1995) EIPASCOPE, 1995/2, 2–9.

127. See the Commission's Communication 'Towards a New Asia Strategy', COM(94)314; Conclusions of the Madrid European Council, Annex 14 (1995); Sutherland (1995), EIPASCOPE, 1995/2, 2–9.

128. There are no sector specific EU-Asia agreements.

129. See 'The Commission's Programme for 1996', COM(95)512 final, Bull-EU, Supp.1/96, p. 29.

130. See A. El-Agraa, 'Japan's Reaction to the Single Internal Market', in Redmond, *The External Relations of the European Community*; C. Hosoya, 'Relations between the European Communities and Japan' (1979) 18 JCMS, 159–74.

restraints.[131] Political dialogue is based on an EU/Japan Joint Declaration of July 1991 and is to be held more regularly.[132] In 1995 the Commission published a communication on 'Europe and Japan – the Next Steps'.[133]

(iv) Russian Federation (formerly the USSR)

We have noted above the international agreements regulating this relationship. A wide-ranging partnership and cooperation agreement was signed in June 1994.[134] An interim agreement concerning the trade provisions was signed on 17 July 1995, after some delay relating to the crisis in the Chechen region. There is some recognition of the relative importance of Russia. The PCA provides for enhanced political dialogue and has more detailed provisions on investments.[135] Respect for human rights and the democratic process is part of the relationship. The EC is Russia's largest trading partner. There are extensive forms of EU-Russia cooperation in the fields of the TACIS programme, transport, energy, telecommunications, education, training, environment, energy, industrial cooperation, research and development. In 1995 the Commission published a Communication on 'The EU and Russia – the Future Relationship'.[136] In November 1995 the Council adopted a strategy on EU-Russia relations.[137]

The EU has also played a major role in food aid, humanitarian assistance and economic aid to Russia. Eleven per cent of the ECHO budget for 1994 went to the Russian Federation.[138]

---

131. See H. Yamane, ' "Grey-Area" Measures, the Uruguay Round and the EC/Japan: Commercial Consensus on Cars', in Emiliou and O'Keeffe, *The European Union and World Trade Law*.
132. See Bull-EU, 6-1995, point 1.4.101. An EU-Japan Summit was held in June 1995.
133. COM(95) 73. For the Council's conclusion see Bull-EU, 5-1995, point 1.4.91.
134. See Council Decision 95/414 on the interim agreement of the trade aspects of that PCA.
135. See S. Peers, 'From Cold War to Lukewarm Embrace: The European Union's Agreements with the CIS States' (1995) 44 ICLQ, 829–47.
136. COM(95) 223. That formed the basis of the Commission's first exercise of its right of initiative under CFSP, namely a draft common position on Russia.
137. Bull-EU, 11-1995, point 2.2.1.
138. Note also the TACIS programme supporting the development of market economies, Regulation 2053/93, [1993] OJ L187/1.

(v) China

There is an economic cooperation agreement with China (1985).[139] Political dialogue is based on an exchange of letters of May 1994. In 1995 the Commission published a Communication on a long-term policy for EU-China relations.[140]

(vi) Mediterranean countries

Concerns relating to the Mediterranean have been regularly on the EC and EPC/CFSP agendas.[141] The EC adopted a 'Global Mediterranean Policy' in 1972 providing for preferential trade relations.[142] There are trade and cooperation agreements with a number of Mediterranean states but these will gradually be replaced by the Euro-Mediterranean association agreements.[143] Three Mediterranean states, Turkey, Malta and Cyprus, are among the current applicants for EU membership.

An important and wide-ranging Euro-Mediterranean Agreement was signed in October 1995. A Euro-Mediterranean Conference was held on 27–28 November 1995 in Barcelona involving the member states and twelve Mediterranean non-member states.[144] It adopted the extensive 'Barcelona Declaration' aimed at a wide-ranging partnership process including political, security, economic, financial, social, cultural and human dimensions.[145]

139. [1985] OJ L250/1.
140. COM(95)279, subsequently approved by the Council. See G. Edwards, 'Common Foreign and Security Policy' (1995) 14 YEL 1994, 541–56, pp. 553–4; F. Snyder, 'Legal Aspects of Trade between the European Union and China: Preliminary Reflections', in Emiliou and O'Keeffe, *The European Union and World Trade Law.*
141. See S. Nuttall, *European Political Cooperation* (Oxford, Clarendon Press, 1992), pp. 93–109; A.J. Figueiredo Lopes, 'La Dimension Méditerranéenne De La Sécurité Européenne', in S.A. Pappas and S. Vanhoonacker (eds) *The European Union's Common Foreign and Security Policy: The Challenges of the Future* (Maastricht, EIPA, 1996).
142. See R. Pomfret, 'The European Community's Relations with the Mediterranean Countries', in Redmond, *The External Relations of the European Community.*
143. See section 1, c above.
144. The twelve included the Palestinian Authority. A Euro-Mediterranean Interim Association Agreement on Trade and Cooperation was signed in December 1996.
145. See Commission Communication on Strengthening the Mediterranean Policy of the European Union: Proposals for Implementing a Euro-Mediterranean Partnership, COM(95)72 final, March 1995; Barcelona Declaration and Work Programme, Bull-EU, 11-1995, point 2.3.1.

(vii) Central and Southern America

There are a number of free trade agreements or framework cooperation agreements with individual states or groups of states.[146] Annual meetings have been held with the countries of Central America since 1985 and with the Rio Group of Latin Amercian states since 1991. In December 1995 a cooperation agreement was signed with MERCOSUR, the common market of Argentina, Brazil, Paraguay and Uruguay.[147]

(viii) Australia and New Zealand

Australia and New Zealand have gradually come to terms with the EU notably in response to the development of the single market.[148] Within the GATT negotiations they have acted within the Cairns Group[149] and exerted substantial pressure on the EU to reform its Common Agricultural Policy. There is political dialogue with Australia based on a Council decision of May 1990. In February 1996 the Commission proposed a framework agreement with Australia. In December 1996, Australia objected to any human rights in the proposal agreement. That with New Zealand's based on a decision of the Political Committee of September 1990.

(ix) Africa

We have already considered the ACP system under the Lome Convention.[150] There are a number of cooperation agrements with individual states. A trade and cooperation agreement with South Africa is being negotiated. The system of generalized trade preferences is also important in this context.[151]

b) International representation/international conferences

Diplomatic representation

This is briefly recalled here because it represents a key factual element in how the EU communicates with the world. Strictly

---

146. See Commissions Communication on a closer relationship with Latin America (1996–2000), COM(95)495; Conclusions of the Madrid European Council, Annex 12 (1995).
147. This was the first international agreement between two customs unions.
148. See J. Lodge, 'New Zealand, Australia and 1992', in Redmond, *The External Relations of the European Community*.
149. Comprising fourteen states.   150. See pp. 189–90 above.
151. See Council Regulations 3281/94, [1994] OJ L348/1; 3282/94, [1994] OJ L348/57.

speaking, the EU does not have diplomatic representatives in the same sense as states.[152] There is no formal EU diplomatic corps. This should not hide the reality that the EU has a massive and growing diplomatic presence in the world.[153] 167 states have missions accredited to the EC/EU.[154] There are EU delegations, representations or offices in over 110 states. In many capitals the EU representative can be more sought after than ambassadors from the member states. This is largely because they may be closer to the EU's purse-strings.

Representation at international conferences[155]

This is done by the Presidency and the Commission or the Commission alone. If EC participation is not possible, then the Presidency and the member states present the Community position.

EU and the UN

We have already observed that the EC is not a member of the UN but has observer status.[156] The member states of the EU have been described as the most regional cohesive grouping in the United Nations. Brinkhorst comments that, 'The current picture corresponds to the Community being a highly developed system of cooperation between states, but it does not correspond to the reality of the Community being an organization in its own right with distinctive characteristics of a supranational nature'.[157]

Community coordination is very highly developed at the UN and 'EU statements' are common.[158] A contemporary example

152. See ch. 2 above.
153. See L.J. Brinkhorst, 'Permanent Missions of the EC in Third Countries: European Diplomacy in the Making' (1984) 1 LIEI, 22–33.
154. See Commission 1996; Bull-EU, 5-1995, point 1.4.115.
155. See Macleod, Hendry and Hyett, op. cit., pp. 175–6, 194–5.
156. See ch. 2, pp. 33–4 above.
157. L.J. Brinkhorst, 'The European Community of UNCED: Lessons to be Drawn for the Future', in Curtin and Henkels, *Institutional Dynamics*, p. 611. This factor must be borne in mind when criticisms are made of the EU by other regional groupings who are not so cohesive.
158. See 'European Union at the UN', Bull-EU, 9-1995, point 2.3.1; B. Lindemann, 'European Political Cooperation at the UN', in D. Allen, R. Rummel and W. Wessels (eds), *European Political Cooperation* (London, Butterworths, 1982); P. Bruckner, 'The EC and the United Nations' (1990) 1/2 EJIL, 174–92; I.J. Thijn, 'The European Political Cooperation in the General Assembly of the United Nations: A Case Study of The Netherlands' (1991) 1 LIEI, 101–25. See also Article J.(5)4 on the Security Council and Declaration No. 25 to the TEU. Security Council resolutions regularly acknowledge the contribution of the EU.

where the Commission was the sole spokesman was the UN Convention on Straddling Stocks (1995).[159] It effectively operated like two conferences. The EC mini-conference took place first thing in the morning. The UN conference then took place. The EC conference resumed at lunch time. The UN conference took over in the afternoon and the EC conference met in the evening. The member states could only speak concerning their dependant territories. This can be very frustrating for the member states. They effectively act through a process of ventriloquism. The Commission exercises responsibilities but may do so very ineffectively. It was very unsatisfactory in practice world experts from member states could say nothing. If the quality of the Commission's representatives is not high then they will be ineffective. The Commission and the member states may have to put so much effort into achieving coordination and common positions, that there is little energy or enthusiasm left for the negotiations with the member states.[160] Third parties may not be very impressed with the EC performance. One of the difficulties with the EC in that so much has to work on the basis of trade offs between the different Councils, for example, between the Fisheries Council and the Agricultural Council. Matters have to be balanced off even if they are entirely dissimilar to each other. This can make the negotiating position of the EU very inflexible. The EC may need to be able to have alternative positions. Assessments of the EU's role in the UNCED Conference have been much more positive about its mediating and conciliatory role.[161] Member states of the EU provide 37 per cent of the UN peacekeeping budget and provides the majority of peacekeeping personnel.

EU and the OSCE

The OSCE (formerly CSCE) was one of the first two areas where EPC was tested.[162] The EU has acted as a fairly cohesive force in the OSCE.[163]

159. See Anderson, op. cit., n. 103. By comparison with UNCLOS there was about 90 per cent member state competence.
160. See J. Sack, 'The European Community's Membership of International Organisations' (1995) 32 CMLRev, 1227–56.
161. See Brinkhorst in Curtin and Heukels, *Institutional Dynamics*, esp. at p. 611.
162. See Nuttall, *European Political Cooperation*, pp. 110–18.
163. See G. von Goll, 'The Nine at the Conference on Security and Cooperation in Europe', in Allen, Rummel and Wessels, *European Political Cooperation*; F. Cameron, 'The European Union and the OSCE: Future Roles and Challenges' (1995) 6(2) Helsinki Monitor, 21–31.

EU and NATO

We have considered this relationship in the context of CFSP.[164]

Competition with other international organizations in Europe

In the last decade the EU has increasingly faced the problem of defining itself, not only internally, but also in relation to other international organizations in Europe. Much has been written on the 'architecture' of the New Europe. If the EU develops a security and defence dimension, how will this affect NATO? How will the relationship with the WEU be developed? How far can human rights developed within the EU be developed without undermining the Council of Europe (ECHR). How are overlaps with the OSCE to be dealt with? Prospective enlargement only underlines the importance of these questions. Their resolution does not solely depend on practical solutions and sophisticated legal texts. It also depends on fundamental issues of identity, values and legitimacy. It is to these matters, among others, that we must turn in the final chapter.

[164.] See ch. 8 above.

CHAPTER ELEVEN

Appraisal and prospectus

Introduction

This final chapter seeks to pull together a few of the themes which emerge in this book and put them into the broad context of the EU's international relations.

The evolution of the EU's international relations

The process of evolution of the international relations of the EU has been complex and confusing. We have considered the international personality of the EC and the issue of the international personality of the EU.[1] The internal structure of the EU is complicated in its own right.[2] Within that structure, the determination of the external relations competence of the EC is, as we have seen, a sophisticated exercise applied to a constant state of evolution and institutional tension.[3] As in other areas, the ECJ has built up a sophisticated jurisprudence on the basis of rather slim legal foundations.[4] It has interpreted the scope of its jurisdiction and its principles of judicial review very widely. It is thus both a cause and effect in the process of political development and integration in the EC. Through the ECJ's judgments, and its opinions under Article 228, the central principles governing international relations have gradually become clearer. The radical ERTA doctrine of parallelism has been politically accepted. It has been refined and extended by the ECJ. The different legal processes by which *exclusive* community competence are generated

[1.] See ch. 1 above. [2.] See ch. 2 above. [3.] See chs. 2–3 above.
[4.] See chs. 3–7 above.

are now much better understood.[5] The difference between common rules and minimum rules is clearly crucial. The phenomenon of mixed agreements has assumed an increasingly important role in the scheme of external relations.[6] They are used for a number of different legal and political reasons. Attention has increasingly focused on the legal problems generated by the use of mixed agreements, rather than questions of their compatibility with EC law.

In addition we have considered the political and legal response of member states that was reflected in the development of EPC from 1970 to 1992, and in the two intergovernmental pillars under the TEU covering 'Common Foreign and Security Policy' and 'Justice and Home Affairs'.[7] Evaluation of the external relations of the EU now requires that the whole of the post-TEU institutional structure be considered, and in particular the relationship between the different pillars. Brief consideration was also given to international human rights and the international aspect of EU citizenship.[8] As the governing principles have become clearer, and the institutional structure has been reformed, so member states, Community institutions and third parties have been able to develop more precise strategies and practices in response.[9]

Legal orders: the EC order

One of the most fascinating questions concerning the evolution of the EC as a legal order has concerned its relationship with international law. Is EC law part of international law? Although the ECJ initially proclaimed EC law as a *'new order of international law'*, this subsequently became simply a *'new legal order'*.[10] Legal principles were developed that coincided with the perceived vision of an internal community legal order rather than being extrapolated from international law. International law doctrines and principles were left far behind as a constitutional system and constitutional principles was being developed.[11] To an outside observer the EC can appear to have been arrogantly and obsessively concerned with the dynamics of its internal evolution

---

[5.] See ch. 4 above.   [6.] See ch. 5 above.   [7.] See chs. 8 and 9 above.
[8.] See ch. 9 above.   [9.] See ch. 6 above.   [10.] See ch. 1 above.
[11.] See L. Hancher, 'Constitutionalism, the Community Court and International Law' (1994) 25 NYIL, 259–98.

and little concerned with its external relations. Questions relating to competence were rebuffed as internal matters of no concern to outsiders.[12] The EEA opinions displayed great concern at protecting the EC system of judicial supervision and dispute settlement.[13] However, the interface between EU law and international law is increasingly evident in the post-TEU era.[14]

However, as the EC increasingly sought to become an international actor and assert its international personality and identity,[15] then it has had to accept that member states and third parties have legitimate interests.[16] EC Treaty practice has become increasingly dominated by mixed agreements.[17] Mixed agreements reflect the political and legal reality that the EC is not a single state for the purposes of international law.[18] The EU's membership of and participation in international organizations is astonishingly variable for an entity which seeks to appear as a single actor.[19] Weiler's comment in 1992 that the EU may not speak with one voice but increasingly speaks like a choir remains close to the truth.[20]

In the analysis above, the concentration has been primarily on the legal instruments which form the sub-structure of the EU's

12. See *Ruling 1/78* (Draft Convention on the Physical Protection of Nuclear Materials, Facilities and Transport) [1978] ECR 2151.
13. *Opinion 1/91* (First EEA Opinion), [1991] ECR 6079; *Opinion 1/92* (Second EEA Opinion), [1992] ECR I-2821. See M-A. Gaudissart, 'La Portée des avis 1/91 et 1/92 de la Cour de justice des Communautés européennes relatif à la création de l'espace économique européen: entre autonomie et homogénéité: L'ordre juridique communautaire en péril . . .' (1992) RMUE, 121–36; H.G. Schermers, 'Opinion 1/91 of 14 Dec. 1991; Opinion 1/92 of 10 Apr. 1992 with annotation' (1992) 29 CMLRev, 991–1010.
14. 'The increasing involvement of the EC in questions of general international law is a relatively new phenomenon . . . The Community is increasingly being forced to take a position on matters of general international law', P.J. Kuyper, 'The Community and State Succession in Respect of Treaties', in D. Curtin and T. Heukels (eds), *Institutional Dynamics of European Integration: Essays in Honour of H.G. Schermers* (Dordrecht, Nijhoff, 1994), vol. II, 619–40, pp. 619–20. See also J. Boulouis, 'Le Droit Des Communautés Européennes Dans Ses Rapports Avec Le Droit International Général' 235 *Receuil Des Cours* (1992–IV), 9–80.
15. See chs. 2 and 10 above.
16. Third States may often appear to be mystified by the EU but then it is a unique experiment in international law and international relations.
17. See ch. 5 above.
18. Nor obviously is the EU, 'it is difficult to see anything short of a major war provoking a transition to statehood', C. Hill, 'The Capability-Expectations Gap, or Conceptualising Europe's International Role' (1993) 31 JCMS, 305–28, p. 325.
19. See chs. 2 and 10 above.
20. See J.H. Weiler, 'The Evolution of Mechanisms and Institutions for a European Foreign Policy. Reflections on the Interaction of Law and Politics' (Florence: European University Institute Research Paper No. 85/202, 1992).

international activities. In addition we have considered the legal basis of the EU's participation in international organizations.[21] To give the full picture we then explained in some detail the operation of the EU's intergovernmental pillars on common foreign and security policy[22] and made brief reference to justice and home affairs, international human rights and the international aspects of citizenship.[23]

Third states have sometimes insisted on specific provisions relating to the different aspects of participation of the EC. The most notorious example is the UNCLOS.[24] While third states may have accepted and recognized the existence of the EC and that member states have transferred Treaty-making powers to it, they of course have sought to bring the EC within the general international law system. They have been suspicious of developing special rules or principles relating to competence, liability, responsibility or dispute settlement that would give the EC or its member states a privileged position.[25]

What must now be considered is how far all of this blends together in a manner that permits the EU to be credibly regarded as a single actor, though playing a variety of roles. The EU is undoubtedly playing an increased number of roles on the international stage.[26] It takes part in a massive array of international activities, both formal and informal. The political commitment of the member states to the EU playing a role seems consistent. Yet there are clear differences between member states in terms of how far they are willing to let the EU displace them as international actors. The contemporary situation is not neat and tidy precisely because it reflects a certain balance of power between the EU and the member states.[27] The formal creation of the essentially intergovernmental pillars for CFSP and JHA epitomizes this tension.

[21.] See ch. 2 above.   [22.] See ch. 8 above.   [23.] See ch. 9 above.
[24.] See K.R. Simmonds, 'The Communities Declaration Upon Signature of the U.N. Convention on the Law of the Sea' (1986) 23 CMLRev, 521–44.
[25.] See D. O'Keeffe and H.G. Schermers (eds), *Essays in European Law and Integration* (Deventer, Kluwer, 1982).
[26.] See ch. 10 above; W. Wessels, 'EC-Europe: An Actor *Sui Generis* in the International System' in B. Nelson, D. Roberts and W. Veit, *The EC in the 1990s* (New York, Berg, 1990), 161–73; R. Rummel (ed.), *The Evolution of an International Actor: Western Europe's New Assertiveness* (Boulder, Col: Westview, 1990); D. Dinan, *An Ever Closer Union?* (London, Macmillan, 1994), pp. 465–501.
[27.] See C. Brewin 'The European Community: A Union of States without Unity of Government' (1987) 26 JCMS, 1–25.

On the basis of the wide interpretation by the ECJ of its international personality and competence, the EC had the potential to play a significant international role, or set of roles. However, whether it could actually do so depended to a substantial extent on the willingness of the rest of the international community to deal with it. Ultimately, the response has been very positive. The EU has a substantial diplomatic presence around the world. Diplomatic cooperation between the embassies of the member states is also very highly developed. Over 170 countries or territories have missions accredited to the EU.[28] The EU enjoys formal economic and political relations with most states in the world and is a member of, participates in, or is an observer at a substantial number of international organizations.[29] The Presidency, the Commission and the EU are day to day actors on the international stage and in international conferences.

Even allowing for the influence of its economic power, it is notable that the rest of the world community has been increasingly willing to let the EU wear the clothes of a major actor.[30] Indeed, their positive responses have heightened the expectations of the roles that the EU can play and exposed its limitations.[31]

The EU as a model for the international community and the international law of the future

Analysts of the EU often seem to lose sight of just how radical and unique a legal and political development it is.[32] Criticisms of the EU's limitations as an international actor, and in particular its CFSP, are routinely made by reference to the supposedly superior model of a single federal state. Though the analogy has merit, it is often pushed too far. As the Reflection Group for the 1996 IGC has commented, 'The Union is not and does not want to be a super-state. Yet it is far more than a market. It is a unique design

---

28. These are described as mission to the EC or to the EU. From a purely legal view only the former is correct.
29. See ch. 2 above.
30. See J. Groux and P. Manin, *The European Communities in the International Order* (European Perspective Series, Brussels, EC Commission, 1985).
31. See Hill, 'The Capability-Expectations Gap, or Conceptualising Europe's International Role'.
32. Cf. Wessels, 'EC-Europe: An Actor *Sui Generis* in the International System', in Nelson, Roberts and Veit, *The EC in the 1990s*.

based on common values'.[33] It is often forgotten just how far the EC, and even the EU, model is in advance of any other regional or universal model of social, political and legal integration.[34] No comparable model even appears to be developing in any other region of the world. None the less, the EU may offer some elements for future international orders.[35]

Mere existence

At a first level of analysis the EU plays an important role simply because it exists as a market and a community. It has an objective physical existence in terms of territory and borders, and a subjective existence in terms of personality, legal system, laws and regulations, and an enormous 'market'. Other international actors are affected by this very existence. It changes lines of communication, working relationships, negotiating processes, diplomatic procedures.[36] By definition the category of member states creates a category of non-EU member states. The concept of citizenship of the Union also creates the category of non-EU citizens. More generally, the creation of a 'community' has both an internal dynamic and an external dynamic. Internally it creates obligations of solidarity, cohesion and consistency. This communitarianism, whether at the level of myth, vision or genuine substance, can contribute to stability and the promotion of the values of the EU. Externally, it changes the perception of Europe. It is perceived a single entity of some kind. The precise kind may be of less importance to third states that the fact of singularity. Thus, third states can partly pull and press the EU towards more coherent international activities. There is enormous world-wide interest in the EU, though just how important Europe is in geo-political, intellectual and cultural terms is increasingly discussed.[37]

33. Reflection Group's Final Report, Doc. SN520/95, Brussels, 5 December 1995, at p. III.
34. See J. Weiler and W. Wessels, 'EPC and the Challenge of Theory', in A. Pijpers, E. Regelsberger and W. Wessels (eds), *European Political Cooperation in the 1980s* (Dordrecht, Nijhoff, 1988), pp. 229–58; J.H. Weiler, 'The Transformation of Europe' (1991) 101 Yale LJ, 2403–83.
35. See P. Allott, *Eunomia – A New World Order for a New World* (Oxford, OUP, 1990); P. Allott, 'The European Community is Not the True European Community' (1991) 101 Yale LJ, 2485–500; M. Hilf, 'The Single European Act and 1992: Legal Implications for Third Countries' (1990) I EJIL, 89–117.
36. See M. Clarke, *British External Policy-making in the 1990s* (Basingstoke: Macmillan, 1992).
37. See D. Brooks, 'Yanks go home, Europe's a bore', *The Sunday Times* (London), 7 July 1996, p. 9.

Economic power and liberal values

In economic terms, the EU has for some time been a superpower. Historically, this has always led to a parallel assertion of political power.[38] The EU likes to present this as benign leadership, and, at least to date, of a civilian rather than a military kind.[39] However, there is no disguising that in its multifold activities the EU is asserting a powerful set of liberal economic and political values.[40] In its various legal and political activities the EU seeks to export its fundamental values and rules. As it is often the dominant legal partner, many agreements are based on substantive EU rules. The increasing range of association agreements are the clearest example of this. Another notable development in the EC's international agreements has been the insertion of human rights clauses and the accompanying possibility of agreements and development aid being suspended.[41]

The EU is a legal organization through which political values – human rights, democracy, economic liberalism based on the centrality of the market – are asserted. Future enlargement will only increase this value process. The EU is a relatively faithful expression of the capitalist ideal which has triumphed over communism and socialism. The EU's hegemony may be preferable to many states than that of the US or the USSR as it was, but is hegemony none the less. If the next century does herald a clash of civilizations then the EU represents a strong expression of western civilization.[42]

[38.] Germany and Japan are in the process of reasserting the political power which goes with their relative economic power.
[39.] See F. Duchene, 'Europe's Role in the World Peace', in R. Mayne (ed.) *Europe Tomorrow: Sixteen Europeans Look Ahead* (London, Fontana/Collins for Chatham House/PEP, 1972) pp. 32–47; H. Bull, 'Civilian Power Europe: A Contradiction in Terms?', in L. Tsoukalis (ed.), *The European Community: Past, Present and Future* (Oxford, Blackwell, 1983), pp. 151–64; A. Pijpers, 'The Twelve Out-of-area: A Civilian Power in an Uncivil World', in Pijpers *et al.*, *European Political Cooperation in the 1980s*, pp. 143–65, C. Hill, 'European Foreign Policy: Power Bloc, Civilian Model – or Flop?', in R. Rummel (ed.), *The Evolution of an International Actor: Western Europe's New Assertiveness* (Boulder, Col., Westview, 1990), pp. 31–55; Commission, *Europe in a Changing World: the External Relations of the European Community* (Luxembourg, Office for Official Publications of the European Communities, 1993).
[40.] See A. Moravcsik, 'Preferences and Power in the EC: A Liberal Inter-governmentalist Approach' (1993) 31 JCMS, 473–524; D. McGoldrick, 'A New International Economic Order for Europe?' (1994) 12 YEL 1992, 434–64. More generally see F. Fukuyama, *The End of History and the Last Man* (London, Macmillan, 1992).
[41.] See ch. 10 above.
[42.] See S.P. Huntingdon, 'The Clash of Civilisations' (1993) 72(3) Foreign Affairs, 22–49 and the critical responses to his article in 72(4) Foreign Affairs, pp. 2–26; F. Fukuyama, *The End of History and the Last Man* (London, Macmillan,1992).

The contribution of the EU to the world economic system

The EC has economic relationships with almost the whole of the world community.[43] It seems to be generally accepted that in economic terms argue the overall effect of the EC on developing countries has been positive.[44] However, it is recognized that given the degree of trade deflection, the effects on terms of trade, and other economic effects, the percentages involved are very small. There have also been identifiable effects on the GATT negotiating system where, all things considered, the EC has become a major force for liberal trading rules and reducing protectionism.[45] The EC's internal progress towards a single market had led it to press for external rules to follow a similar path.[46]

Moreover, the relative economic success of the EU is often forgotten. It is perhaps the leading world model of a market-led community. This may have stimulated other markets and reduced overall protectionism. The single market legislation brought new areas into international negotiations, especially services.[47] The feared threat of a 'fortress Europe' to a multilateral system does not appear to have transpired. However, the EU is not a philanthropist. It has its own interests and uses its economic and political power to pursue them. In the not too distant future it may also be able to pursue through a coherent European military identity.

The credibility of the EU as a major international actor

In recent decades the EU has been increasingly put under the microscope for its international activities. Their coherence and

---

43. See ch. 10 above.
44. See M. Davenport and S. Page, *Europe: 1992 and the Developing World* (London, Overseas Development Institute, 1991).
45. See E.L.M. Völker (ed.), *Protectionism and the European Community*, 2nd edn (Deventer, Kluwer, 1986); M. Hilf, F.G. Jacobs and E.-U. Petersman (eds), *The European Community and GATT*, 2nd edn (Deventer, Kluwer, 1989), pp. 125–54; J. Pelkman, 'Europe 1992: A Handmaiden to GATT', in F. Laursen (ed.), *Europe 1992: World Partner? The Internal Market and the World Political Economy* (Maastricht, EIPA, 1991); F. Laursen (ed.), *Europe 1992: World Partner?* (1991). The EU is currently taking the initiative at the WTO to open up world telecommunications markets.
46. See Hilf, 'The Single European Act and 1992: Legal Implications for Third Countries'.
47. See *Opinion 1/94* (WTO).

credibility have been questioned.[48] It is assimilated to an inter-national actor somewhere between a state and a superpower. With the demise of the USSR it is increasingly a counterpoint to the US. Hill notes that –

> the EC remains the principal interlocutor with the poor majority in the UN. With the inclusion of the Lome system, the Mediterranean preferences, and its agreements with ASEAN and the Contadora countries, the EC enjoys institutional relationships with at least 90 per cent of the world's poorer countries, who in turn constitute around 80 per cent of the membership of the United Nations.[49]

The EU can be perceived as at the centre of a series of concentric economic circles reflecting levels of privilege.[50]

In some recent situations the EU has been singled out as the most appropriate actor. It has taken a central role in the reconstruction of Central and Eastern Europe and the former USSR.[51] The EU is the largest provider of humanitarian aid in the world. The conflict in the former Yugoslavia since 1990 was for a long time perception of as a European problem that the EU should deal with.[52] The EU did in fact play a variety of roles in that conflict.[53] These included establishing an international conference to deal with it,[54] appointing an EC mediator,[55] establishing recognition guidelines,[56] making the dominant military contribution (from the member states of the EU), diplomatic and political support for the peaceful resolution of the conflict,[57]

48. See Hill, 'The Capability-Expectations Gap, or Conceptualising Europe's Inter-national Role'; M. Holland, 'Bridging the Credibility-Expectations Gap; A Case Study of the CFSP Joint Action on South Africa' (1995) 33 JCMS, 555–72.
49. Hill, 'The Capability-Expectations Gap, or Conceptualising Europe's International Role', p. 311.
50. See the range of agreements considered in ch. 10 above.
51. See L. Kramer, 'The EC's Response to the "New Eastern Europe"' (1993) 31 JCMS, 211–44; M. Maresceau and E. Montaguti, 'The Relations Between the European Union and Central and Eastern Europe: A Legal Appraisal' (1995) 32 CMLRev, 1327–67.
52. See S. Nuttall, 'The EC and Yugoslavia – *Deus ex Machina* or *Machina sine Deo*?' (1994) 32 JCMS, 11–25.
53. See G. Edwards, 'European Responses to the Yugoslav Crisis – An Interim Assessment', in Rummel (ed.), *The Evolution of an International Actor*; J. Gow, 'The Use of Coercion in the Yugoslav Crisis' (1992) The World Today, vol. 48, no. 11; T.C. Salmon, 'Testing Times for European Political Cooperation: the Gulf and Yugoslavia, 1990–92' (1992) 68(2) Int. Affairs, 233–53; Nuttall, 'The EC and Yugoslavia'.
54. See D. Owen, *Balkan Odyssey* (London, Gollancz, 1995).
55. Lord Carrington, Lord Owen and Carl Bildt in turn.
56. See C. Warbrick, 'Recognition of States' (1992) 41 ICLQ, 473–82.
57. See under CFSP, ch. 8 above.

administration of the city of Mostar.[58] Under the peace agreement of November 1994 on the former Yugoslavia, member states of the EU have played a crucial military role.[59] If the agreement works then the EU will also play a central role in the reconstruction there.[60]

Limits to the roles the EU can play

Perceived limitations tend to be derived from analogies with federal states. CFSP is a concept of enormous potential. Although it is at an early stage in its own right the member states of the EU possess between them massive diplomatic, military and financial assets that could be harnessed to it. However, given the variety of views of the member states on the evolution of the military aspects of CFSP, it may be that the EU could achieve most by resort to both internal and external institutional flexibility.[61] As the deeper identity.of the EU, if any, becomes clearer this will afford a clearer reflection of its long term objectives and interests. The EU has claimed credit for leadership in some areas, for example, in the GATT Uruguay Round and in setting the agenda for the Non-Proliferation Review. It sought to lead in resolving the crises in the former Yugoslavia and invested enormous diplomatic, economic and military resources in doing so.[62] However, the messy complexities of international relations make it unlikely that any scientific purity of foreign policy will ever be achieved by the EU, no more than it is achieved by states. Whatever the EU decides it is trying to achieve in its international relations roles, major limitations on financing and resources remain.[63] Paradoxically, it may be that constraints on national budgets compel the member states to a greater pooling and sharing of the international resources through the EU.

[58.] See M. Levy, *L'Administration De La Ville De Mostar Par L'Union Européenne* (Bruges, 1995).

[59.] See 35 ILM (1996) pp. 75–183.

[60.] In December 1994 the Commission and the World Bank held a conference to discuss reconstruction.

[61.] See. R. Rummel (ed.), *Toward Political Union: Planning a Common Foreign and Security Policy in the European Community* (Baden-Baden, Nomos, 1992).

[62.] See D. McGoldrick, 'Yugoslavia – The Responses of the International Community and of International Law' (1996) 49(2) Current Legal Problems, 375–92.

[63.] See, e.g., ch. 8, pp. 157–8 above on the difficulties raised on financing CFSP.

Reform of the EU's international relations

Issues on the agenda of the IGC which relate to the EU's international relations will include according legal personality to the EU, reform of CFSP. We have considered these matters above.[64] Reform of the principles relating to competence appears unlikely. The Reflection Group was not in favour of incorporating a catalogue of the Union's powers in the Treaty. It preferred to maintain the present system which establishes the legal basis for the Unions's actions and policies in each individual case.[65] Some members of the Reflection Group have suggested extending Article 113 to cover commercial policy as a whole and therefore including services and intellectual property. Other members regarded it as important to maintain the division of competence reflected in *Opinion 1/94*.[66] If this option is followed it has been suggested that procedures should be established to facilitate the EC and the member states speaking with one voice in international fora.[67] The procedure could be based on a Treaty provision or a ·code of conduct. Amendments have also been suggested to Article 228 concerning the possibility of swiftly giving effect to international agreements, the suspension of the application of such agreements and the procedure for establishing the Community position within joint bodies set up by such agreements.[68] Some member states have suggested incorporating the EP assent requirement in Treaty changes (Article N), Article 235 and agreements with third countries.[69] Consideration is being given to establishing a new legal basis for general agreements which are neither association agreements nor development cooperation agreements.[70] Any significant changes in the institutional balance as it affects the EU's international relations seems unlikely.

---

64. See chs. 2 and 8 respectively. See also 'General Outline'.
65. Reflection Group's Final Report, pr. 125; Progress Report on IGC, Presidency Conclusions, European Council in Florence, 21–22 June 1996, Doc. SN 300/96, Annexes, p. 5; European Parliament, Report on the Functioning of the Treaty on European Union, 19 May 1995, EP Doc. A4-0102/95, pr. 12.
66. Reflection Group's Final Report, pr. 143. See 'General Outline', ch. 11.
67. Progress Report on IGC, p. 38.
68. Ibid.
69. Reflection Group's Final Report, pr. 85; Progress Report on IGC, p. 21.
70. Progress Report on IGC, p. 39.

Identity and legitimacy

As the EC, and now the EU, has expanded and assumed a greater internal and external competence,[71] and become much more than an economic organization, it has become subject to more critical scrutiny. Indeed, in the 1990s there has developed what has been described as a 'crisis of legitimacy'.[72] Part of this takes the from of a practical and critical assessment of the EU by reference to broad standards of democratic control. Narrow discussion in terms of sovereignty has been broadened by terms such as accountability, transparency, openness, accessability, subsidiarity, the role and value of citizenship, and the role of national Parliaments.[73] However, there is also a wider consideration of some deeper philosophical issues of identity, values and constitutionalization.[74] What does the EU stand for? What does it stand against? What are its fundamental values? To what extent does the EU have a substantive social dimension? What rights, obligations, or privileges go with being a European citizen? What implications

---

[71.] See ch. 1 above.

[72.] See G. De Burca, 'The Quest for Legitimacy' (1996) 59 MLR, 349–76.

[73.] See Commission Report on the Operation of the Treaty on European Union, Brussels, 10 May 1995, SEC (95) 731 final, Preface and Part One; Progress Report on IGC, chs. I–II; N. MacCormick, 'Beyond the Sovereign State' (1993) 56 MLR, 1–18.

[74.] See F. Snyder, *New Directions in European Community Law* (London, Weidenfeld and Nicolson, 1990); J. Derrida, *The Other Heading: Reflections on Today's Europe* (Bloomington: Indiana Press, 1992); U. Hudetoft, 'National Identities and European Integration from Below: Bringing People Back In' (1994) 18 Journal of European Integration, 1–28; E.-U. Petersmann, 'The External Powers of the Community and the Union', in *The Treaty on European Union: Suggestions for Revision* (The Hague, TMC Asser Instituut Conference on European Law, Sept 1995) and 'Proposals for a New Constitution for the European Union: Building Blocks for a Constitutional Theory and Constitutionalised Law of the EU' (1995) 32 CMLRev, 1123–75; De Burca, 'The Quest for Legitimacy'; J. Shaw and G. More (eds), *New Legal Dynamics of European Union* (Oxford, OUP, 1995); I. Ward, 'In Search of European Identity' (1994) 57 MLR, 315–29; I. Ward, 'Identity and Difference: The European Union and Postmodernism', in J. Shaw and G. More (eds), *New Legal Dynamics of European Union* (Oxford, OUP, 1995); D. Wincott, 'Political Theory, Law and European Union', in Shaw and More (eds), *New Legal Dynamics of European Union*, pp. 293–311; I. Ward, *A Critical Introduction to European Law* (London, Butterworths, 1996), especially at pp. 138–72 on 'The Morality of European Law'; N. Walker, 'European Constitutionalism and European Integration' (1996) PL, 266–90; Reflection Group's Final Report, pp. I–X.

does this have for the treatment of non-EU citizens.[75] Does the EU have a heart and a soul?

As and when the EU has made progress on some of these issues of identity and values then it will inevitably be able to externalize them to much greater effect.

[75.] See D. Curtin and M. Guerts, 'Race Discrimination and the European Union Anno 1996: From Rhetoric to Legal Remedy?' (1996) 14/2 Netherlands Quarterly of Human Rights, 147–71; S. Peers, 'Towards Equality: Actual and Potential Rights of Third-Country Nationals in the European Union' (1996) 33 CMLRev, 7–50.

Further reading

Carlsnaes, W. and Smith, S., *European Foreign Policy – The EC and Changing Perspectives in Europe*, London, Sage, 1994

Commission, *Relations between the European Community and International Organizations*, Luxembourg, Office for Official Publications of the European Communities, 1989

Cremona, M., 'The Doctrine of Exclusivity and the Position of Mixed Agreements in the External Relations of the European Community' (1982) 2 OJLS, 393–428

Emiliou, N. and O'Keeffe, D. (eds), *The European Union and World Trade Law – After the GATT Uruguay Round*, Chichester, Wiley, 1996

Groux, J. and Manin, P., *The European Communities in the International Order*, Brussels, EC Commission, European Perspective Series, 1985

Macleod, I., Hendry, I. and Hyett, S., *The External Relations of the European Communities: A Manual of Law and Practice*, Oxford, OUP, 1996

Maresceau, M. (ed.), *The European Community's Commercial Policy after 1992: The Legal Dimension*, Dordrecht, Nijhoff, 1993

Megret, J. *et al.* (eds), *Le droit de la Communauté économique européenne, vol. xii: relations extérieures*, by Louis, J.V. and Bruckner, P., Brussels, Editions de l'Université de Bruxelles, 1980

Neuwahl, N., 'Joint Participation in International Treaties and the exercise of power by the EEC and its Member States: Mixed Agreements' (1991) 28 CMLRev, 717–40

Nuttall, S., *European Political Cooperation*, Oxford, Clarendon Press, 1992

O'Keeffe, D. and Schermers, H.G. (eds), *Mixed Agreements*, Dordrecht, Nijhoff, 1983

O'Keeffe, D. and Twomey, P. (eds) *Legal Issues of the Maastricht Treaty*, Chichester, Wiley Chancery, 1994

Pappas, S.A. and Vanhoonacker, S. (eds), *The European Union's Common Foreign and Security Policy: The Challenges of the Future*, Maastricht, EIPA, 1996

Pescatore, P., 'External Relations in the Case Law of the Court of Justice of the European Communities' (1979) 16 CMLRev, 615–45

Pescatore, P., 'Les Relations Extèrieures des Communautes Européennes', 103 *Recueil Des Cours* (1961–II), 1-244

Timmermans, C.W.A. and Völker, E.L.M. (eds), *Division of Powers between the European Communities and their Member States in the Field of External Relations*, Deventer, Kluwer, 1981

Useful Websites

European Commission, EUROPA: on European Union Institutions:
  http://europa.eu.int

European Commission, DGI:
  http://europa.eu.int/en/comm/dg01/dg.htm

European Commission, DGIA:
  http://europa.eu.int/en/comm/dg1a/dg1ahome.htm

European Commission, DGIB
  http://europa.eu.int/en/comm/dg1b/index.htm

European Court of Justice:
  http://www.europa.eu.int/cj/en

Presidency:
  If a Presidency has a home page the website will be available from the Presidency Information Service.

Bibliography

Addo, M., 'A Critical Analysis of the Perennial International Economic Law Problems of the EEC-ACP Relationship' (1990) 33 GYIL 1990, 37–68

Allen, D., 'Foreign Policy at the European Level: Beyond the Nation-State?', in W. Wallace and W. Paterson (eds), *Foreign Policy Making in Western Europe*, Farnborough, Saxon House, 1978, pp. 135–54

Allen, D., Rummel, R. and Wessels, W. (eds), *European Political Cooporation*, London, Butterworths, 1982

Allott, P., 'Adherence To and Withdrawal From Mixed Agreements', in D. O'Keeffe and H.G. Schermers (eds), *Mixed Agreements*, Dordrecht, Nijhoff, 1983, pp. 97–121

Allott, P., *Eunomia – A New World Order for a New World*, Oxford, OUP, 1990

Allott, P., 'The European Community is Not the True European Community' (1991) 101 Yale LJ, 2485–500

Anderson, D., 'The Straddling Stocks Agreement of 1995 – An Initial Assessment' (1996) 45 ICLQ, 463–75

Anon., Editorial, 'The Aftermath of Opinion 1/94 or How to Ensure Unity of Representation for Joint Competences' (1995) 32 CMLRev, 385–90

Appella, A., 'Constitutional Aspects of Opinion 1/94 of the ECJ Concerning the WTO Agreement' (1996) 45 ICLQ, 440–62

Arnull, A., 'The European Court and Judicial Objectivity: A Reply to Professor Hartley' (1996) 112 LQR, 411–23

Arnull, A., 'The Scope of the Common Commercial Policy: A Coda on Opinion 1/94', in N. Emiliou and D. O'Keeffe (eds), *The European Union and World Trade Law – After the GATT Uruguay Round*, Chichester, Wiley, 1996, pp. 343–60

Auvret-Finck, J., 'L'Avis Relatifs A La Convention No. 170 De L'OIT' (1995) 31 CDE, 443–60

Balekjian, W.H., 'Mixed Agreements: Complementary and Concurrent Competencies', in D. O'Keeffe and H.G. Schermers (eds), *Mixed Agreements*, Dordrecht, Nijhoff, 1983, pp. 141–51

Balfour, J., 'Freedom to Provide Air Transport Services in the EEC' (1989) 14 ELRev, 30–46

Barav, A., 'The Division of External Relations Powers between the European Community and the Member States in the Case-law of the Court of Justice, in C.W.A. Timmermans and E.L.M. Völker (eds), *Division of Powers between the European Communities and their Member States in the Field of External Relations*, Deventer, Kluwer, 1981, pp. 29–64

Baring, A. (ed.), *Germany's Position in the New Europe*, Oxford, Berg, 1994

Barnard, C., 'The External Dimension of Community Social Policy: The Ugly Duckling of External Relations', in N. Emiliou and D. O'Keeffe (eds), *The European Union and World Trade Law – After the GATT Uruguay Round*, Chichester, Wiley, 1996, pp. 149–64

Beaumont, P. and Moir, G., 'Brussels Convention II: A New Private International Law Instrument in Family Matters for the European Union or the European Community' (1995) 20 ELRev, 268–88

Bebr, G., 'Agreements Concluded by the Community and their Possible Direct Effect: From International Fruit Company to Kupferberg' (1983) 20 CMLRev, 35–73

Bengoetxea, J., *The Legal Reasoning of the European Court of Justice: Towards a European Jurisprudence*, Oxford, OUP, 1993

Bercusson, B., *European Labour Law*, London, Butterworths, 1996

Bermann, G.A., Goebel, R.J., Davey, W.J. and Fox, E.M., *Cases and Materials on European Community Law*, St Paul, Minnesota, West, 1993

Bieber, R., 'Democratic Control of European Foreign Policy' (1990) 1/2 EJIL, 148–73

Bieber, R. and Monar, J., *Justice and Home Affairs in the European Union: The Development of the Third Pillar*, Brussels, European Inter-University Press, 1994

Bindman, G., 'The Starting Point' (1995) 145 NLJ, 62–3

Bleckmann, A., 'The Mixed Agreements of the EEC in Public International Law', in D. O'Keeffe and H.G. Schermers (eds), *Mixed Agreements*, Dordrecht, Nijhoff, 1983, pp. 155–65

Bleckmann, A., 'The Personal Jurisdiction of the European Community' (1980) 17 CMLRev, 467–85

Bohr, S., 'Sanctions by the United Nations Security Council and the European Community' (1993) 4 EJIL, 256–68

Booss, D. and Forman, J., 'Enlargement: Legal and Procedural Aspects' (1995) 32 CMLRev, 95–130

Bot, B.R., 'Cooperation in the Missions of the EC in Third Countries: European Diplomacy in the making' (1984) 1 LIEI, 149–69

Bot, B.R., 'Negotiating Community Agreements: Procedure and Practice' (1970) 7 CMLRev, 286–310

Boulouis, J., 'Le Droit Des Communautés Européennes Dans Ses Rapports Avec Le Droit International Général' (1992) 235 *Receuil Des Cours* (1992–IV), 9–80

Bourgeois, J., 'Some Comments on the Practice', in C.W.A. Timmermans and E.L.M. Völker (eds), *Division of Powers between the European Communities and their Member States in the Field of External Relations*, Deventer, Kluwer, 1981, pp. 97–110

Bourgeois, J., 'Effects of International Agreements in European Community Law: Are the Dice Cast?' (1984) 82 MichLRev., 1250–73

Bourgeois, J., 'The Common Commercial Policy: Scope and Nature of the Powers', in E.L.M. Völker (ed.) *Protectionism and the European Community*, 2nd edn, Deventer, Kluwer, 1986, pp. 1–16

Bourgeois, J., 'The EC in the WTO and Advisory Opinion 1/94: An Echternach Procession' (1995) 32 CMLRev, 763–87

Bradley, K., 'The European Court and the Legal Basis of Community Legislation' (1988) 13 ELRev, 379–402

Brewin, C., 'The European Community: A Union of States without Unity of Government' (1987) 26 JCMS, 1–25

Brinkhorst, L.J., 'Permanent Missions of the EC in Third Countries: European Diplomacy in the Making' (1984) 1 LIEI, 23–33

Brinkhorst, L.J., 'The European Community at UNCED: Lessons to be Drawn for the Future', in D. Curtin and T. Heukels (eds), *Institutional Dynamics of European Integration: Essays in Honour of H.G. Schermers*, vol. II, Dordrecht, Nijhoff, 1994, pp. 609–17

Brooks, D., 'Yanks go home, Europe's a bore', *The Sunday Times*, 7 July 1996, News Review, p. 9

Bruckner, P., 'The EC and the United Nations' (1990) 1/2 EJIL, 174–92

Bruggemann, W., 'Europol: Wanted or Tolerated?' in *The Treaty on European Union: Suggestions for Revision*, TMC Asser Instituut Conference on European Law, The Hague, September 1995

Bull, H., 'Civilian Power Europe: A Contradiction in Terms?', in L. Tsoukalis (ed.), *The European Community: Past, Present and Future*, Oxford, Blackwell, 1983, pp. 151–64

Burrows, F., 'The effects of the main cases of the Court of Justice in the field of the external competences on the conduct of member states', in C.W.A. Timmermans and E.L.M. Völker (eds), *Division of Powers between the European Communities and their Member States in the Field of External Relations*, Deventer, Kluwer, 1981, pp. 111–25

Cameron, F., 'The European Union and the OSCE: Future Roles and Challenges' (1995) 6(2) Helsinki Monitor, 21–31

Campbell, I., 'From the "Personal Union" between England and Scotland in 1603 to the European Communities Act 1972 and Beyond – Enduring Legal Problems from an Historical Viewpoint', in B.S. Jackson and D. McGoldrick, *Legal Visions of the New Europe*, London, Graham and Trotman/Nijhoff, 1993, pp. 37–104

Carlsnaes, W. and Smith, S., *European Foreign Policy – The EC and Changing Perspectives in Europe*, London, Sage, 1994

Chalmers, D., 'Legal Basis and External Relations of the European Community', in N. Emiliou and D. O'Keeffe (eds), *The European Union and World Trade Law – After the GATT Uruguay Round*, Chichester, Wiley, 1996, pp. 46–61

Charles Le Bihan, D. and Lebullenger, J., 'Common Maritime Transport Policy: Bilateral Agreements and the Freedom to Provide Services' (1990) 9 YEL 1989, 209–23

Checcini, P., *Research on the Cost of 'Non-Europe'*, Luxembourg, Office for Official Publications, 1988

Cheyne, I., 'International Agreements and the European Community Legal System' (1994) 18 ELRev, 581–98

Churchill, R. and Foster, N., 'European Community Law and Prior Treaty Obligations of Member States: The Spanish Fisherman's Cases' (1987) 36 ICLQ, 504–24

Clarke, M., *British External Policy-making in the 1990s*, Basingstoke, Macmillan, 1992

Clarke, M., 'Future Security Threats and Challenges', in S.A. Pappas and S. Vanhoonacker (eds), *The European Union's Common Foreign and Security Policy: The Challenges of the Future*, Maastricht, EIPA, 1996

Close, G., 'Harmonisation of Laws: Use or Abuse of the Powers under the EEC Treaty?' (1978) 3 ELRev, 461–81

Close, G., 'Self-restraint by the EEC in the Exercise of its External Powers' (1982) 1 YEL 1981, 45–68

Close, G., 'Subordination Clauses in Mixed Agreements' (1985) 34 ICLQ, 382–91

Close, G., 'External Relations in the Air Transport Sector: Air Transport Policy or the Common Commercial Policy?' (1990) 27 CMLRev, 108–27

Commission, 'Completing the Internal Market' (1985) COM(85) 310

Commission, *Relations between the European Community and International Organizations*, Luxembourg, Office for Official Publications of the European Communities, 1989

Commission, *Europe in a Changing World: the External Relations of the European Community*, Luxembourg, Office for the Official Publications of the European Communities, 1993

Commission, Report on the Operation of the Treaty on European Union, Brussels, 10 May 1995, SEC (95) 731 final

Commission, *Corps Diplomatique accrédité auprès des Communautés européennes et representations auprès de la Commission*, Brussels, June 1996

Corbett, R., Jacobs, F. and Shackleton, M., *The European Parliament*, 3rd edn, London, Cartermill, 1995

Coreu, G., *Taming Commodity Markets*, Manchester, MUP, 1992

Cosgrove, C. and Laurent, P.H., 'The Unique Relationship: The European Community and the ACP', in J. Redmond, *The External Relations of the European Community: the International Response to 1992*, Basingstoke, Macmillan, 1992, pp. 120–37

Costonis, J.J., 'The Treaty Making Power of the EEC: The Perception of a Decade' (1967–68) 5 CMLRev, 421–57

Council, Report of the Council of Ministers on the Functioning of the TEU, Luxembourg/Brussels, 10 April 1995, Doc. 5082/95

Craig, P. and De Burca, G., *EC Law – Text, Cases and Materials*, Oxford, OUP, 1995

Cremona, M., 'The Doctrine of Exclusivity and the Position of Mixed Agreements in the External Relations of the European Community' (1982) 2 OJLS, 393–428

Cremona, M., 'The Completion of the Internal Market and the Incomplete Commercial Policy of the European Community' (1990) 15 ELRev, 283–97

Cremona, M., 'The Common Foreign and Security Policy of the European Union and the External Relations Power of the European Community', in D. O'Keeffe and P. Twomey (eds), *Legal Issues of the Maastricht Treaty*, Chichester, Wiley Chancery, 1994, pp. 247–58

Cremona, M., 'The "Dynamic and Homogenous" EEA: Byzantine Structures and Variable Geometry' (1994) 19 ELRev, 508–26

Cremona, M., 'Human Rights and Democracy Clauses in the EC's Trade Agreements', in N. Emiliou and D. O'Keeffe (eds), *The European Union and World Trade Law – After the GATT Uruguay Round*, Chichester, Wiley, 1996, pp. 62–77

Cross, E.D., 'Pre-Emption of Member State Law in the European Community: A Framework for Analysis' (1992) 29 CMLRev, 447–72

Curtin, D., 'The Constitutional Structure of the Union: A Europe of Bits and Pieces' (1993) 30 CMLRev, 17–69

Curtin, D. and Guerts, M., 'Race Discrimination and the European Union Anno 1996: From Rhetoric to Legal Remedy?' (1996) 14/2 Netherlands Quarterly of Human Rights, 147–71

Curtin, D. and Heukels, T. (eds), *Institutional Dynamics of European Integration: Essays in Honour of H.G. Schermers*, vol. II, Dordrecht, Nijhoff, 1994

Curtin, D. and van Ooik, R., 'Denmark and the Edinburgh Summit: Maastricht Without Tears: A Legal Analysis', in D. O'Keeffe and P. Twomey (eds), *Legal Issues of the Maastricht Treaty*, Chichester, Wiley Chancery, 1994, pp. 349–65

Cutileiro, J., 'CFSP and the Role of the Western European Union (WEU)', in S.A. Pappas and S. Vanhoonacker (eds), *The European Union's Common Foreign and Security Policy: The Challenges of the Future*, Maastricht, EIPA, 1996

Dashwood, A., *Reviewing Maastricht: Issues for the 1996 IGC*, London, Sweet and Maxwell/Law Books in Europe, 1996

Dashwood, A., 'The Limits of European Community Powers' (1996) 21 ELRev, 113–28

Davenport, M. with Page, S., *Europe: 1992 and the Developing World*, London, Overseas Development Institute, 1991

Davies, P., 'The EC/Canadian Fisheries Dispute in the Northwest Atlantic' (1995) 44 ICLQ, 927–39

Davies, P., 'The European Environment Agency' (1995) 14 YEL 1994, 313–49

De Burca, G., 'The Quest for Legitimacy' (1996) 59 MLR, 349–76

Dehousse, R. (ed.), *Europe After Maastricht: An Ever Closer Union?*, Munich, Law Books in Europe, 1994

Dehousse, F. and Katelyne, G., 'Le Traité De Maastricht et les Relations Extérieures de la Communauté Européenne' (1994) 5 EJIL, 151–72

Demaret, P., 'Environmental Policy and Commercial Policy: The Emergence of Trade-Related Environmental Measures', in M. Maresceau (ed.), *The European Community's Commercial Policy after 1992: The Legal Dimension*, Dordrecht, Nijhoff, 1993, pp. 305–86

Demaret, P., 'The Treaty Framework', in D. O'Keeffe and P. Twomey (eds), *Legal Issues of the Maastricht Treaty*, Chichester, Wiley Chancery, 1994, pp. 3–11

Demiray, P., 'Intellectual Property and the External Power of the European Community: The New Dimension' (1994) 16 Mich.JIL, 187–239

Den Boer, M., 'Justice and Home Affairs Cooperation in the European Union: Current Issues', 1996/1 EIPASCOPE, 12–16, Maastricht, EIPA

Denza, E., 'Groping Towards Europe's Foreign Policy', in D. Curtin and T. Heukels (eds), *Institutional Dynamics of European Integration: Essays in Honour of H.G. Schermers*, vol. II, Dordrecht, Nijhoff (1994), pp. 575–93

Denza, E., 'The Community as a Member of International Organizations', in N. Emiliou and D. O'Keeffe (eds), *The European Union and World Trade Law – After the GATT Uruguay Round*, Chichester, Wiley, 1996, pp. 3–15

Derrida, J., *The Other Heading: Reflections on Today's Europe*, translated by P.A. Brault and M. Naas, Bloomington, Indiana University Press, 1992

Dinan, D., *An Ever Closer Union?*, London, Macmillan, 1994

Dolmans, J.F.M., *Problems of Mixed Agreements*, The Hague, Asser Instituut, 1985

Duchene, F., 'Europe's Role in the World Peace', in R. Mayne (ed.), *Europe Tomorrow: Sixteen Europeans Look Ahead*, London, Fontana/Collins for Chatham House/PEP, 1972, pp. 32–47

Duff, A., Pinder J. and Pryce R. (eds), *Maastricht and Beyond: Building the European Union*, London, Routledge, 1994

Duke, S., 'The Second Death (or the Second Coming?) of the WEU' (1996) 34(2) JCMS, 167–90

Duthiel, J. De La Rochere, 'L'ère des compétences partagées a propos de l'entendue des compétences extérieures de la communauté européenne', (1995) RMC, 461–70

Eaton, M.R., 'Common Foreign and Security Policy', in D. O'Keeffe and P. Twomey (eds), *Legal Issues of the Maastricht Treaty*, Chichester, Wiley Chancery, 1994, pp. 215–25

Eaton, M.R., 'Common Foreign and Security Policy (non-security aspects)', in *The Treaty on European Union: Suggestions for Revision*, TMC Asser Instituut Conference on European Law, The Hague, September 1995

Edwards, G., 'Europe and the Falklands Crisis' (1984) 22 JCMS, 295–313

Edwards, G., 'Interaction Between European Political Cooperation and the European Community' (1988) 7 YEL 1987, 211–49

Edwards, G., 'European Responses to the Yugoslav Crisis – an Interim Assessment', in R. Rummel (ed.), *The Evolution of an International Actor: Western Europe's New Assertiveness*, Boulder, Col., Westview, 1990

Edwards, G., 'Common Foreign and Security Policy' (1994) 13 YEL 1993, 497–509

Edwards, G., 'Common Foreign and Security Policy' (1995) 14 YEL 1994, 541–56

Edwards, G. and Nuttall, S., 'Common Foreign and Security Policy', in A. Duff, J. Pinder and R. Pryce (eds), *Maastricht and Beyond: Building the European Union*, London, Routledge, 1994, pp. 84–103

Edwards, G. and Regelsberger, E. (eds), *Europe's Global Links*, London, St. Martin's, 1990

Eeckhout, P., *The European Internal Market and International Trade*, Oxford, Clarendon Press, 1994

Ehlermann, C.-D., 'Mixed Agreements: A List of Problems', in D. O'Keeffe and H.G. Schermers (eds), *Mixed Agreements*, Dordrecht, Nijhoff, 1983, pp. 3–21

Ehlermann, C.-D., 'The Scope of Article 113 of the EEC Treaty', in *Mélanges offerts à Pierre-Henri Teitgen*, Paris, Pedone, 1984, 148–69

EIPA, 'The European Union's Common Foreign and Security Policy: The Positions of the Main Actors', Documentary Collection from Conference on The European Union's Common Foreign and Security Policy: The Challenges of the Future, held at EIPA, Maastricht, 19–20 October 1995

El-Agraa, A., 'Japan's Reaction to the Single Internal Market', in J. Redmond, *The External Relations of the European Community: the International Response to 1992*, Basingstoke, Macmillan, 1992, pp. 12–30

Elles, Baroness, 'The Role of EU Institutions in External Trade Policy', in N. Emiliou and D. O'Keeffe (eds), *The European Union and World*

Trade Law – After the GATT Uruguay Round, Chichester, Wiley, 1996, pp. 19–30

Emiliou, N., 'Subsidiarity: Panacea or Fig Leaf?', in D. O'Keeffe and P. Twomey (eds), *Legal Issues of the Maastricht Treaty*, Chichester, Wiley Chancery, 1994, pp. 65–83

Emiliou, N., 'Towards a clearer demarcation line? The division of external relations power between the Community and the Member States' (1994) 18 ELRev, 76–86

Emiliou, N., 'The Allocation of Competence Between the EC and its Member States in the Sphere of External Relations', in N. Emiliou and D. O'Keeffe (eds), *The European Union and World Trade Law – After the GATT Uruguay Round*, Chichester, Wiley, 1996, pp. 31–45

Emiliou, N. and O'Keeffe, D. (eds), *The European Union and World Trade Law – After the GATT Uruguay Round*, Chichester, Wiley, 1996

European Parliament, Report of the European Parliament on the Functioning of the Treaty on European Union with a View to the 1996 Inter-governmental Conference – Implementation and Development of the Union, 19 May 1995, EP Doc.A4–0102/95

European Political Cooperation Documentation Bulletin, Bonn, European Commission, 8 vols to date

Everling, U., 'Reflections on the Structure of the European Union' (1992) 29 CMLRev, 1053–77

Feenstra, J.J., 'A Survey of the Mixed Agreements and their Participation Clauses' in D. O'Keeffe and H.G. Schermers (eds), *Mixed Agreements*, Dordrecht, Nijhoff, 1983, pp. 207–49

Figueiredo Lopes, A.J., 'La Dimension Méditerranéenne De La Sécurité Européenne', in S.A. Pappas and S. Vanhoonacker (eds), *The European Union's Common Foreign and Security Policy: The Challenges of the Future*, Maastricht, EIPA, 1996

Fink-Hooijer, F., 'The CFSP of the EU' (1994) 5 EJIL, 173–98

Fischer, T.C. and Neff, S., 'Some Thoughts About European "Federalism" ' (1995) 44 ICLQ, 904–15

Freeman, E., 'The Division of Powers Between the European Communities and the Member States' (1977) 30 Current Legal Problems, 159–73

Freestone, D. and Davidson, S., 'Community Competence and Part III of the Single European Act' (1986) 23 CMLRev, 793–801

Frid, R., 'The EEC: A Member of a Specialized Agency of the UN' (1993) 4 EJIL, 239–55

Fukuyama, F., *The End of History and the Last Man*, London, Macmillan, 1992

Gabriel, J.M., 'The Integration of European Security: A Functionalist Analysis' (1995) 50 Aussen-Wirtschaft, 135–59

Gaja, G., 'The European Community's Rights and Obligations under Mixed Agreements', in D. O'Keeffe and H.G. Schermers (eds), *Mixed Agreements*, Dordrecht, Nijhoff, 1983, pp. 133–40

Gaudissart, M-A., 'La Portée des avis 1/91 et 1/92 de la Cour de justice des Communautés européennes relatif à la création de l'espace économique européen: entre autonomie et homogénéité: L'ordre juridique communautaire en péril . . .' (1992) RMUE, 121–36

'General Outline for a draft revision of the Treaties', prepared by the Irish Presidency, CONF 2500/96, Brussels, 5 December 1996

Gosalbo Bono, R., 'The International Powers of the European Parliament, The Democratic Deficit and the Treaty on European Union' (1994) 12 YEL 1992, 85–138

Govaere, I., 'Intellectual Property Protection and Commercial Policy', in M. Maresceau (ed.) *The European Community's Commercial Policy after 1992: The Legal Dimension*, Dordrecht, Nijhoff, 1993, pp. 197–222

Govaere, I. and Eeckhout, P., 'On Dual Use Goods and Dualist Case Law: The *Aimé Richardt* Judgment on Export Controls' (1992) 29 CMLRev, 941–66

Gow, J., 'The Use of Coercion in the Yugoslav Crisis', *The World Today*, vol. 48, 1992, No. 11

Grimes, J.M., 'Conflicts Between EC Law and International Treaty Obligations: A Case Study of the German Telecommunications Dispute' (1994) 35 Harv.ILJ, 535–64

Group of Experts on CFSP, High Level Group of Experts on the CFSP, First Report, 'European Security Policy Towards 2000: Ways and Means to Establish Genuine Creditability', Brussels, 19 December 1994

Groux, J., 'Le parallèlisme des compétences internes et externes de la Communauté économique européenne' (1978) Cahiers de droit européenne', 3–32

Groux, J., 'Mixed Negotiations', in D. O'Keeffe and H.G. Schermers (eds), *Mixed Agreements*, Dordrecht, Nijhoff, 1983, pp. 87–96

Groux, J. and Manin, P., *The European Communities in the International Order*, Brussels, EC Commission, European Perspective Series, 1985

Haanappel, P., 'The External Aviation Relations of the European Economic Community and of EEC Member States into the Twenty-First Century' (1989) 14 Air Law, 122–46

Hagleitner, T., 'Financing the Common Foreign and Security Policy – A Step Towards Communitarisation or Institutional Deadlock' (1995) CFSP Forum 2, 6

Haigh, N., 'The EC and International Environmental Policy', in A. Hurrell and B. Kingsbury, *The International Politics of the Environment*, Oxford, OUP, 1992

Halsbury's Laws of England, 4th edn, 'External Relations', vol. 51, pp. 477–98

Ham, A.D., 'International Cooperation in the Anti-Trust Field and in particular between the United States of America and the Commission of the European Communities' (1993) 30 CMLRev, 571–98

Hancher, L., 'Constitutionalism, the Community Court and International Law' (1994) 25 NYIL, 259–98

Hardy, M., 'Opinion 1/76 of the Court of Justice' (1977) 14 CMLRev, 561–600

Harris, D.J., O'Boyle, M. and Warbrick, C., *Law of the European Convention on Human Rights*, London, Butterworths, 1995

Harrison, V., 'Subsidiarity in Article 3b of the EC Treaty – Gobbledegook or Justiciable Principle' (1996) 45 ICLQ, 431–9

Hartley, T.C., 'International Agreements and the Community Legal System: Some Recent Developments' (1983) 8 ELRev, 383–92

Hartley, T.C., *The Foundations of European Community Law*, 2nd edn, Oxford, Clarendon Press, 1988

Hartley, T.C., 'Constitutional and Legal Aspects of the Maastricht Agreement' (1993) 42 ICLQ, 213–37

Hartley, T.C., *The Foundations of European Community Law*, 3rd edn, Oxford, Clarendon Press, 1994

Hartley, T.C., 'The European Court, Judicial Objectivity and the Constitution of the European Union' (1996) 112 LQR, 95–109

Hendry, I., 'The Third Pillar of Maastricht: Cooperation in the Fields of Justice and Home Affairs' (1993) 36 GYIL 1993, 295–327

Higgins, R., *Problems and Process – International Law and How We Use It*, Oxford, OUP, 1994

Hilf, M., 'The Single European Act and 1992: Legal Implications for Third Countries' (1990) 1 EJIL, 89–117

Hilf, M., 'The ECJ's Opinion on the WTO – No Surprise, but Wise?' (1995) 6 EJIL, 245–59

Hilf, M., Jacobs, F.G. and Petersmann, E.-U. (eds), *The European Community and GATT*, 2nd edn, Deventer, Kluwer, 1989

Hill, C. (ed.), *National Foreign Policies and European Political Cooperation*, London, Allen and Unwin, 1983

Hill, C., 'European Foreign Policy: Power Bloc, Civilian Model – or Flop?', in R. Rummel (ed.), *The Evolution of an International Actor: Western Europe's New Assertiveness*, Boulder, Co. Westview 1990, pp. 31–55

Hill, C., 'The Capability-Expectations Gap, or Conceptualising Europe's International Role' (1993) 31 JCMS, 305–28

Hirsh, M., 'The 1995 Trade Agreement between the European Communities and Israel: Three Unresolved Issues' (1996) I EFARev, 87–123

Holland, M. (ed.), *The Future of European Political Cooperation*, London, Macmillan, 1991

Holland, M., 'Bridging the Credibility-Expectations Gap: A Case Study of the CFSP Joint Action on South Africa' (1995) 33 JCMS, 555–72

Holland, M. (ed.), *Common Foreign and Security Policy: The Record and the Reforms*, London, Pinter, forthcoming 1997

Hosoya, C., 'Relations between the European Communities and Japan' (1979) 18 JCMS, 159–74

House of Lords Select Committee on the European Communities, *External Competence of the European Communities*, 16th Report, HL 236, 1984–85

House of Lords Select Committee on the European Communities, *Conduct of the Community's External Aviation Relations*, 9th Report, HL 39, 1990–91

House of Lords Select Committee on the European Communities, *Human Rights Reexamined*, 3rd Report, HL 10, 1992–93

Hudetoft, U., 'National Identities and European Integration from Below: Bringing People Back In' (1994) 18 Journal of European Integration, 1–28

Hufbauer, G.C. (ed.), *Europe 1992: An American Perspective*, Washington, DC, The Brookings Institute, 1990

Huntingdon, S.P., 'The Clash of Civilisations' (1993) 72(3) Foreign Affairs, 22–49

Hurd, D., 'Developing the CFSP' (1994) 70(3) Int. Affairs, 421–8

Ifestos, P., *European Political Corporation*, Aldershot, Avebery, 1987

Jackson, J., 'Status of Treaties in Domestic Legal Systems: A Policy Analysis' (1992) 86 AJIL, 310–40

Jackson, B.S. and McGoldrick, D., *Legal Visions of the New Europe*, London, Graham and Trotman/ Nijhoff, 1993

Jacobs, F., *Human Rights in the European Union*', Durham, Durham Law Institute, 1994

Jacobs, F., 'Judicial Review of Commercial Policy Measures After the Uruguay Round', in N. Emiliou and D. O'Keeffe (eds), *The European Union and World Trade Law – After the GATT Uruguay Round*, Chichester, Wiley 1996, pp. 329–42

Jacobs, F. and Roberts, S. (eds), *The Effect of Treaties in Domestic Law*, London, Sweet and Maxwell, 1987, pp. 171–95

Jennings, R.Y. and Watts, A. (eds), *Oppenheim's International Law*, 9th edn, 2 vols, Harlow, Longman, 1992

Justus Lipsius (a pseudonym), 'The 1996 Intergovernmental Conference' (1995) 20 ELRev, 235–67

Kapteyn, P.J.G. and Verloren Van Themaat, P., *Introduction to the Law of the European Communities*, 2nd edn, Lawrence W. Gormley (ed.), Deventer, Kluwer, 1990

Kennedy, D. and Webb, D., 'The Limits of Integration: Eastern Europe and the European Communities' (1993) 30 CMLRev, 1095–117

Kingston, J. 'External Relations of the European Community – External Capacity versus Internal Competence' (1995) 44 ICLQ, 659–70

Kissinger, H., *Diplomacy*, New York, Simon and Schuster, 1994

Klabbers, J., 'Informal Instruments Before the European Court of Justice' (1994) 31 CMLRev, 997–1023

Koers, A.W., 'The External Authority of the EEC in Regard to Marine Fisheries' (1977) 14 CMLRev, 269–301

Kramer, H., 'The EC's Response to the "New Eastern Europe" ' (1993) 31 JCMS, 211–44

Kramer, L., *EC Treaty and Environmental Law*, 2nd edn, London, Sweet and Maxwell, 1994

Krenzler, H.G. and Schomaker, A., 'A New Transatlantic Agenda' (1996) 1 EFARev, 9–28

Kronenberger, V., 'Does the EFTA Court Interpret the EEA Agreement as if it were the EC Treaty? Some questions raised by the Restamark Judgment' (1996) 45 ICLQ, 198–212

Kuijper, P.J., 'Community Sanctions against Argentina: Lawfulness under Community and International Law', in D. O'Keeffe and H.G. Schermers (eds), *Essays in European Law and Integration*, Deventer, Kluwer, 1982, pp. 141–66

Kuijper, P.J., 'Trade Sanctions, Security and Human Rights and Commercial Policy', in M. Maresceau (ed.), *The European Community's Commercial Policy after 1992: The Legal Dimension*, Dordrecht, Nijhoff, 1993, pp. 387–422

Kuijper, P.J., 'The Conclusion and Implementation of the Uruguay Round Results by the EC' (1995) 6 EJIL, 222–44

Kuyper, P.J., 'The Community and State Succession in Respect of Treaties', in D. Curtin and T. Heukels (eds), *Institutional Dynamics of European Integration: Essays in Honour of H.G. Schermers*, vol II, Dordrecht, Nijhoff, 1994, pp. 619–40

Lasok, K.P.E., *The European Court of Justice*, London, Butterworths, 1994

Laursen, F. (ed.), *Europe 1992: World Partner? The Internal Market and the World Political Economy*, Maastricht, European Institute of Public Administration, 1991

Levy, M., *L'Administration De La Ville De Mostar Par L'Union Européenne*, Bruges, 1995

Lindemann, B., 'European Political Cooperation at the UN', in D. Allen, R. Rummel and W. Wessels (eds), *European Political Cooperation*, London, Butterworths, 1982, pp. 110–33

Lodge, J., 'New Zealand, Australia and 1992', in J. Redmond, *The External Relations of the European Community: the International Response to 1992*, Basingstoke, Macmillan, 1992, 161–76

London Report, 'Report on European Political Cooperation', adopted by the Foreign Ministers of the Ten Member States of the European Community, 1981.

Louis, J.V., *The Community Legal Order*, 2nd edn, Brussels, European Commission, 1990

Ludlow, P. and Ersboell, N., *Towards 1996: the Agenda of the Intergovernmental Conference*, Brussels, Centre for European Policy Studies, 1994

MacCormick, N., 'Beyond the Sovereign State' (1993) 56 MLR, 1–18

Macleod, I., Hendry, I. and Hyett, S., *The External Relations of the European Communities: A Manual of Law and Practice*, Oxford, OUP, 1996

Manin, P., 'The European Communities and the Vienna Convention on the Law of Treaties between States and International Organizations or between International Organizations' (1987) 24 CMLRev, 457–81

Mansfield, E. and Snyder, J., 'Democratization and War' (1995) 74(3) Foreign Affairs, 79–97

Marais, E.A. (ed.), *European Citizenship*, Maastricht, EIPA, 1994

Maresceau, M. (ed.), *The Political and Legal Framework of Trade Relations Between the European Community and Eastern Europe*, Dordrecht, Nijhoff, 1989

Maresceau, M., 'The European Community, Eastern Europe and the ACP', in J. Redmond, *The External Relations of the European Community: the International Response to 1992*, Basingstoke, Macmillan, 1992, pp. 93–119

Maresceau, M. (ed.), *The European Community's Commercial Policy after 1992: The Legal Dimension*, Dordrecht, Nijhoff, 1993

Maresceau, M. and Montaguti, E., 'The Relations Between the European Union and Central and Eastern Europe: A Legal Appraisal' (1995) 32 CMLRev, 1327–67

Martin, L. and Roper, J. (eds), *Towards a Common Defence Policy*, Paris, WEU/ Institute for Strategic Studies, 1994

Mathijsen, P.S.R.F., *A Guide to European Union Law*, 6th edn, London, Sweet and Maxwell, 1995

McGoldrick, D., *The Human Rights Committee*, Oxford, OUP, 1991 and 1994

McGoldrick, D., 'The Development of the Conference on Security and Cooperation in Europe – from Process to Institution', in B.S. Jackson and D. McGoldrick, *Legal Visions of the New Europe*, London, Graham and Trotman/Nijhoff, 1993, pp. 135–82

McGoldrick, D., 'A New International Economic Order for Europe?' (1994) 12 YEL 1992, 434–64

McGoldrick, D., 'Yugoslavia – The Responses of the International Community and of International Law' (1996) 49(2) Current Legal Problems, 375–92

Meessen, K., 'The Application of Rules of Public International Law within Community Law' (1976) 13 CMLRev, 485–501

Megret, J. *et al.* (eds), *Le droit de la Communauté économique européenne, vol. xii: relations extérieures*, by Louis, J.V. and Bruckner, P., Brussels, Editions de l'Université de Bruxelles, 1980

Mengozzi, P., *EC Law*, London, Graham and Trotman/Kluwer, 1992

Mengozzi, P., 'Trade in Services and Commercial Policy', in M. Maresceau (ed.), *The European Community's Commercial Policy after 1992: The Legal Dimension*, Dordrecht, Nijhoff, 1993, pp. 223–47

Merrills, J.G., *International Dispute Settlement*, 2nd edn, Cambridge, Grotius, 1991

Monar, J., 'Interinstitutional Agreements: The Phenomenon and its New Dynamics After Maastricht' (1994) 31 CMLRev, 693–719

Monar, J., 'The Financial Dimension of the Common Foreign and Security Policy', in M. Holland (ed.), *Joint Actions*, London, Macmillan, 1996

Moravcsik, A., 'Preferences and Power in the EC: A Liberal Intergovernmentalist Approach' (1993) 31 JCMS, 473–524

Morawiecki, W., 'Actors and Interests in the Process of Negotiations between the CMEA and the EEC', 1989/2 LIEI, 1–38

Muller-Graff, P.-C., 'The Legal Basis of the Third Pillar and its Position in the Framework of the Union Treaty' (1995) 31 CMLRev, 493–510

Napoli, D., 'The European Union's Foreign Policy and Human Rights', in N. Neuwahl and A. Rosas (eds), *The European Union and Human Rights*, The Hague, Nijhoff, 1995, pp. 297–312

Neuwahl, N., 'Joint Participation in International Treaties and the exercise of power by the EEC and its Member States: Mixed Agreements' (1991) 28 CMLRev, 717–40

Neuwahl, N., 'Comment on Opinion 2/91' (1993) 30 CMLRev, 1185–95

Neuwahl, N., 'Foreign and Security Policy and the Implementation of the Requirement of "Consistency" under the Treaty on European Union', in D. O'Keeffe and P. Twomey (eds), *Legal Issues of the Maastricht Treaty*, Chichester, Wiley Chancery, 1994, pp. 227–46

Neuwahl, N., 'Individuals and the GATT: Direct Effect and Indirect Effects of the General Agreement on Tariffs and Trade in Community Law', in N. Emiliou and D. O'Keeffe (eds), *The European Union and World Trade Law – After the GATT Uruguay Round*, Chichester, Wiley, 1996, pp. 313–28

Neuwahl, N., 'Shared powers or combined incompetence'? Move on mixity' (1996) 33 CMLRev, 667–87

Neuwahl, N., 'The European Parliament and Association Council Decision 1/95 of the EC/Turkey Association Council' (1996) 33 CMLRev, 51–68

Neuwahl, N., 'The WTO Opinion and the Implied External Powers of the Community – A Hidden Agenda?', 1996, unpublished

Neuwahl, N. and Rosas, A. (eds), *The European Union and Human Rights*, The Hague, Nijhoff, 1995

Neville-Brown, L. and Kennedy, T., *The Court of Justice of the European Communities*, 4th edn, London, Sweet and Maxwell, 1994

Nicoll, W., 'Note the Hour – and File the Minute' (1993) 32 JCMS, 558–66

Nicoll, W., 'The European Parliament's Post-Maastricht Rules of Procedure' (1994) 32 JCMS, 403–10

Noirfalisse, C., 'The Community System of Fisheries Management and the *Factortame* Case' (1994) 12 YEL 1992, 325–51

Norberg, S., 'The Agreement on a European Economic Area' (1992) 29 CMLRev, 1171–98

Nuttall, S., *European Political Cooperation*, Oxford, Clarendon Press, 1992

Nuttall, S., 'The Commission and Foreign Policy Making', in G. Edwards and D. Spence (eds), *The European Commission*, London, Longman, 1994, pp. 287–302

Nuttall, S., 'The EC and Yugoslavia – *Deus ex Machina* or *Machina sine Deo?*, (1994) 32 JCMS, 11–25

Nuttall, S., 'The European Commission's Internal Arrangements for Foreign Affairs and External Relations' (1995) CFSP Forum 2

O'Keeffe, D., 'Union Citizenship' in D. O'Keeffe and P. Twomey (eds), *Legal Issues of the Maastricht Treaty*, Chichester, Wiley Chancery, 1994, pp. 87–107

O'Keeffe, D., 'Recasting the Third Pillar' (1995) 32 CMLRev, 893–920

O'Keeffe, D. and Schermers, H.G. (eds), *Essays in European Law and Integration*, Deventer, Kluwer, 1982, pp. 141–66

O'Keeffe, D. and Schermers, H.G. (eds), *Mixed Agreements*, Dordrecht, Nijhoff, 1983

O'Keeffe, D. and Twomey, P. (eds), *Legal Issues of the Maastricht Treaty*, Chichester, Wiley Chancery, 1994

O'Leary, S., 'Nationality Law and Community Citizenship: A Tale of Two Uneasy Bedfellows' (1994) 12 YEL 1992, 353–84

Oppenheimer, A., *The Relationship Between EC Law and National Law: The Cases*, Cambridge, CUP, 1995

Owen, D., *Balkan Odyssey*, Gollancz, London, 1995

Pappas, S.A. and Vanhoonacker, S. (eds), *The European Union's Common Foreign and Security Policy: The Challenges of the Future*, Maastricht, EIPA, 1996

Peers, S., 'An Ever Closer Waiting Room: the Case for Eastern European Accession to the EEA' (1995) 32 CMLRev, 187–200

Peers, S., 'From Cold War to Lukewarm Embrace: The European Union's Agreements with the CIS States' (1995) 44 ICLQ, 829–47

Peers, S., 'The Visa Regulation: Free Movement Blocked Indefinitely' (1996) 21 ELRev, 150–5

Peers, S., 'Towards Equality: Actual and Potential Rights of Third-Country Nationals in the European Union' (1996) 33 CMLRev, 7–50

Pelkman, J., 'Europe 1992: A Handmaiden to GATT', in F. Laursen (ed.), *Europe 1992: World Partner? The Internal Market and the World Political Economy*, Maastricht, European Institute of Public Administration, 1991, pp. 125–54

Pescatore, P., 'Les Relations Extèrieures des Communautes Européennes', 103 *Recueil Des Cours* (1961–II), 1-244

Pescatore, P., 'External Relations in the Case Law of the Court of Justice of the European Communities' (1979) 16 CMLRev, 615–45

Pescatore, P., 'The Doctrine of Direct Effect – An Infant Disease of Community Law' (1983) 8 ELRev, 155–77

Pescatore, P., 'Treaty-making by the European Communities', in F. Jacobs and S. Roberts (eds), *The Effect of Treaties in Domestic Law*, London, Sweet and Maxwell, 1987, pp. 171–95

Petersmann, E.-U., 'Participation of the European Communities in the GATT: International Law and Community Law Aspects', in D. O'Keeffe and H.G. Schermers (eds), *Mixed Agreements*, Dordrecht, Nijhoff, 1983, pp. 167–98

Petersmann, E.-U., 'Grey Area Trade Policy and the Rule of Law' (1988) 22 JWTL, 23–44

Petersmann, E.-U., 'The EEC as a GATT Member: Legal Conflicts between GATT Law and European Community Law', in M. Hilf, F.G. Jacobs and E.-U. Petersmann (eds), *The European Community and GATT*, 2nd edn, Deventer, Kluwer, 1989, pp. 23–72

Petersmann, E.-U., 'The External Powers of the Community and the Union', in *The Treaty on European Union: Suggestions for Revision*, TMC Asser Instituut Conference on European Law, The Hague, September 1995

Petersmann, E.-U., 'Proposals for a New Constitution for the European Union: Building Blocks for a Constitutional Theory and Constitutionalised Law of the EU' (1995) 32 CMLRev, 1123–75

Pfetsch, F., 'Tensions in Sovereignty – Foreign Policies of EC Members Compared', in W. Carlsnaes and S. Smith, *European Foreign Policy – The EC and Changing Perspectives in Europe*, London, Sage, 1994, pp. 120–37

Pijpers, A., 'European Political Cooperation and the CSCE Process' (1984) 1 LIEI, 135–48

Pijpers, A., 'The Twelve Out-of area: a Civilian Power in an Uncivil World', in A. Pijpers, E. Regelsberger and W. Wessels (eds), *European Political Cooperation in the 1980s*, Dordrecht, Nijhoff, 1988, pp. 143–65

Pijpers, A., *The European Community At The Crossroads*, Dordrecht, Nijhoff, 1992

Pijpers, A., Regelsberger, E. and Wessels, W. (eds), *European Political Cooperation in the 1980s*, Dordrecht, Nijhoff, 1988

Pinder, J., *The European Community and Eastern Europe*, London, Pinter, 1991

Piontek, E., 'European Integration and International Law of Economic Interdependence' 236 *Receuil Des Cours* (1992–V), 9–126

Pomfret, R., 'The European Community's Relations with the Mediterranean Countries', in J. Redmond, *The External Relations of the European Community: the International Response to 1992*, Basingstoke, Macmillan, 1992, pp. 77–92

Progress Report on IGC, Presidency Conclusions, European Council in Florence, 21–22 June 1996, Doc. SN 300/96, Annexes

Qureshi, A., *The World Trade Organization*, Manchester, MUP, 1996

Redmond, J., 'The European Community and ASEAN', in J. Redmond, *The External Relations of the European Community: the International Response to 1992*, Basingstoke, Macmillan, 1992, pp. 138–60

Redmond, J., *The External Relations of the European Community: the International Response to 1992*, Basingstoke, Macmillan, 1992

Reflection Group's Progress Report (RGP), Doc. SN509/1/95, Rev. 1 (Reflex 10), 1 September 1995, Brussels

Reflection Group's Final Report (RG), Doc. SN520/95, 5 December 1995, Brussels

Regelsberger, E., 'Reforming the CFSP – An Alibi Debate or More', in S.A. Pappas and S. Vanhoonacker (eds), *The European Union's Common Foreign and Security Policy: The Challenges of the Future*, Maastricht, EIPA, 1996

Regelsberger E. and Wessels, W., 'The CFSP Institutions and Procedures: A Third Way for the Second Pillar' (1996) 1 EFARev, 29–54

Rifkind, M., 'Principles and Practice of British Foreign Policy', Speech Delivered at the Royal Institute of International Affairs, Chatham House, London, 21 September 1995

Rosenne, S., *Breach of Treaty*, Cambridge, CUP, 1985

Rummel, R. (ed.), *The Evolution of an International Actor: Western Europe's New Assertiveness*, Boulder, Col., Westview, 1990

Rummel, R., (ed.), *Toward Political Union: Planning a Common Foreign and Security Policy in the European Community*, Baden-Baden, Nomos, 1992

Ryba, B.C., 'La Politique Etrangère Et De Sécurité Commune (PESC) – Mode D'Emploi Et Bilan D'Une Année D'Application (Fin 1993/94), 384 Revue Du Marche Commun Et De L'Union Européenne, 1995, 14–35

Sack, J., 'The European Community's Membership of International Organisations' (1995) 32 CMLRev, 1227–56

Salmon, T.C., 'Ireland: A Neutral in the Community?' (1982) 3 JCMS, 205–27

Salmon, T.C., 'Testing Times for European Political Cooperation: The Gulf and Yugoslavia, 1990–92' (1992) 68(2) Int. Affairs, 233–53

Sands, P., *Principles of International Environmental Law*, Manchester, MUP, 1995

Sands, P. and Tarasofsky, R.G., *Documents in European Community Environmental Law*, Manchester, MUP, 1995

Sands, P., Tarasofsky, R.G. and Weiss, W., *Documents in International Environmental Law*, 2 vols, Manchester, MUP, 1995

Schermers, H.G., 'Community Law and International Law' (1975) 12 CMLRev, 77–90

Schermers, H.G., 'The Direct Application of Treaties with Third States: Note Concerning the Polydor and Pabst Cases' (1982) 19 CMLRev, 563–69

Schermers, H.G., 'A Typology of Mixed Agreements', in D. O'Keeffe and H.G. Schermers (eds), *Mixed Agreements*, Dordrecht, Nijhoff, 1983, pp. 23–33

Schermers, H.G., 'Opinion 1/91 of 14 Dec. 1991; Opinion 1/92 of 10 April 1992 with annotation' (1992) 29 CMLRev, 991–1010

Schermers, H.G. and Blokker, N.M., *International Institutional Law*, 3rd edn, The Hague, Nijhoff, 1995

Schermers, H.G. and Waelbroeck, D., *Judicial Protection in the European Communities*, 5th edn, Deventer, Kluwer, 1992

Schoutheete, P. de, *La Coopération Politique Européenne*, 2nd edn, Brussels, Editions Labor, 1986

Schoutheete, P. de, 'The Presidency and the Management of Political Cooperation' in A. Pijpers, E. Regelsberger and W. Wessels (eds), *European Political Cooperation in the 1980s*, Dordrecht, Nijhoff, 1988, pp. 71–83

Schoutheete, P. de, 'The Creation of the CFSP in the Maastricht Treaty', in E. Regelsberger *et al.* (eds), *Foreign Policy of the European Union: From EPC to CFSP and Beyond*, Boulder, Lynne Reinner publishers, 1996

Schwarze, J., *The External Relations of the European Community, in particular EC-US Relations*, Baden-Baden, Nomos, 1989

Schwok, R., 'The European Free Trade Association: Revival or Collapse?' in J. Redmond, *The External Relations of the European Community: the International Response to 1992*, Basingstoke, Macmillan, 1992, pp. 55–76

Scott, J., 'The GATT and Community Law: Rethinking the Regulatory Gap', in J. Shaw and G. More (eds), *New Legal Dynamics of European Union*, Oxford, OUP, 1995, pp. 147–64

Scott, J. and Mansell, W., 'Trading Partners: The European Community Trade Agreements with Poland, Hungary and Czech and Slovak Republics' (1993) 64 BYIL, 391–408

Sedivy, J., 'Common Foreign and Security Policy – A Central European View', in S.A. Pappas and S. Vanhoonacker (eds), *The European Union's Common Foreign and Security Policy: The Challenges of the Future*, Maastricht, EIPA, 1996

Shaw, J., 'Twin-Track Social Europe – The Inside Track', in D. O'Keeffe and P. Twomey (eds), *Legal Issues of the Maastricht Treaty*, Chichester, Wiley Chancery, 1994, pp. 295–11

Shaw, J. and More, G. (eds), *New Legal Dynamics of European Union*, Oxford, OUP, 1995

Simmonds, K.R., 'The Evolution of the External Relations Law of the European Economic Community' (1979) 28 ICLQ, 644–68

Simmonds, K.R., 'The Communities Declaration Upon Signature of the U.N. Convention on the Law of the Sea' (1986) 23 CMLRev, 521–44

Simmonds, K.R., 'The Fourth Lome Convention' (1991) 28 CMLRev, 521–47

Slaughter-Burley, A.-M., 'International Law and International Relations Theory' (1993) 87 AJIL, 205–39

Slynn, G., *Introducing a European Legal Order*, London, Stevens/Sweet and Maxwell, 1992

Smit, H. and Herzog, P., *The Law of the European Economic Community*, New York, Bender, 1976

Smith, M., 'The United States and 1992: Responses to a Changing European Community', in J. Redmond, *The External Relations of the European Community: the International Response to 1992*, Basingstoke, Macmillan, 1992, pp. 31–54

Snyder, F., *New Directions in European Community Law*, London, Weidenfeld and Nicolson, 1990

Snyder, F., 'Legal Aspects of Trade between the European Union and China: Preliminary Reflections', in N. Emiliou and D. O'Keeffe (eds), *The European Union and World Trade Law – After the GATT Uruguay Round*, Chichester, Wiley, 1996, pp. 363–77

Soetendorp, B., 'The Evolution of the EC/EU as a Single Foreign Policy Actor', in W. Carlsneas and S. Smith, *European Foreign Policy – The EC and Changing Perspectives in Europe*, London, Sage, 1994, pp. 103–19

Spaak, P.-H., *Rapport des chefs de Délégations aux Ministries des Affaires Etrangères*, Brussels, Secretariat of the Intergovernmental Conference, 1956

Stein, E., 'External Relations of the European Community: Structure and Process', Academy of European Law, European University Institute, Florence, 1990, vol. I, 115–88

Steiner, J., 'Subsidiarity under the Maastricht Treaty', in D. O'Keeffe and P. Twomey (eds) *Legal Issues of the Maastricht Treaty*, Chichester, Wiley Chancery, 1994, pp. 49–64

Subedi, S.P., 'The Common Foreign and Security Policy of the European Union and Neutrality' (1996) XLII NILR, 399–412

Sutherland, P., 'The European Union – A Stage of Transition', EIPASCOPE, 1995/2, 2–9

Taylor, P., *When Europe speaks with one voice: the external relations of the European Community*, London, Aldwych Press, 1979

Taylor, P., 'The European Communities as an Actor in International Society' (1982) 6(1) Journal of European Integration

Temple Lang, J., 'The Ozone Layer Convention: A New Solution to the Question of Community Participation in "Mixed" International Agreements' (1986) 23 CMLRev, 157–76

Temple Lang, J., 'The ERTA Judgement and the Court's Case-Law on Competence and Conflict' (1987) 6 YEL 1986, 183–218

Temple Lang, J., 'Community Constitutional Law: Article 5 EEC Treaty' (1990) 27 CMLRev, 645–81

Thijn, I.J., 'The European Political Cooperation in the General Assembly of the United Nations: A Case Study of the Netherlands' (1991) 1 LIEI, 101–25

Timmermans, C.W.A., 'Division of External Powers between Community and Member States in the Fields of Harmonization of National Law: A Case Study' in C.W.A. Timmermans and E.L.M. Völker (eds), *Division of Powers between the European Communities and their Member States in the Field of External Relations*, Deventer, Kluwer, 1981, pp. 15–28

Timmermans, C.W.A. and Völker, E.L.M. (eds), *Division of Powers between the European Communities and their Member States in the Field of External Relations*, Deventer, Kluwer, 1981

Toledano-Laredo, A., 'The EEA Agreement: An Overall View' (1992) 29 CMLRev, 1199–213

Tomuschat, C., 'Liability for Mixed Agreements', in D. O'Keeffe and H.G. Schermers (eds), *Mixed Agreements*, Dordrecht, Nijhoff, 1983, pp. 125–32

Torre, F.C. de la, 'The Status of GATT in EC Law, Revisited' (1995) 29(1) JWTL, 53–68

Toth, A.G., *Oxford Encyclopedia of European Community Law*, Oxford, OUP, 1990

Toth, A.G., 'Is Subsidiarity Justiciable?' (1994) 19 ELRev, 268–85

Tridimas, T. and Eeckhout, P., 'The External Competence of the Community and the Case-Law of the Court of Justice: Principle versus Pragmatism' (1995) 14 YEL 1994, 143–77

Tsakaloyannis, P., 'Risks and Opportunities in the East and South', in A. Pijpers, *The European Community at The Crossroads*, Dordrecht, Nijhoff, 1992

Tsoukalis, L. (ed.), *The European Community: Past, Present and Future*, Oxford, Blackwell, 1983

United Kingdom Government White Paper, *A Partnership of Nations* (Cm. 3181), London, HMSO, 1996

United Nations Secretary-General, *Agenda For Peace*, New York, UN, 1992

Usher, J.A., *European Community Law and National Law – the Irreversible Transfer*, London, Allen and Unwin, 1981

Usher, J.A., 'The Scope of Community Competence – Its Recognition and Enforcement' (1985) 24 JCMS, 121–36

van den Broek, H., 'The Common Foreign and Security Policy: The Challenges of the Future', in S.A. Pappas and S. Vanhoonacker (eds), *The European Union's Common Foreign and Security Policy: The Challenges of the Future*, Maastricht, EIPA, 1996

Van Eekelen, W.F., 'The Common Foreign and Security Policy', in *The Treaty on European Union: Suggestions for Revision*, TMC Asser Instituut Conference on European Law, The Hague, September 1995

Van Forrest, H., 'NATO and the New European Security Landscape', in S.A. Pappas and S. Vanhoonacker (eds), *The European Union's*

Common Foreign and Security Policy: The Challenges of the Future, Maastricht, EIPA, 1996

Vedder, C., 'A Survey of the Principal Decisions of the ECJ Pertaining to International Law' (1990) 1/2 EJIL, 365–77

Völker, E.L.M., 'The Direct Effect of International Agreements in the Community's Legal Order', LIEI, 1983/1, 131–45

Völker, E.L.M. (ed.), *Protectionism and the European Community*, 2nd edn, Deventer, Kluwer, 1986

von Goll, G., 'The Nine at the Conference on Security and Cooperation in Europe', in D. Allen, R. Rummel and W. Wessels (eds), *European Political Cooperation*, London, Butterworths, 1982, pp. 60–8

Waever, O., 'European Security Identities' (1996) 34(2) JCMS, 103–32

Walker, N., 'European Constitutionalism and European Integration' (1996) PL, 266–90

Wallace, W. and Paterson, W. (eds), *Foreign Policy Making in Western Europe*, Farnborough, Saxon House, 1978

Warbrick, C., 'Recognition of States' (1992) 41 ICLQ, 473–82

Ward, I., 'In Search of a European Identity' (1994) 57 MLR, 315–29

Ward, I., 'Identity and Difference: The European Union and Postmodernism', in J. Shaw and G. More (eds), *New Legal Dynamics of European Union*, Oxford, OUP, 1995, pp. 15–28

Ward, I., *A Critical Introduction to European Law*, London, Butterworths, 1996

Weatherill, S., 'Beyond Pre-Emption? Shared Competence and Constitutional Change in the European Community', in D. O'Keeffe and P. Twomey (eds), *Legal Issues of the Maastricht Treaty*, Chichester, Wiley Chancery, 1994, pp. 13–33

Weatherill, S., *Law and Integration in the European Union*, Oxford, OUP, 1995

Weatherill, S. and Beaumont, P., *EC Law*, 2nd edn, London, Penguin, 1995

Weiler, J., 'The External Relations of Non-Unitary Actors: Mixity and the Federal Principle', in D. O'Keeffe and H.G. Schermers (eds), *Mixed Agreements*, Dordrecht, Nijhoff, 1983, pp. 35–83

Weiler, J. and Wessels, W., 'EPC and the Challenge of Theory', in A. Pijpers, E. Regelsberger and W. Wessels (eds), *European Political Cooperation in the 1980s*, Dordrecht, Nijhoff, 1988, pp. 229–58

Weiler, J.H., 'The Transformation of Europe' (1991) 101 Yale LJ, 2403–83

Weiler, J.H., 'The Evolution of Mechanisms and Institutions for a European Foreign Policy: Reflections on the Interaction of Law and Politics', Florence, European University Institute Research Paper, No. 85/202, 1992

Weiss, F., 'The Oporto Agreement on the EEA – A Legal Still Life' (1994) 12 YEL 1992, 385–431

Wellenstein, E., 'Participation of the Community in International Commodity Agreements', in *In Memoriam J.D.B. Mitchell*, St. John Bates and others (eds), London, Sweet and Maxwell, 1983, 65–73

Wessels, W., 'EC-Europe: An Actor *Sui Generis* in the International System', in B. Nelson, D. Roberts and W. Veit, *The EC in the 1990s*, New York, Berg, 1990, pp. 161–73

Westlake, M., *A Modern Guide to the European Parliament*, London, Pinter, 1994

White, N., *The Law of International Organisations*, Manchester, MUP, 1996

Wincott, D., 'Political Theory, Law and European Union', in J. Shaw and G. More (eds), *New Legal Dynamics of European Union*, Oxford, OUP, 1995, pp. 293–311

Wood, M., 'Security Council Working Methods and Procedure: Recent Developments' (1996) 45 ICLQ, 150–61

Wyatt, D., 'New Legal Order, or Old?' (1982) 7 ELRev, 147–66

Wyatt, D., 'The United States of Europe' (1984) 4 OJLS, 256–65

Wyatt, D., and Dashwood, A., *European Community Law*, 3rd edn, London, Sweet and Maxwell, 1993

Wyn-Rees, G., *International Politics in Europe – The New Agenda*, London, Routledge, 1993

Yamane, H., ' "Grey-Area" Measures, the Uruguay Round and the EC/Japan: Commercial Consensus on Cars', in N. Emiliou and D. O'Keeffe (eds), *The European Union and World Trade Law – After the GATT Uruguay Round*, Chichester, Wiley, 1996, pp. 278–92

Index

EC competence and, interpretation
of, 43–7, 67
international agreements, role as to,
94–9, 107, 113, 117–37
mixed agreements, interpretation of,
88
policy considerations, 133–5
preliminary rulings, 30–1
role of, generally, 24, 43, 67, 107,
116, 170, 206
subsidiarity principle and, 16
European Defence Community, 10
European Parliament –
association agreements, role as to,
92, 93, 184
CFSP, role as to, 148, 157–8, 168
Commission and, 16, 114
committees of, 114
Council and, 17, 114
ECJ and, 114
human rights, resolutions on, 192
international agreements, role as to,
17, 91–4
JHA and, 176
powers of, 113–14
Presidency and, 148
role of, 67, 135
European political co-operation –
CFSP and, 13, 139–43, 146, 161
development of, 10, 138–9, 141,
182, 207
institutions' roles, 144–7
JHA and, 174
OSCE and, 204
provision for, 10, 138
European Union –
meaning, 3
Africa, relations with, 189–90
appraisal and prospectus, 6, 206–18
ASEAN and, 198, 214
Australia, relations with, 198, 202
Caribbean, relations with, 189–90
Central America, relations with,
198, 202
CFSP. See common foreign and
security policy
China, relations with, 198–201
citizenship of. See Citizenship of
Union
diplomatic representation, 179–80,
202–3
economic power and liberal values,
212
EFTA, relations with, 186–7

evolution of, 3–4, 7–13
human rights and. *See* human rights
humanitarian aid. *See* humanitarian
assistance
identity and legitimacy, 217–18
international actor, as, 2, 3, 5, 6,
181–205, 209, 210, 213–15
international relations. *See*
international relations
international responsibilities, 35–6
Japan, relations with, 198–200
JHA. *See* justice and home affairs
legal personality. *See* legal personality
limits to role of, 215
Mediterranean countries, relations
with, 198, 201
membership of, 11, 162, 182, 183,
187
model, as, 210–12
NATO and, 170–1, 205
New Zealand, relations with, 198,
202
OSCE and, 204, 205
Russian Federation, relations with,
198, 200, 212, 213
South America, relations with, 198,
202
structured dialogue with states,
198–205
TEU, effect of. *See* TEU
third states and. *See* third states
United Nations and, 31, 36, 203–4
United States, relations with, 198–9,
212
WEU and, 170–1
world economic system, contribution
to, 213
extradition, co-operation as to, 177

federalism, 8
fisheries –
exclusive competence of EC, 69,
70
international agreements on,
195–6
foreign policy, common. *See* common
foreign and security policy
'Fortress Europe', 11, 114, 213
free trade agreements, 128, 130, 134,
191
functionalists, aims of, 8–9
fundamental freedoms, 101, 142,
191–3
further reading, 219–20